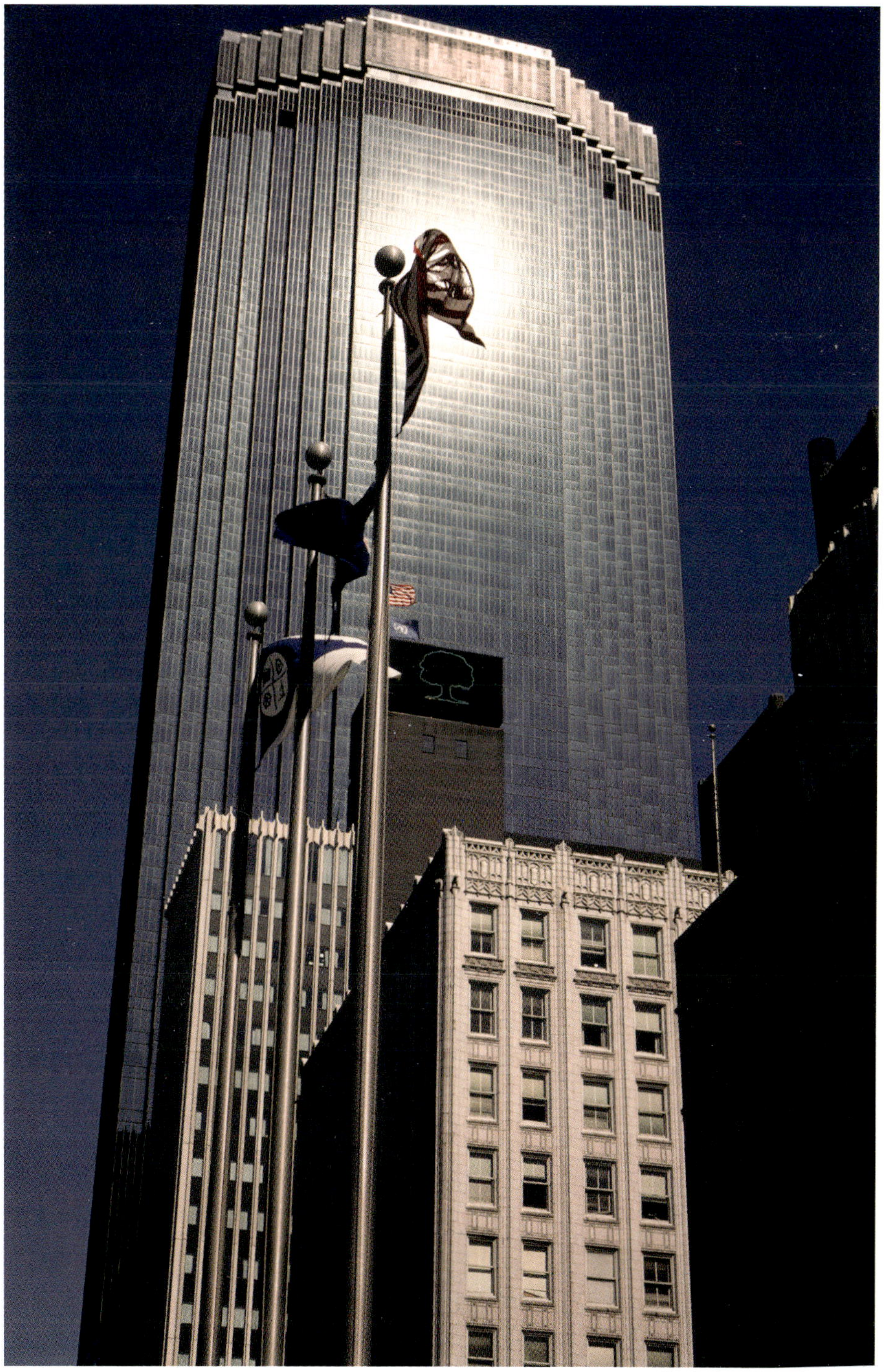

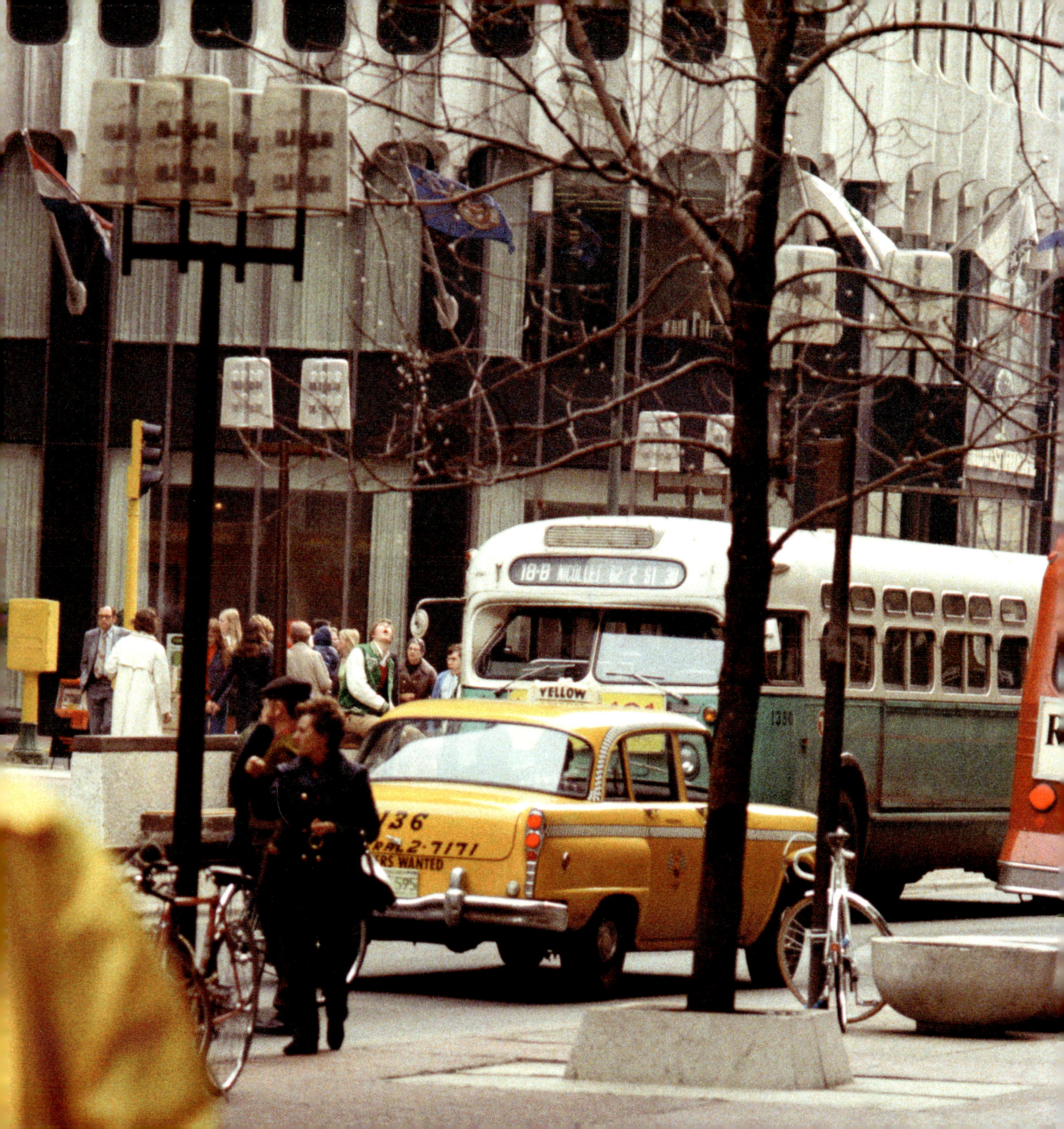
YELLOW
WANTED

DOWNTOWN
MINNEAPOLIS IN THE 1970s

PHOTOGRAPHS BY
MIKE EVANGELIST

WITH TEXT BY
ANDY STURDEVANT

MINNESOTA HISTORICAL SOCIETY PRESS

On the frontispiece: The Midwest Federal building and its new neighbor, the IDS Tower, as seen from Nicollet Mall

On the title page: Old and new buses on Nicollet Mall

www.mnhspress.org

The Minnesota Historical Society Press is a member of the Association of American University Presses.

Manufactured in India

10 9 8 7 6 5 4 3 2

∞ The paper used in this publication meets the minimum requirements of the American National Standard for Information Sciences—Permanence for Printed Library Materials, ANSI Z39.48-1984.

International Standard Book Number
ISBN: 978-1-68134-117-0 (paper)

Library of Congress Cataloging-in-Publication Data available upon request.

Downtown was designed and set in type by Chris Long at Mighty Media, Minneapolis.

THIS COLLECTION OF PHOTOS is dedicated to the late John Croft. John was a staff photographer at the *Minneapolis Star Tribune* for forty years, starting in 1957. As a young photographer I would often notice his images in the newspaper and admire his skill at capturing the moment. I aspired to learn the art and craft of photography as well as he obviously had. I've been trying ever since.

MIKE EVANGELIST

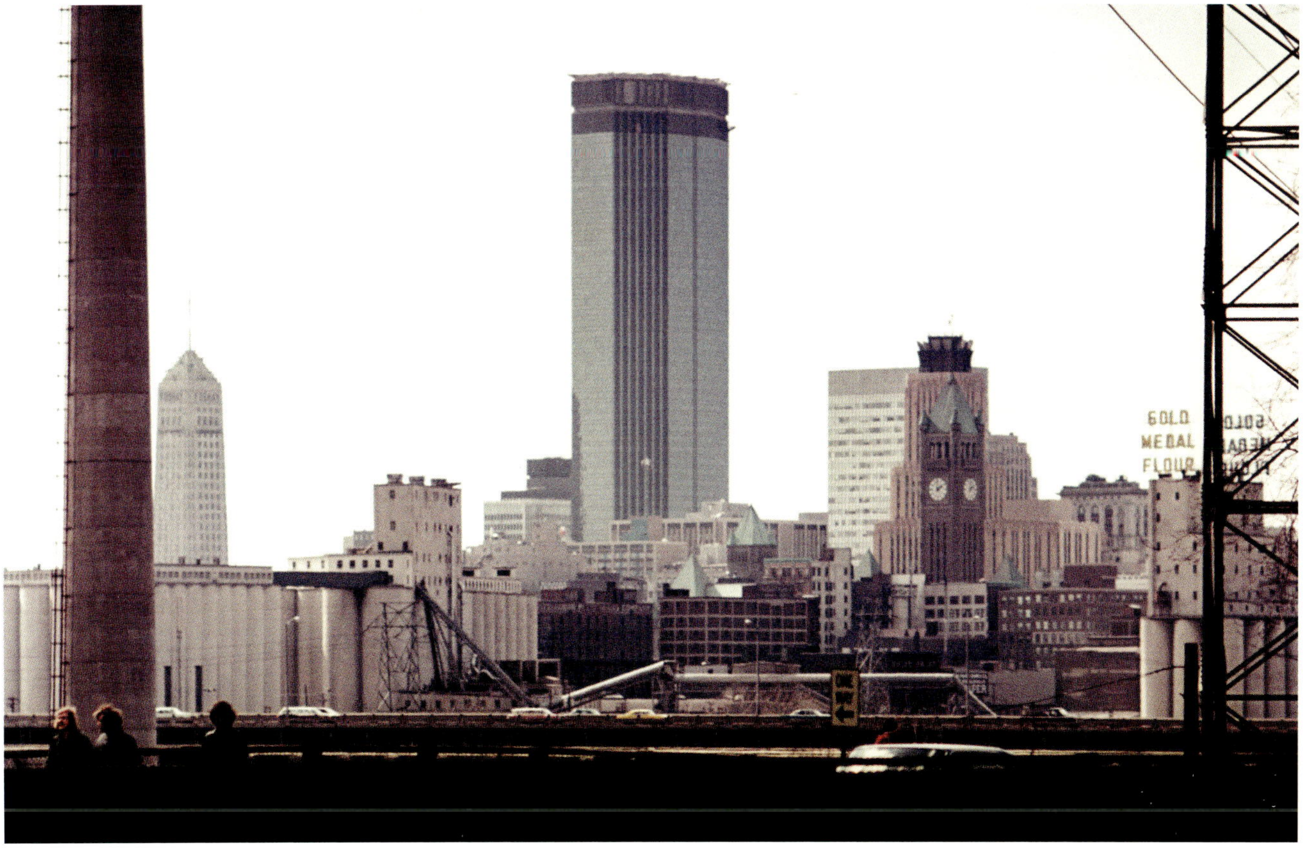

PREFACE

THIS BOOK IS FILLED WITH PHOTOGRAPHS that I made for my own education and enjoyment. I never imagined that anyone besides me would ever see them, much less actually like them. But thanks to the combined effects of several seemingly unrelated events, you are now holding a collection of these images in your hands.

First, the advent of affordable high-quality photo scanners made it possible for me to begin to digitize and sort my old negatives and slides, which had long languished in my closet. In fact, many of them had never been printed before, so in some cases I was essentially seeing the images for the first time.

Second, as I began to go through the images, I realized that the passage of time had been good to them. The ordinary things I photographed had gained new meaning and relevance in the intervening forty years. Even as they sat in my closet, the images were changing. They were no longer just a bunch of separate photos of miscellaneous stuff; they were coalescing into a collection, an unintentional chronicle of places and people and things and times that were very important to me—and, as I learned later, to others as well.

Third, serendipity and Facebook led me to share a few of these vintage images with my friends and family.

Fourth, after seeing some of my photos, my cousin Bill Ojile encouraged me to check out the "Old Minneapolis" Facebook community. I'm very glad I did; it seemed an ideal place to share my images, and founder Jesse Jamison agreed. He began posting

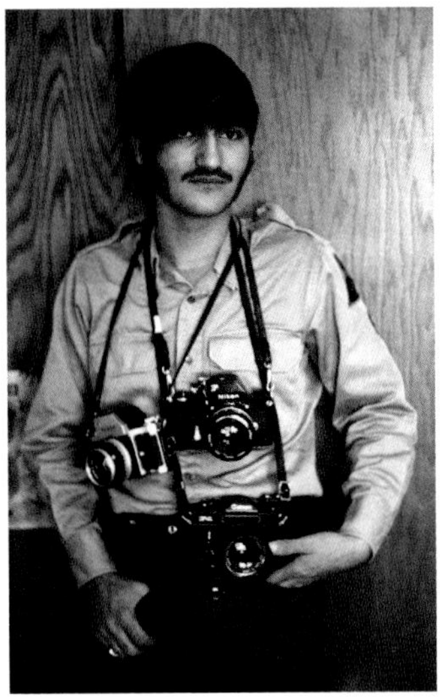

"With my tools of the trade, in 1971"

an image every day or so, and the immediate and enthusiastic response from the community was most gratifying. I especially loved how the ensuing conversations often revealed new details and context for an image or a scene.

Fifth, I met Andy Sturdevant, who was working on a piece for *MinnPost* about the phenomenal growth of the Old Minneapolis community. This embarrassingly flattering article also included commentary on some of my photos, which caught the eyes of the good folks at the Minnesota Historical Society Press. Their interest ultimately led to the creation of this book.

Speaking of the historical society, I'd like to express my deepest thanks to Ann Regan, for thinking this was a good idea, and to Josh Leventhal, for making it happen and making it better. Further thanks go to Andy Sturdevant for his illuminating text, and finally to Jesse Jamison, whose creation of the Old Minneapolis Facebook page is a tremendous gift to the whole community.

Finally, thank *you* for choosing this book. I could not be happier about being able to share my work with you. I hope you enjoy it as much as I enjoyed creating it.

MIKE EVANGELIST

Besides everyone that Mike thanked, I'd also like to send a special thanks to the staff of the Minneapolis Central Library generally, and the Special Collections specifically, for their assistance. Also thanks to Stuart Klipper, Paul Shambroom, and David Little for their expertise, the Amalgamates for their feedback early in the writing process, and my editor Susan Albright at *MinnPost*. I dedicate the text to Fatuma Mohamud, in whose capable hands the tradition of Minneapolis street photography continues into the twenty-first century.

ANDY STURDEVANT

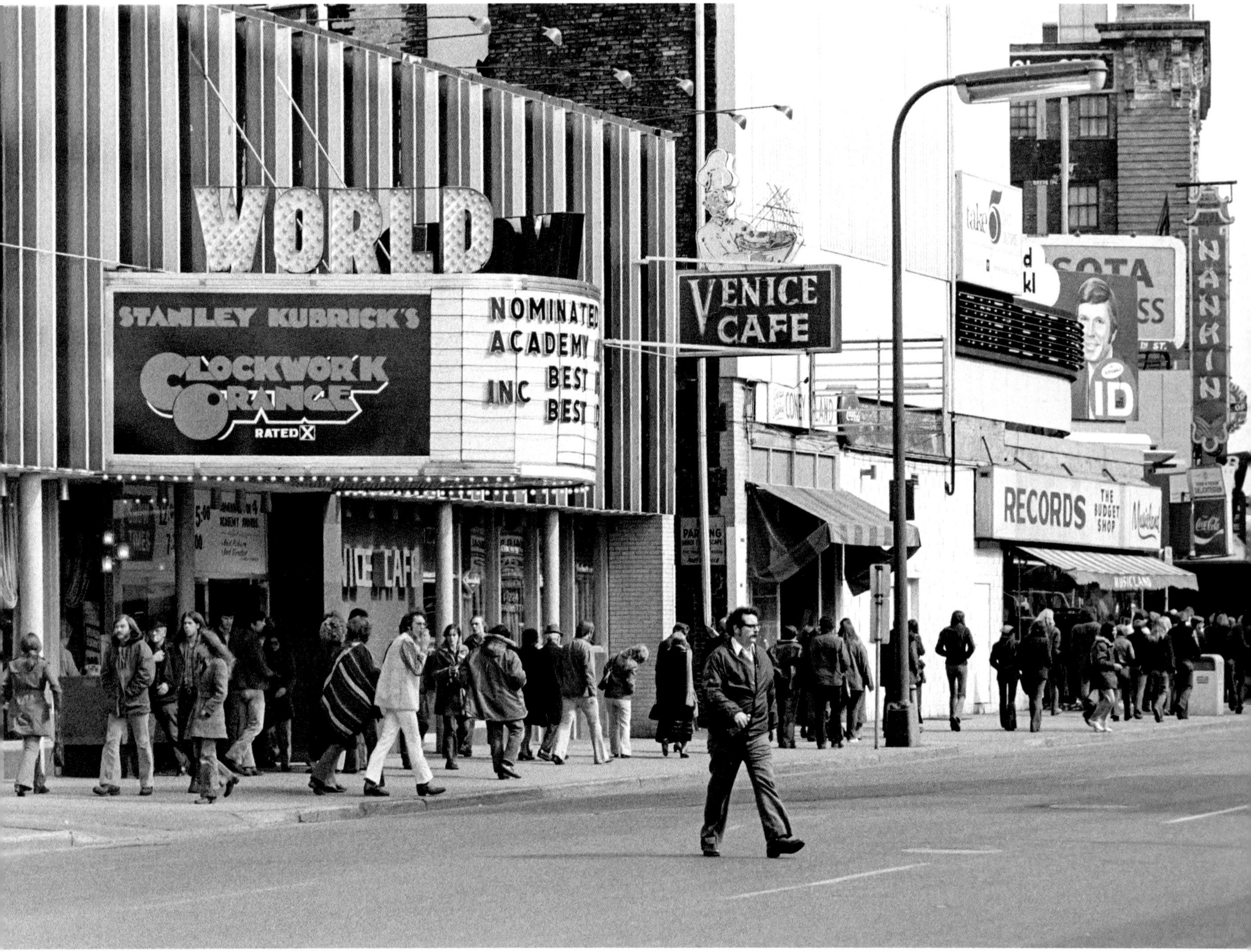

A Clockwork Orange lets out at the World Theater on Seventh Street, March 1972

INTRODUCTION

by ANDY STURDEVANT

On the first day of March in 1972, a midweek cold snap was ending a run of unseasonably warm weather in Minneapolis. At the end of the previous week, an employee of the Downtown World Theater on the Seventh Street side of Block E had pasted up a new marquee banner for the theater's current offering: Stanley Kubrick's *A Clockwork Orange*. It had been released at the end of 1971 in larger markets and was finally making its Minneapolis debut. In a decade where X-rated films were becoming a regular part of the cinematic landscape, the World had a different approach with this particular specimen: "Nominated for two Academy Awards," it pointed out helpfully.

That afternoon, the early edition of the *Minneapolis Star* was hitting the green newspaper boxes along the city's streets. It included a review of the film from the paper's longtime chief critic, Don Morrison. Morrison was a sharp, goateed dandy, a native of Texas via New York City—"a philosopher," according to the *Star*'s sidebar ads, "who enjoys fine food and conversation." He was less enthused than the Academy was about the British film import. "Kubrick does things so well," Morrison noted, "you aren't permitted to forget the cool technician at work." If you picked up the morning paper that weekend, you'd have found another pan from Morrison's colleague Ben Kern. "I don't really look forward to a nudist Nicollet Mall," he noted wryly, taking Kubrick's dystopian vision to its logical and most extreme local conclusion.

In spite of Morrison and Kern's misgivings, *A Clockwork Orange* would be a blockbuster among Twin Cities moviegoers, playing for a solid three months at the World, well into spring.

During its run, *A Clockwork Orange*'s first evening showing was at 5:00 PM. Right about that time, a kid from the northern suburbs named Mike Evangelist was making his way up Nicollet Mall to get to his job sorting mail at the downtown post office on First Street. He had arrived downtown earlier in the afternoon, taking the 4A bus after school from New Brighton. He typically would spend the hour and a half before his shift wandering the streets with a camera around his neck, with other things on his mind than movies on these weekday afternoons. It shouldn't have been possible for Mike to see *A Clockwork Orange*. For one, he was only seventeen years old, but more importantly, his shift at the post office started at 4:30, and an afternoon matinee would have left him little time to hustle up Nicollet Mall and clock in on time.

Still, he managed to see *A Clockwork Orange* anyway.

On his way out of the theater, Mike—seldom without his camera—snapped a photo of the scene, cut across Hennepin Avenue on Seventh Street, and headed up

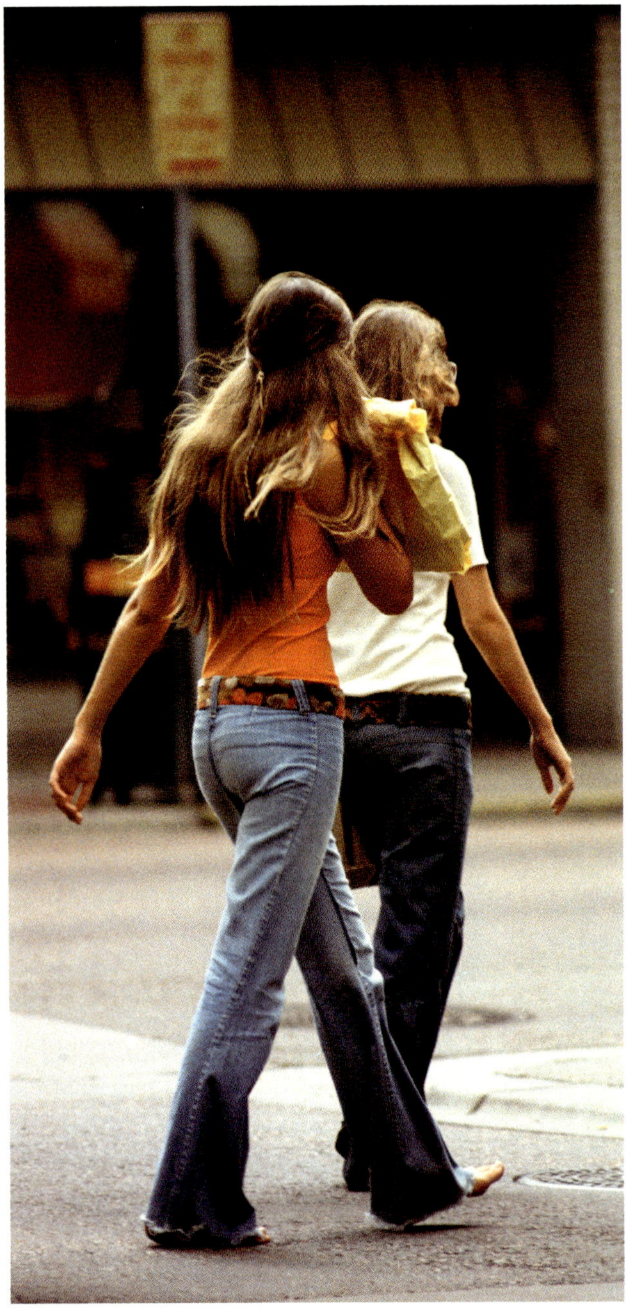

Seventies style on display in downtown Minneapolis

the mall to work. The image could be from the week if not the exact day that Morrison's review ran. The outfits here make one think of the dreary dregs of late winter.

Mike would shoot a dozen or more photos like that over the course of the afternoon, something he would do almost every weekday for years.

This was Mike Evangelist's routine, from the time he began working at the post office in January 1972 to when he left the job in early 1974: arrive downtown after school at about 3:00 PM and spend the intervening hour and a half before his shift walking around, taking pictures on a Mamiya or Nikon or Leica of whatever he'd see around him. The images were mostly people (and, befitting a seventeen-year-old boy, lots of girls), but also restaurants, businesses, sidewalk vendors, buses, and the interactions between people that occur in all of these venues. For years, Mike spent his weekday afternoons walking through the city, shooting roll after roll of film. He'd been coming downtown to shoot pictures semi-regularly since 1969, but the job at the post office gave him two additional advantages: one, a regular schedule that brought him downtown nearly every day, and two, the disposable income necessary to invest in more and better equipment. During his jaunts before work, Mike could pop into Jay's Cameras or Brown Photo or Century Camera, all located within a few blocks of one another around Nicollet Mall, and get whatever he needed. It was all downtown.

Many photos were shot as test images—trying out a new filter or lens, taking a look at the negatives, and then throwing them in a storage box. But the vast majority of Mike's photos capture the enthusiasm of a young suburban boy making his way through an American city—an enthusiasm for the places, the bustling

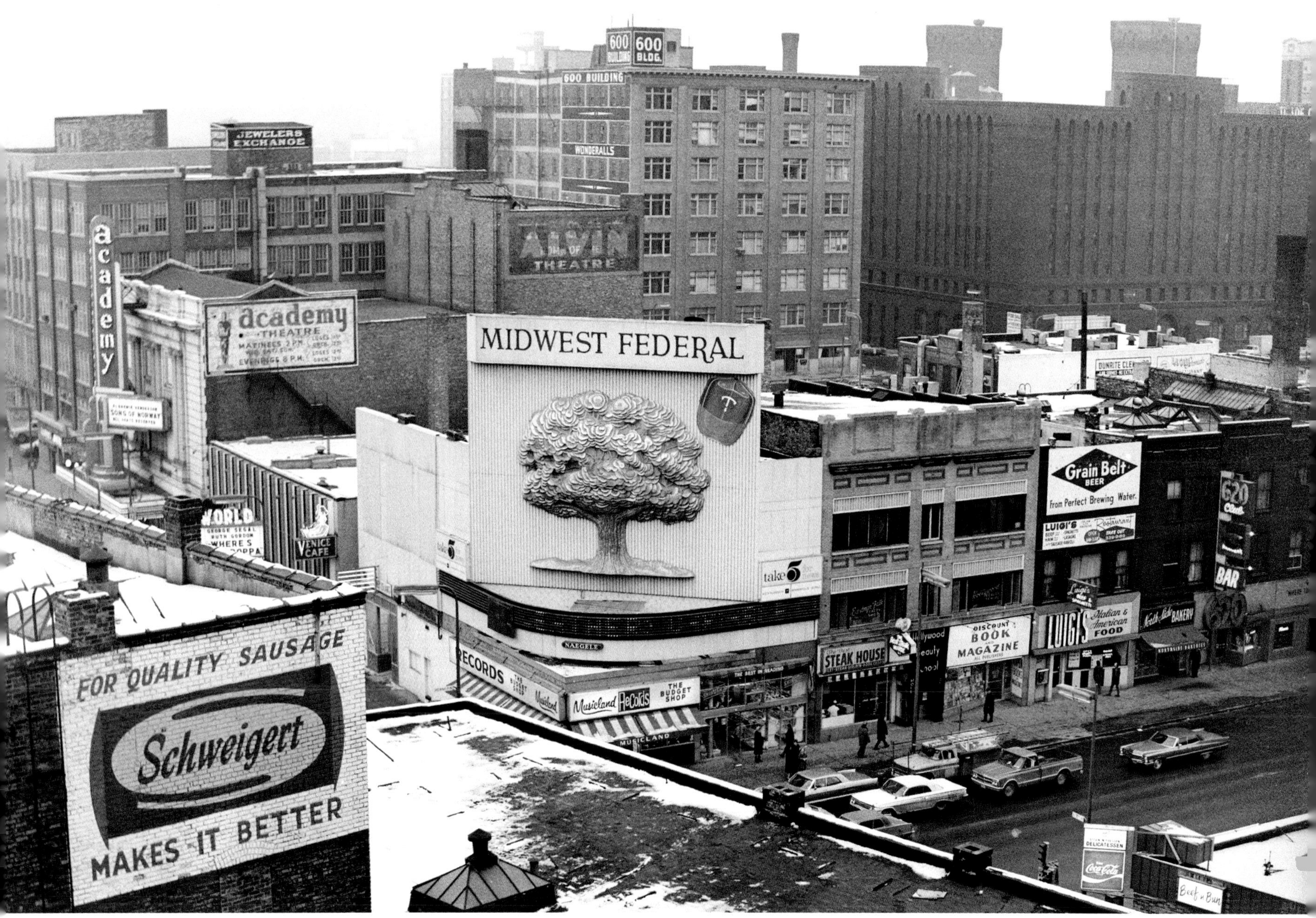

Block E viewed from the top floor of the Dayton's parking ramp

crowds, the scenes on the streets and on the buses, the outfits, the faces. It seems to be the work of a fairly shy kid, looking for connections, looking to be a part of the world. The scenes that he captured, viewed forty years later, give us a feel for the way the city looked and felt to a young man. "I could pretty much go wherever I wanted and do what I felt like doing," he wrote later. "And what I felt like doing was taking pictures."

Seen from the perspective of many years, these photos have a universal quality that the photographer may not have anticipated as a young man. The type of scene outside the Downtown World Theater that March afternoon, the opening week of *A Clockwork Orange*, is interesting to us not in spite of its unremarkable, workaday character but *because* of it. It's a scene of everyday life, the type that, for most of history, goes unchronicled. We're out on Seventh Street with Mike, looking up at a marquee. The block is shot from the perspective of this lowly old cross street, just off the main drag; we see the Venice Café, an advertisement for KSTP Channel 5, and a shuttered Coney Island joint.

In the early 1970s, Nicollet Mall, only two blocks away, was the crown jewel of downtown development. Its glamorous, tourist brochure–ready vistas appeared regularly in promotional literature.

Seventh Street isn't that. Unlike celebrated thoroughfares such as Nicollet Mall or Hennepin Avenue, its name barely registers.

A few blocks away from the city's main commercial drag, we see a side of Minneapolis not captured in glossy magazine spreads or celebrated by civic boosters and tourism bureaus. Not because it's dirty or unattractive. It's just—well, it's just *regular*. The awnings sag a little bit, as awnings do. The neon looks like it might be buzzing a little too loudly. The Venice Café, a red sauce and square-cut pizza joint, was a well-loved restaurant of the era, but not the sort of place that got rave reviews in the local press or garnered a cult following. It was just a place owned by a local Italian family where downtowners could go to get a good plate of spaghetti and meatballs at all hours without much fuss. There are no shoppers with bags from glamorous department stores on the scene, no tourists craning their necks to glimpse the IDS Tower rising to the top of the skyline. Mike has plenty of shots of the mall that the tourism bureau would have happily signed off on. But that's only a small part of his Minneapolis images.

This scene reveals a city gearing up for the evening commute. Businessmen, shoppers, students, commuters, and other downtown types all stream by. Some are getting off work, making their way to their buses or cars; others are headed to work; and not more than a few are probably out of work. Certainly a lot of these people will have read Morrison's pan in the *Star*—the paper's average daily circulation is close to half a million at this time—and will formulate their own opinions about Kubrick's film. The air is cool. Maybe we can detect that energy that pervades the streets of upper

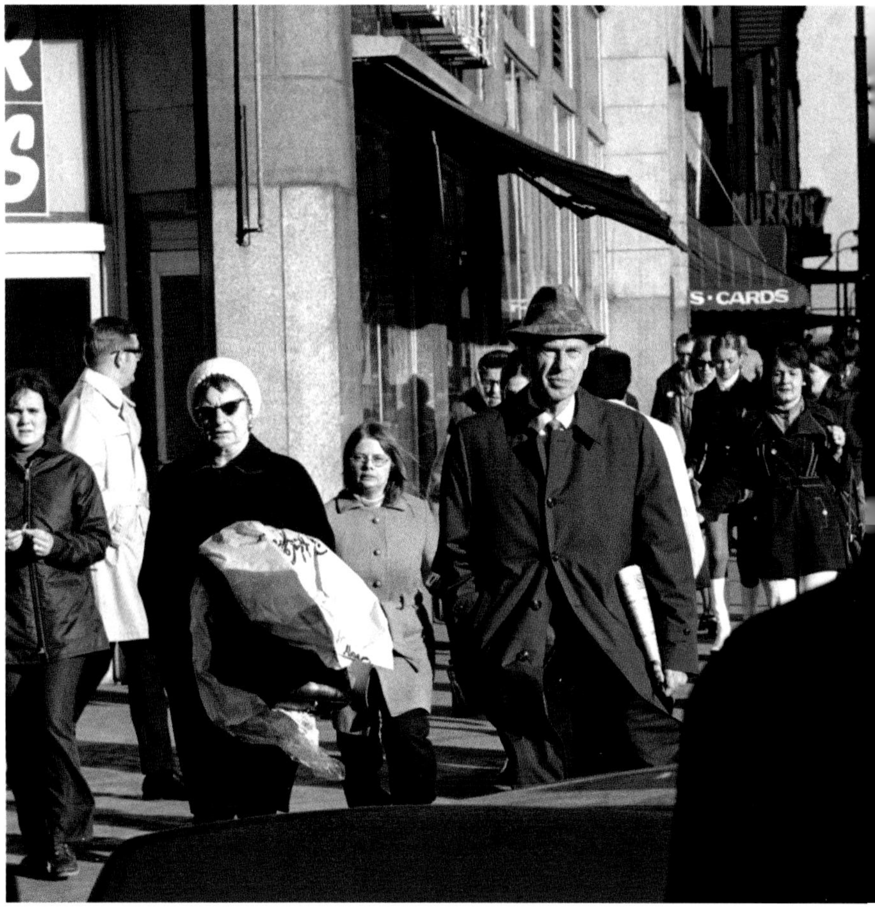

Pedestrians coming and going at the corner of Hennepin and Sixth

midwestern cities when the winter weather shows signs of finally letting up and gives a quick preview of the coming attractions of spring. We see Minneapolitans outfitted in suits, hip-huggers, long hair, short hair, a poncho, thigh-high boots. Most of them shuffle by, unaware of the camera.

Mike's lens is interested in all of it.

Of all the wonderful photos collected in this book, there are a few pragmatic reasons to linger a bit longer on this particular image of a crowd leaving a movie theater on Seventh Street. For one, it allows us to timestamp the scene to around March 1972 and affords us the opportunity to play detective by working out when the movie opened in Minneapolis. There'll be much more on this type of amateur sleuthing work to come. It's an important part of this story.

It's worth thinking, as well, about the name up on that marquee, and how it relates to this scene: Stanley Kubrick, the filmmaker that Don Morrison refers to as a "cool technician." Kubrick began his career twenty years earlier as a New York street photographer, particularly around the Bronx, snapping the sorts of scenes on black-and-white film that Evangelist would later chase down himself. Street photography, as a medium, relies on maintaining a delicate balance between an empathic enthusiasm for people and places on one hand and, on the other, keeping a certain distant quality. There must be a willingness to remove oneself from the action, to work at arm's length. Kubrick's work as a Bronx street photographer tended to the chillier side of that spectrum, qualities that later defined his work as a filmmaker. Evangelist, in his sense of post-adolescent abandon, edges toward the more enthusiastic end.

Mike, too, is a technician—not a cool technician, but a warm one. Much of this body of work is about taking advantage of contemporary technical advances, an eagerness for tools and gadgetry and new ways of doing things. A telling early self-portrait of Mike from that time (and included with the preface of this book) shows him displaying three different late-model cameras draped around his neck like medallions. This enthusiasm for technology has, in fact, defined his professional life. Mike would leave his job at the post office in the early seventies and enter the world of consumer electronics in earnest by taking a job at Schaak Electronics in LaSalle Court (also downtown), the Minneapolis-based hi-fi retailer that later sold some of the first PCs in the region. Retaining a deep interest in technology, Mike would eventually go on to serve as director of product marketing at Apple under Steve Jobs, during the period that the iPod was introduced. It's Mike's enthusiasm that makes this story, in part, also about technology—not just about the tools themselves but about how people use these tools to discover and remember parts of their lives, to make connections to one another and to the places they live.

But before all that, Mike Evangelist was just a kid with a camera and a passion for photography. The rolls and rolls of negatives that he shot during the early 1970s sat in a box in his closet for decades, untouched, mostly unseen, and only sporadically thought about by the photographer who made them. Mike's life continued—marriage, kids, work, the usual way stations of adulthood. He kept making photos throughout all of it, but you only get a few chances in life to devote hours and hours a day to a time-consuming undertaking like photography and to pursue it at the expense of all other things. "It was my most intense period of exploration and creativity," he later recalled. "It was the period for me between sort of becoming an adult and the onset of actual adult responsibilities."

Only in the last few years has the technology made it practical for him to retrieve these images from their shoebox purgatory and scan them one by one to see how they looked on a computer screen after the passage of so much time. As soon as the opportunity presented itself, that's exactly what Mike did. He was pleased with what he found and thought others might be as well.

Not until recently have there been venues for sharing images like this with the world at large, for putting these images into a context where interested people—those who remember the Minneapolis of this era and others who don't—can peruse them. Here they are also able to tell personal anecdotes about the photos or ask follow-up questions of the original photographer and each other. Occasionally, someone will find another person they know pictured in the image—a person who may in fact be long dead, and who'd never seen this particular image of themselves—and tag them.

It is at least partially a story, like so many contemporary stories, about Facebook.

Smartphones today have made amateur photography as ubiquitous as any form of creative expression in human history. It's easy to forget, however, that in the prosperous years of the postwar period leading up to the 1970s, photography may have seemed as ubiquitous then as it does to us now. Cameras were both better and more affordable than they'd ever been before, and getting prints made—once an expensive process usually carried out by mail order—was as easy as ducking into a neighborhood developer and waiting a few days. "A new pervasiveness to photographic imagery characterizes these decades," writes photographic curator Matthew Witkovsky of the period beginning in the late 1960s, "spurred by widening affluence and the advent of television as well as a perhaps unprecedentedly casual attitude towards picture making." The technology of picture making, he continues, "becomes an extension of daily living, accompanying people not just on birthdays or family trips but to the bathroom, to the store—in short, everywhere." Whether wielded by professionals or amateurs, the camera, it seemed, was everywhere.

Minneapolis was among the vanguard in this surge of photography. In the late 1950s, at the beginning of a period of enormous growth in the local advertising industry, one regional publication estimated that "any national publication will carry from six to a dozen advertisements carrying pictures from Minneapolis photographers, featuring Minneapolis products with Minneapolis models." These numbers would continue to grow through the 1960s and early '70s.

Mike took up photography in 1968, at the age of fourteen. "I happened to borrow an old Argus C3 camera from a friend's dad," he recalls. "I was already an unapologetic gadget nerd, and the look of this camera really grabbed me. I wanted to learn about it and understand how it worked." It was a good time to be making these inquiries. By the late 1960s, "The Brick," as the C3 was affectionately known from its introduction in 1939, was no longer in production. The equipment that replaced it was infinitely more sophisticated. As mass-market photo equipment grew easier and easier to use—this era marked the advent of the Instamatic, a multimillion-selling camera that simplified the photographic process to "press the button"—higher-end equipment geared to professionals grew more accessible. What would have been unwieldy (or unobtainable) to anyone besides a *Life* magazine photographer thirty years earlier was now available to anyone with a few hundred dollars squirreled away. An aspiring photographer like Mike, looking to take up photography as a hobby (and, perhaps, an avocation), had plenty of resources to turn to in the Twin Cities of the 1970s to learn about this new universe of equipment. Most of these resources were in the form of full-service, locally owned photo shops. And most of these were located in downtown Minneapolis.

The 1970 city directory lists no fewer than ten photographic supply shops within perhaps a twenty-block radius. They varied in terms of their particular clientele's wants and needs, and in the general environment. Photographer Stuart Klipper, whose career in the Twin Cities began in the late 1960s, remembers some of the shops in downtown as being "like walking up a flight of stairs into a Reginald Marsh painting." They were places full of "real old-time gearheads," arguing and cackling and debating the finer points of operating photographic equipment.

Mike haunted three shops in particular, all located within a few blocks of each other around Nicollet Mall: Brown Photo at Ninth Street and Nicollet, Century Camera on Ninth Street and a block off Nicollet, and Jay's Cameras at Fifth Street and Nicollet. Mike's downtown perambulations would take him by each of these—sometimes to buy, sometimes to browse.

Each of the three had a distinct personality, based on its clientele and the sort of equipment they sold. They served the full array of photographers at work in the Twin Cities in the early 1970s. This ran the gamut from weekend enthusiasts shooting birds for their camera clubs, to professionals shooting products made by Minneapolis corporations for spreads in national magazines, to young artists whose work was being exhibited at the Minneapolis Institute of Arts, under the auspices of the new Photo Department, established in 1972 by curator Ted Hartwell. Between these and other downtown sales, repair, and print shops like Brand's Camera Craft, Gopher Camera, Pako Photo, and Film Shops Camera Store, photographers at any level had plenty of options.

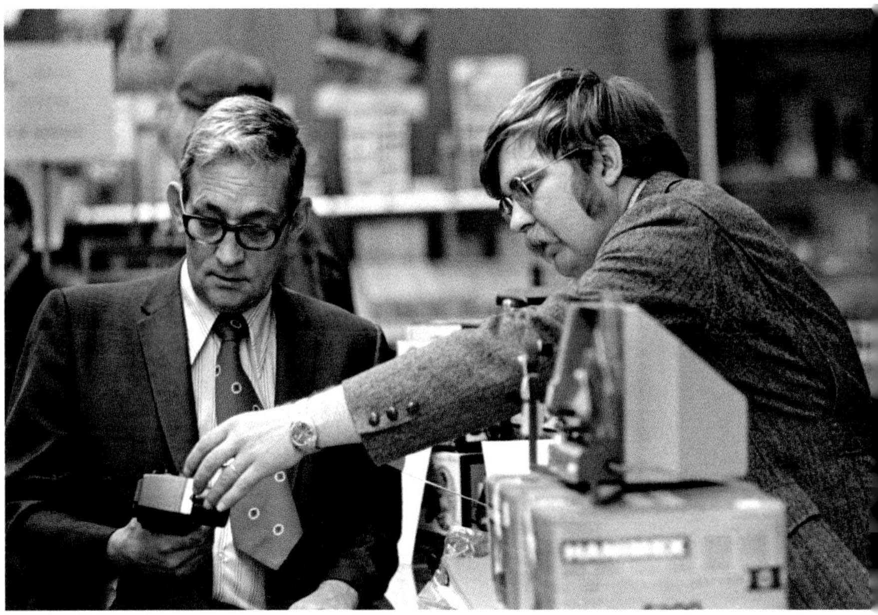

A helpful salesman at Century Camera

"An all-weather business," Century Camera founder Harvey Goldstein called photography, one that can be "an inexpensive hobby using up idle hours" in lean times and also one that "doesn't slack off during good times because equipment can run to a wide range of cost." These shops operated like clubhouses, with eager salespeople showing off newly arrived gear to regulars ("known haunters," Goldstein called them). Mike's photos of the shops' interiors show neatly dressed clerks in suits and ties, giving hands-on demos to customers, pointing to floor models, and chatting about shutter speeds and interchangeable viewfinders and 500mm telephoto lenses and ASA dials. The technology was changing rapidly. "There has never been an up-to-date photograph made of the Nikon System," boasted one advertisement in 1971, reminding the consumer of the constant churn of new accessories available to the contemporary photographer. The staff at the photo stores could be counted on to help navigate it all.

Local amateur enthusiasts had the additional option of joining as many as fourteen photo clubs. By the mid-1970s, there was a camera or photo club meeting somewhere in the metro nearly every weekday, ranging from the Nature Camera Club to the Women's Color Photo Club (these clubs were still fairly segregated not only by color versus black and white but also by gender, even at that late date). The photo supply shops sponsored a Twin Cities Area Council of Camera Clubs, which kept a steady stream of perhaps hundreds of members coming in regularly for equipment, parts, advice, and general socializing. The local papers were filled not only with glowing accounts of the hometown winners of national photo contests but also with stories and profiles of local photo enthusiasts, ranging from precocious teens to enthusiastic retirees, building out darkrooms in their basements and shooting for both fun and profit. "He likes his pictures to have a message for the viewer," beamed one such profile of a high school boy about Mike's age in Brooklyn Center. The young man's stated aim: "a career in industrial photography."

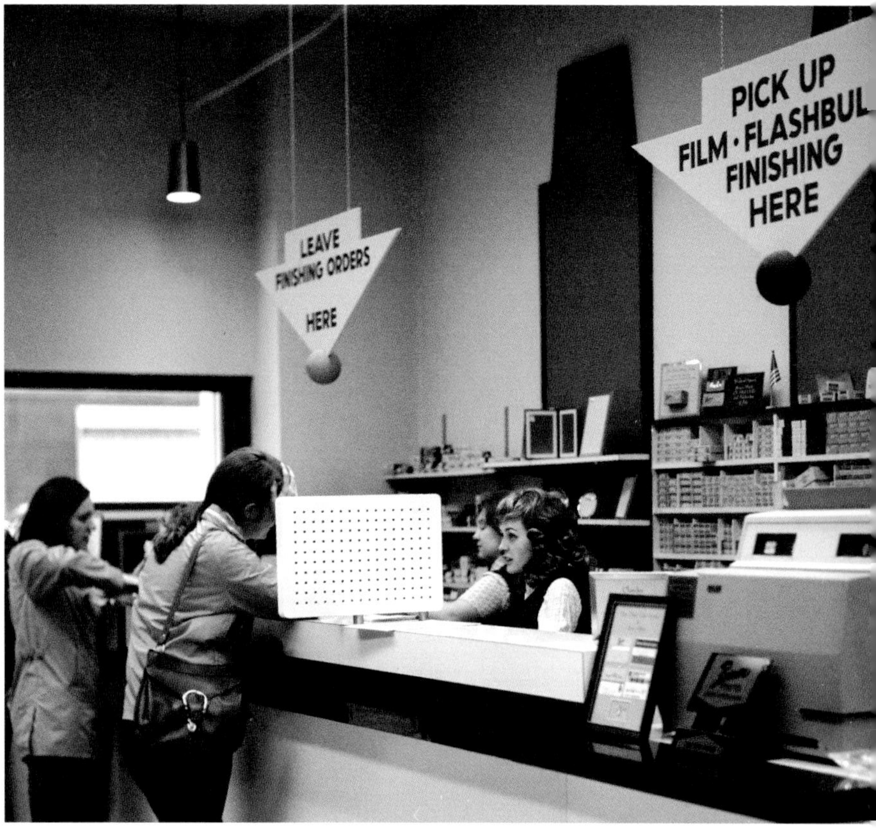

The photofinishing counter at Brown Photo

Mike was both of and apart from this world; he wasn't a member of any photo clubs, nor did he ever show his work professionally. But he was, as his photos of the store interiors show, a part of the larger community, on friendly terms with the various clerks. A select few would even, on occasion, loan Mike equipment to take out and try.

To those who didn't live through it—I count myself in this number—the downtown Minneapolis of the 1970s may seem quite unfamiliar.

It doesn't, however, seem *alien.*

I've seen footage of the *old* old Minneapolis from after World War II, the street scenes best captured in Johnny Rex's 1950s-era Super 8 movies of the old skid row, which you may have come across at some point. That's a Minneapolis that looks completely alien today, as vanished as Pompeii.

As unfamiliar as the Minneapolis of the 1970s looks, it is still broadly recognizable as a very early version of the contemporary city of today. It's recognizable in the same way photos of your mom and dad at age twenty-two are today. Sure, they're a little grayer and more wrinkled now, but you can still see it's them in the brow line and the bone structure and in the eyes.

In many of these Minneapolis scenes, the names on the stores are different, but much of the infrastructure is the same. Demographically, the city seems whiter and older than it seems today—or maybe older people just looked older back then—but there is much that is unchanged. People cluster under shelters waiting not for streetcars but for buses. Nicollet Mall, despite some cosmetic differences, is firmly in place by this time. Although Dayton's is now Macy's and Young-Quinlan is now a jewelry store, the buildings are the same. The IDS Center towers over everything, and though its two 1990s-era skyscraping siblings aren't on the scene yet, we can look at a photo of Nicollet Mall in the early 1970s, presided over by the fifty-five-story building, and still generally orient ourselves. As I said: unfamiliar, but not alien.

Downtown of that era still retains many of its mid-century neon lights and hand-painted signage, but these seem to be disappearing quickly, edged out by digital displays and more contemporary-looking billboards. The architecture seems caught between eras. The Gateway District of Johnny Rex's skid row movies is a decade gone, and the more modern glass-and-concrete skyscraper architecture we associate with downtown today is already starting to crowd out brick storefronts and ornate stone facades.

Take a shot like the one of Seventh Street near Hennepin Avenue depicting three somewhat worse-for-the-wear businesses: the Greeting Card Center, Millie Owens' Wigs and Things, and the Adonis Tie Shop. Aside from the psychedelic displays in the window of the card shop (and the bell-bottom jeans and long hair on the waiting customers), it looks right out of the 1940s. That is, until you look to the left of the frame and see the cast concrete tower looming there. It's that "Park and Shop" garage that now has the Foot Locker and the Team Liquor Wine and Spirits shop.

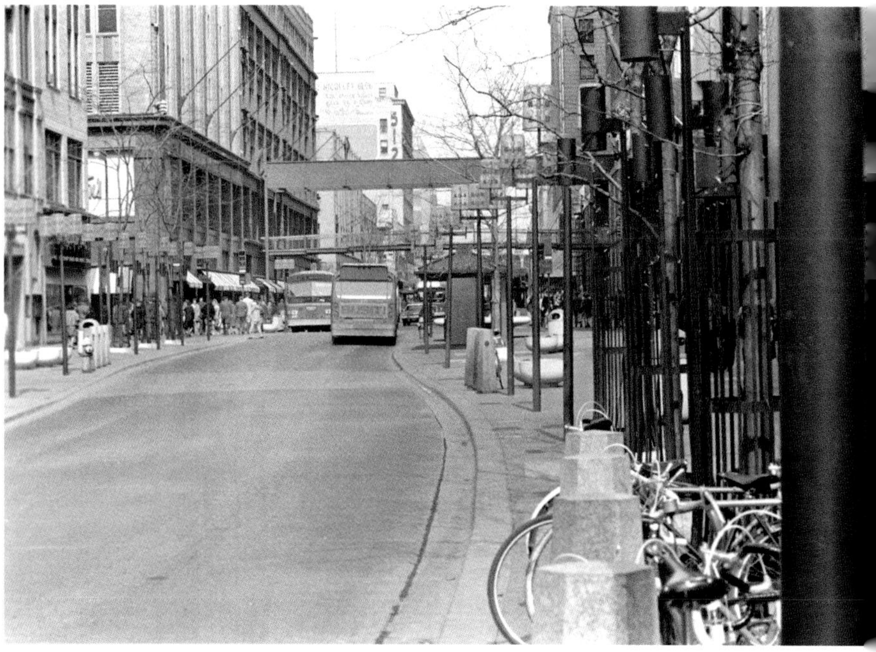

Looking north on Nicollet Mall from Ninth Street

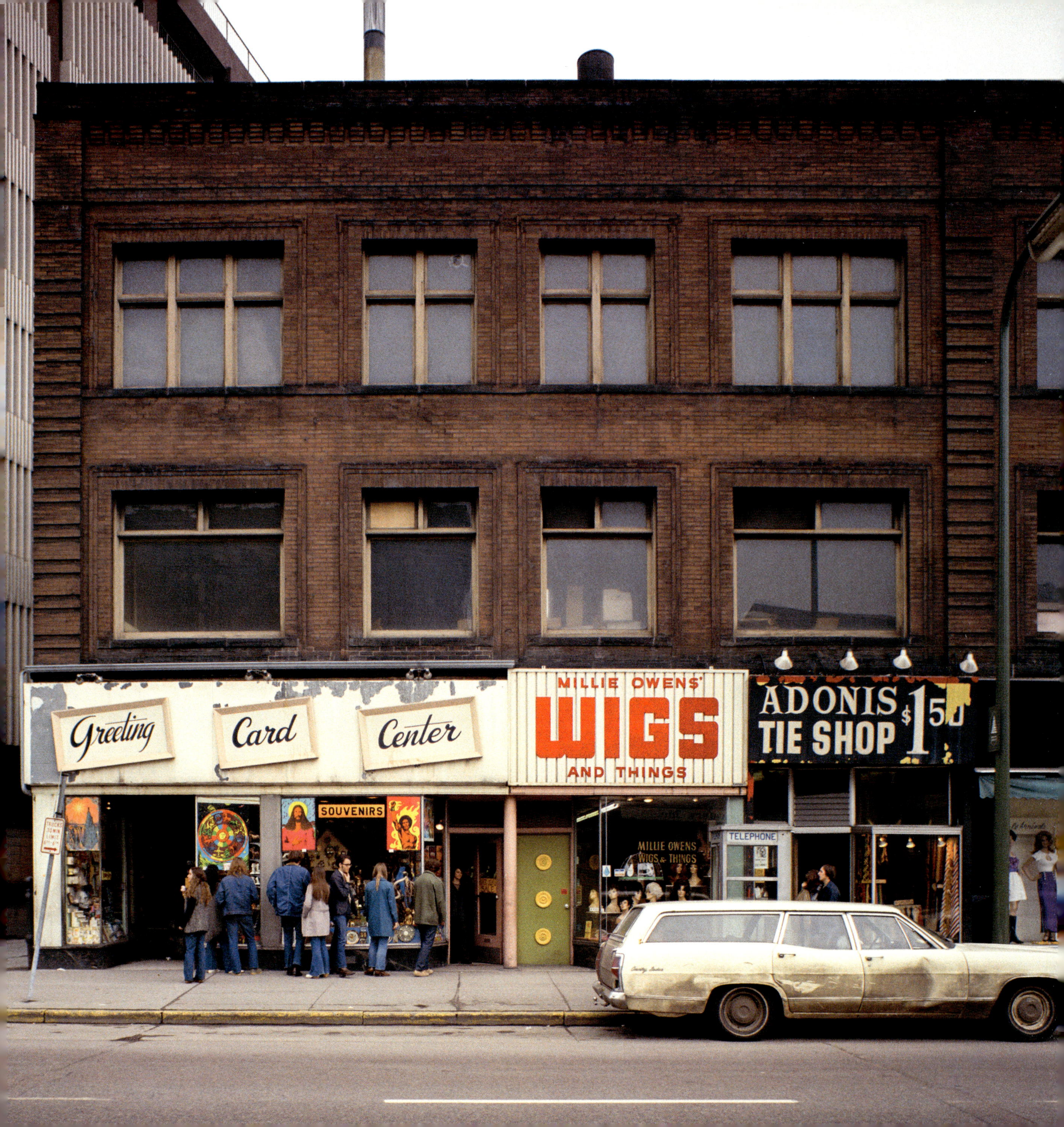
Greeting Card Center
SOUVENIRS
MILLIE OWENS'
WIGS
AND THINGS
ADONIS
TIE SHOP
MILLIE OWENS
WIGS & THINGS
TELEPHONE

You may know the one. It's still there today.

In the end, it's the Park and Shops that defeat the Millie Owens' Wigs and Things and Adonis Tie Shops of the world. Some of the buildings depicted in these pages would be torn down post-1970: Donaldson's (replaced by Gaviidae Common after it burned down in 1982), the World Theater, Venice Café, and all the rest of the old Block E (torn down in 1988 and turned into a surface parking lot before being replaced by the new Block E structure in 2001, transformed into Mayo Clinic Square in 2015), and Powers department store (replaced by Dain Rauscher Plaza in 1992).

However, upon some reflection on Millie Owens' and Adonis, you can also see that while those businesses are gone, the charming brick building that housed them still stands. This building was home to the Taste of Thailand restaurant for many years, until it closed in 2015. There's little doubt that a new restaurant will open in that space in short order. As a piece of real estate, it's too valuable for anything else to happen. While the signage has changed, it's unmistakably the same building, and vacant or not, it's most likely not going anywhere. Despite the obvious exceptions noted above, by 1970 most of the physical infrastructure that was going to be torn down had already been torn down. The vast majority of that was done in the 1950s and '60s. By the early 1970s, if you were an old building downtown and you'd managed to avoid the wrecking ball up to that point, you had a fighting chance at sticking around for another forty years.

This isn't to downplay the incredible out-of-time quality of the photos collected here. The city has transformed greatly since these images were snapped. But it's also that very quality of these images seeming *just* out of reach that makes them so appealing. I used to catch a bus at Eighth and Hennepin, a streetscape captured in one of Mike's photos. I used to stare down this same vista, past the Orpheum and State Theater to the Plymouth Building on Sixth Street. I look at this photo, and while the signage and billboards are unfamiliar, the underlying bones of the buildings and city streets are not. It's like peering at a recognizable scene through a thick veil of fog.

In many respects, the early 1970s were a sort of early Monday morning for the city. It was waking up with a rotten hangover after a weekend of ostentatious, furniture-smashing abandon. Beginning around 1955, when General Mills fled the downtown core for the western suburbs, the city's leaders feared that the postwar suburban exodus of businesses, corporations, and residents would leave downtown empty and economically unviable, a desiccated husk left to crumble into the Mississippi River. The modern downtown, it was decided, would have to look and function more like a suburban campus than a crowded, filthy, nineteenth-century cityscape. "Creating a corporate city required new modern buildings to serve the needs of financial institutions and the emerging information industries," wrote Judith Martin and Antony Goddard in their 1989 account of the Twin Cities' urban renewal efforts, *Past Choices/Present Landscapes*. "If downtown Minneapolis . . . had to be completely rebuilt to accommodate those new functions, then that is what would be done." Ground zero for this transformation was a seedy, perpetually down-on-its-luck neighborhood of bars and flophouses variously known as the Lower Loop and the Gateway District—the blocks around Hennepin Avenue

Opposite: Retail shops on Seventh Street, just off Hennepin Avenue

and Washington Avenue, not far from the post office where Mike worked.

With a few notable exceptions, the dozen or so blocks of the Gateway District were very rundown areas in the mid-twentieth century, populated primarily by transient day laborers (of the more than seventeen hundred residents that had to be relocated, only forty were women). Very little new construction had happened in this area since the 1920s, and much of what was left from that time had aged badly. *It looks rotten*, city fathers said, from both an economic and aesthetic perspective. *No wonder everyone wants to drive to the suburbs and do their shopping there.*

The work of urban renewal happened quickly. All said, in a single decade, one hundred eighty buildings, housing about three hundred businesses—a lot of liquor stores, missions, and bars but also some independent businesses catering to lonely, unattached men, like one-chair barbershops, hardware stores, and tailors—were leveled. When it was over, the area was unrecognizable. "It used to be that I never had to look at a street sign down there," wrote *Star* columnist Bob Murphy after the extensive urban renewal efforts utterly transformed the streetscape. "There were always plenty of landmarks. The landmarks are practically all gone now, though, and I find myself gaping at street signs to figure out just exactly where I am."

The project was capped by perhaps the most notorious architectural destruction in the city's annals: the demolition of the stately old Metropolitan Building, located at Second Avenue South and Third Street, in 1961. "A monstrosity," declared one city attorney, "in the eyes of most observers." The building was structurally sound and even had tenants; it was just old, very unfashionable, and in the way. Architectural critic and historian Larry Millett reported that the doomed building's engineer, Wally Marotzke, made the following invocation on the evening of the Metropolitan's destruction: "The future generations are gonna read about this building and they'll see some of the buildings they're putting up here and they'll damn us, they will, for tearing down the Met." Marotzke was prescient. Two generations on, and we do damn them. (Ironically, perhaps, the offices of the Minneapolis Housing and Redevelopment Authority, which oversaw the Gateway project, were located in the Metropolitan Building.)

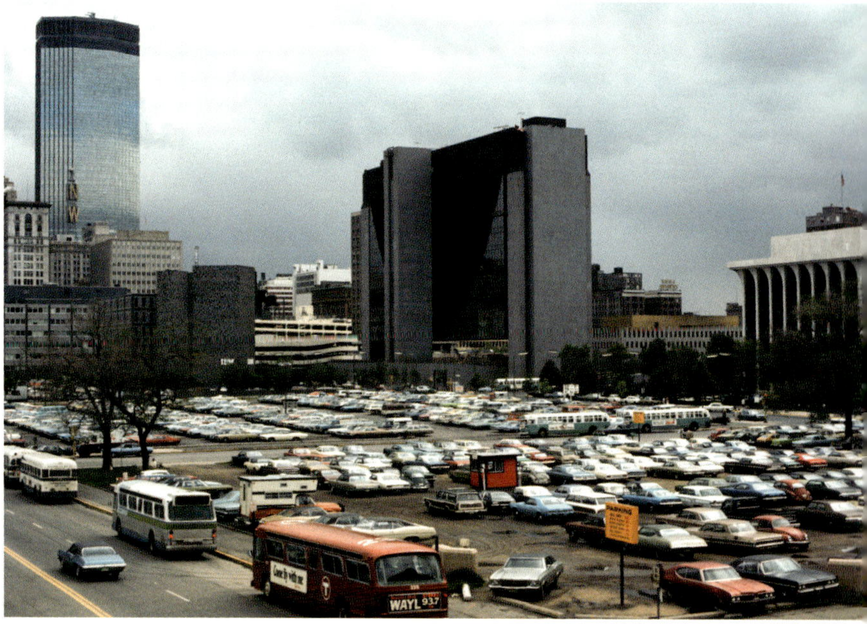

Downtown landmarks—the IDS Tower, the Federal Reserve, and the Northwestern National Life building—viewed from the post office on First Street

The area of most radical change also happens to

be the one in which Mike primarily made his photos. "Nearly all of these images were taken within a rectangular area of Minneapolis between Hennepin Avenue and Nicollet Mall, bounded on the north by the post office and on the south by Ninth Street," he writes. "I rarely strayed outside that area. Further, the photos can be divided pretty clearly into those taken on or near Hennepin, and those taken on the mall. The former tend to be grittier and perhaps more 'historical' in nature, while the latter are more about people and shopping and community. Essentially, these photos are a walk through time and space, within that very interesting rectangle."

Mike's carefully defined zone of interest—his interesting rectangle—is the space in which the most drastic efforts of the urban renewal era took place. But his photos do not tell the story of that era. The redevelopment efforts were "dramatic and they were heralded by city officials, and by most residents," write Goddard and Martin. "Few complained when slums left from the nineteenth century were removed. But by the late 1960s the ideas that had fostered urban renewal were being questioned by residents. . . . Urban renewal, in its traditional guise, was abandoned as a tool for civic improvement in the early 1970s."

That is, abandoned right about the time Mike stepped off the 4A bus with his camera to document the city around him. His photos tell the story of this era, often overshadowed by the extremes of the 1960s.

The flashy new buildings that sprang up on the ruins of the old Gateway District—the Northwestern National Life building, the Sheraton-Ritz Hotel, the first skyways—were already in place; others, like the new Federal Reserve building, were completing their

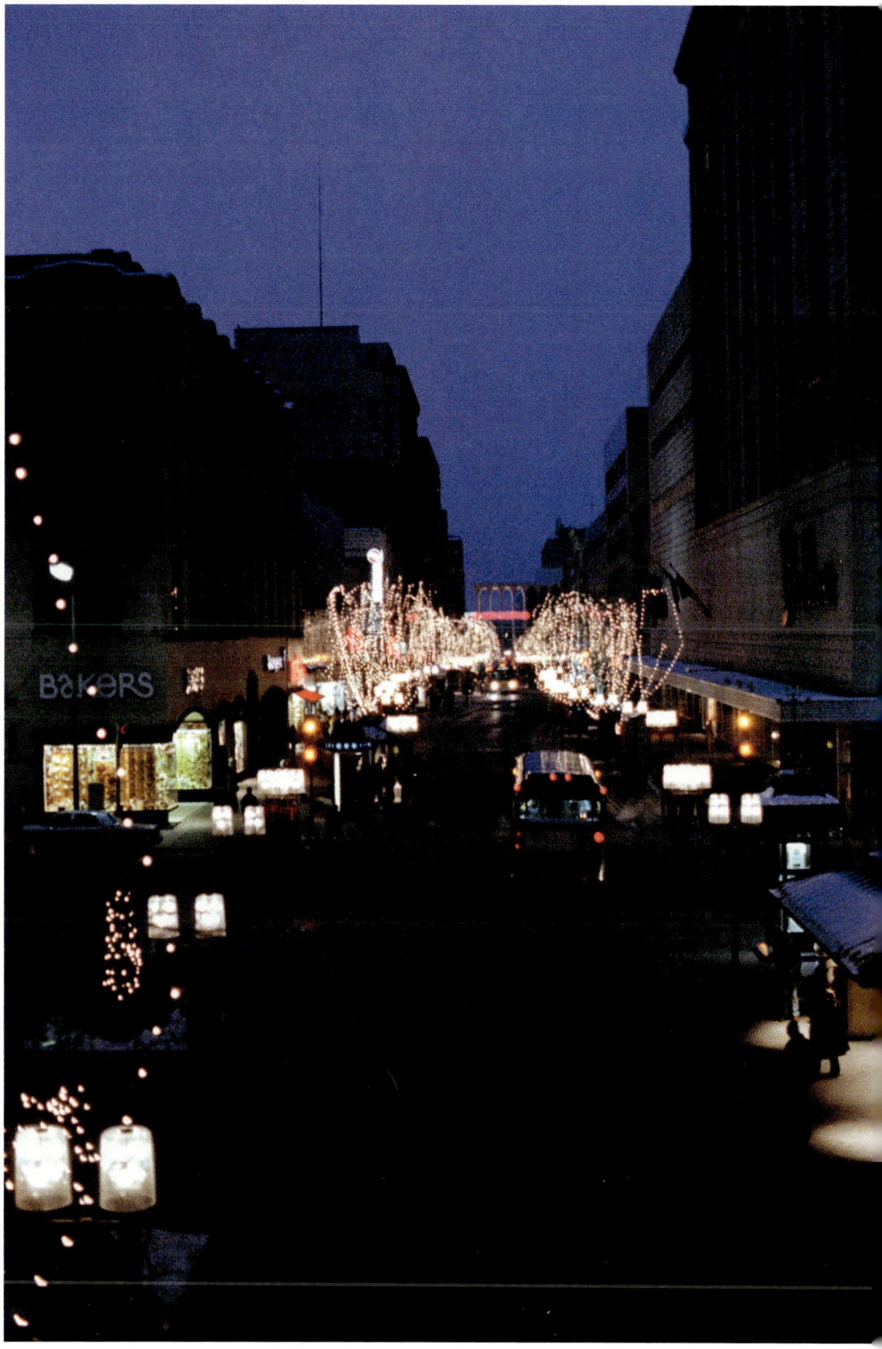

Nicollet Mall decorated for Christmas

ascent as Mike photo-documented their construction. Mike's Minneapolis is one that had organized itself around a less drastic large-scale development project: Nicollet Mall. Although, as Goddard and Martin point out, there was already a growing sense that perhaps the more extreme urban renewal efforts of the 1960s had been a mistake, Nicollet Mall was as popular as ever with Minneapolitans.

Nicollet Mall forms the heart and soul of Mike's photos from this period. As much as you can tell that young Mike enjoys the buses and side streets and raucous stretches of Hennepin Avenue, he truly comes alive on Nicollet. Which makes sense: it's everything a city in the 1970s was supposed to be. It was lively, it was clean, and it was modern. The mall, created in the mid-1960s by a group of downtown merchants and city leaders and spearheaded by the Dayton family, was perhaps the most celebrated local public space of the day. The fact is, it *did* succeed in bringing shoppers and tourists downtown in large numbers. For the first time since the

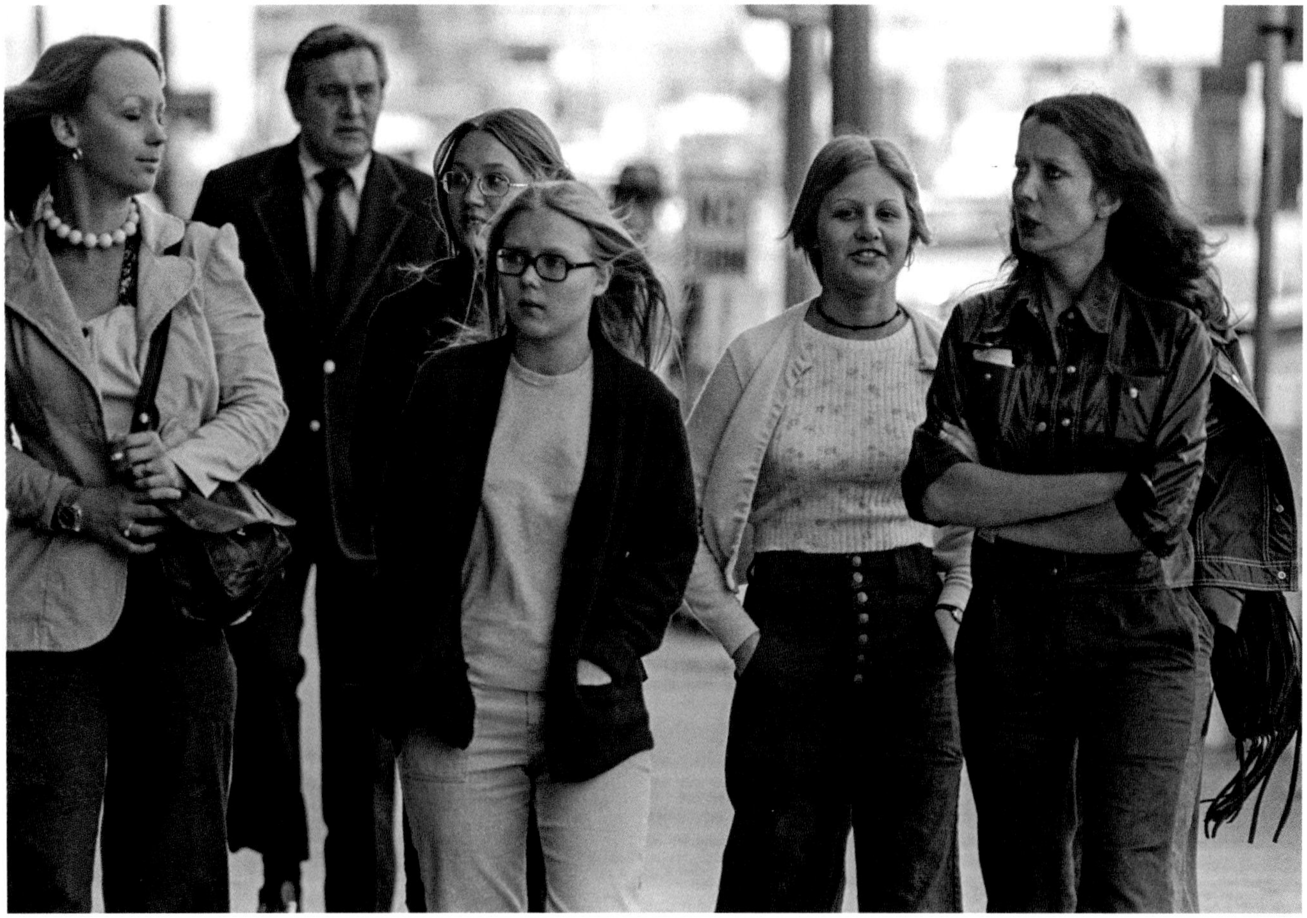

Pedestrian activity downtown

early twentieth century, Nicollet Avenue was the commercial and spiritual center of the city.

Pictorial spreads of people out on the mall were a regular feature in the region's newspapers and magazines. "There are always people watchers and IDS building watchers, bench sitters and newspaper readers, walkers and strollers," read one such account in the *Tribune* from 1971. "The music from the bus stops invites toe-tapping as well as just listening. The store windows invite window shopping." (It reads, in fact, like a catalog of Mike's images.) Barbara Flanagan made note of a whole constellation of amenities in her 1973 book, *Minneapolis:* "Note as you walk that the Mall is dotted in every block with fountains, benches, flower beds, trees, heated bus shelters, sculptures, and regularly, special events such as art shows, concerts and folk festivals." It was, she proclaimed, an "answer to the suburban shopping center."

The praise and attention for Nicollet Mall also came from outside the state. In 1973, as a sort of victory lap, the *Star* reprinted an editorial from the *New York Times* singing the praises of urban pedestrian and transit malls generally and of Nicollet Mall specifically. These sorts of projects, the Paper of Record begrudgingly conceded, were "working well in, of all places, Minneapolis."

"Nicollet Mall, designed by San Francisco architect Lawrence Halprin," the editorial continued, "has helped make Minneapolis the place to visit nowadays if you're interested in really understanding how architecture and urban design (inseparable processes, really) can revive a downtown."

Sadly, this lively period of pedestrianism may have been more of a last gasp than a harbinger of things to come. When British writer Jonathan Raban visited Minneapolis only a few years later, in 1979, he found a city whose street life had been sucked dry by the skyway system—still nascent in the early 1970s but vastly expanded to cover nearly all of downtown by the end of the decade. "No wonder the streets had seemed empty," he wrote. "The city had gone somewhere else and cunningly hid itself inside its own façade. To go shopping, one had to take the elevator up to this other Minneapolis. It was a completely synthetic urban space."

Left behind in the enthusiasm for Nicollet Mall, perhaps, was Hennepin Avenue. Up until the 1950s, it had been the heart of downtown's theater and entertainment district. By the 1970s, Hennepin Avenue—specifically Block E, between Sixth and Seventh Streets—had settled comfortably into its role as the city's vice district. Even after the redevelopment of the Gateway, Hennepin retained a kind of gritty glamour that even the most concentrated urban renewal efforts couldn't totally erase. A coworker who'd grown up in the Catholic parishes of South Minneapolis once told me the most egregious insult that could be levied against a local kid in the 1970s was "your mother works on Hennepin."

Paeans to Hennepin Avenue (or Block E) don't turn up much in the mainstream media of the day, in the way that one finds them about Nicollet Mall. Mostly it's crime reports, or editorial handwringing about violence, prostitution, porn, and vice. You can thumb through a whole stack of tourist brochures and restaurant guides from the period—running the gamut from 1971's *The Twin Cities Explored* to 1976's *Whitman's Restaurant Guide to Minnesota*—and it's as if Hennepin Avenue between Ninth Street and Washington Avenue doesn't exist. Not a single listing for any restaurant or attraction anywhere in the area. There are no explicit warnings,

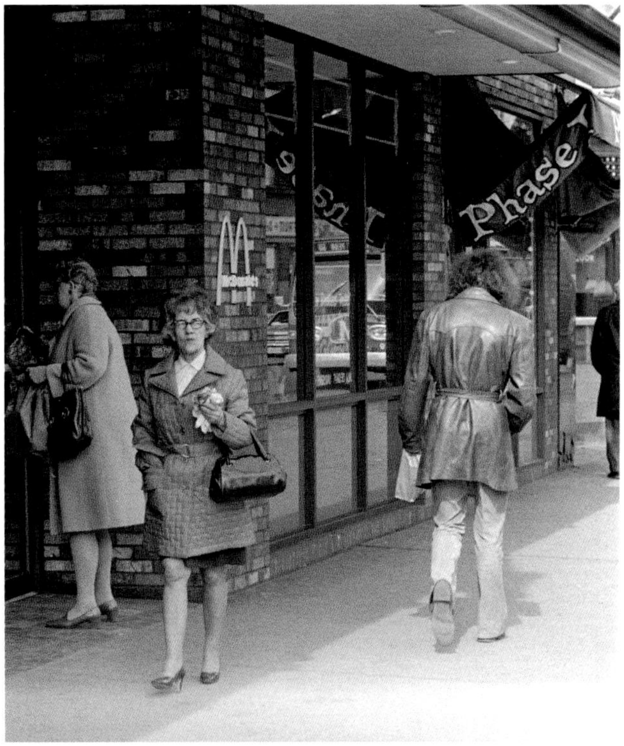

Old and young outside the McDonald's on Hennepin

but the message is pretty clear: *Stay away, tourists and conventioneers!* For the purposes of civic boosterism, Hennepin Avenue may as well not have existed.

Comedian Lizz Winstead, who as a teenager in the mid-1970s would hang around downtown, gives a taste of the scene when she recalls in her memoir, *Lizz Free or Die*, that her mother described the stretch of Hennepin Avenue around Block E as "a morality-free zone." The area was made up of "a few flophouses, a pinball arcade, and a headshop. And, of course, a McDonald's." Moby Dick's, a bar most famous for its six hundred or so police calls a year, was the center of the action. It was, Winstead writes, a venue frequented by "bikers, pimps, hookers, and a lot of other folks with lesser ambitious career aspirations. . . . Moby's had a big clear jar on one end of the bar filled with AA chips, because at Moby's if you came in and dropped your AA chip in the jar, you drank all day for free."

When Block E was razed in 1988—the final step in a process that began with the demolition of the Gateway District three decades earlier—the old buildings were replaced by a parking lot, which held the spot for more than a decade. Then, in 2001, a new suburban-style development went up to house a series of chain businesses, including a multiplex cinema, the first downtown movie house in years. Each of these businesses died undignified deaths, one by one, until there were virtually no tenants left by the middle of the 2010s. Compared to that sad story, the cultural memory of the old Block E has softened in recent years into something almost resembling nostalgia: the city's last bastion of authenticity, a public space that, compared to the niceties of Nicollet Mall, was resolutely *not* clean and *not* modern. Winstead's passages about Hennepin voice her teenage enthusiasm for the place loud and clear, positing it as a thrilling alternative to the rest of the city, which she dismissively termed "Lutheran-occupied territory."

Mike's shots capture this quality, but also something more complex. The photos along Hennepin depict a city much less fresh scrubbed, but it's not necessarily the tourist-scaring hellhole we've come to expect from contemporary accounts or latter-day recollections. It's business as usual: a menagerie of commuters, buses, signage, panhandlers, pedestrians, storefronts, and bars. Mostly, it looks how we expect a city to look, even if cities looked less and less like this over the last few decades of the twentieth century.

The consensus today about this earlier period of urban renewal—especially as relates to the Gateway—is that it was unnecessarily ruinous, ripping out an important piece of the urban fabric and replacing it with parking lots and bland, modern high-rises. However, at the time, these types of large-scale projects—both in the Gateway District and on Nicollet Mall—gave Minneapolis a reputation as a progressive, forward-thinking city. It was a corporate city, one that was "willing to take big risks," as one contemporary commentator noted. That's still the Minneapolis we sometimes brag about today: the clean, high-functioning, and progressive land of charitable giving, corporate volunteerism, and the 5% Club.

When Mike mentions the Hennepin/Nicollet split in his photos—the grittier and more historic on the Hennepin side, the commercial and community focused on the Nicollet side—he's reflecting the split in the city's spirit, perhaps true now but certainly very true at the dawn of the 1970s.

He's moving through the city at a time when "urban renewal," in the 1960s sense, is mostly finished, a completed project. Minneapolis is caught up in the bright and lively spirit consistent with the opening credits of *The Mary Tyler Moore Show*, a place where shoppers find whatever they need on the mall, and crane their necks heavenward to see the top of the mighty IDS Tower, the tallest building between Lake Superior and the Pacific Ocean. This is the Minneapolis of the triumphalist *Time* magazine cover of 1973, declaring that "The Good Life" had an address, and that address was Minnesota. Right at the heart of the so-called Minnesota Miracle was Minneapolis, *a city*, it was said, *that worked.*

At the same time, it's a city that's neither totally scrubbed nor divested of its wilder roughneck qualities. Old-timers used to refer to the western edge of the area Mike walked as "the real avenue": the heart of an authentic, hardscrabble city that civic leadership wanted to scrub away. In Mike's photos, there's a lingering quality of urban grit. "Action almost 24 hours a day," is how Dick Chapman described it in a 1977 eulogy for the old days, a *wink-wink* embedded in his use of the word *action*. "Always humming," he continued, "as the melting pot, as the center of the universe for every bindlestiff, Working-Joe or Bon Vivant of the times." Mike's photos probably don't feature any actual bindlestiffs—that's like a hobo with a sack over his shoulder, I'm pretty certain—but there are plenty of Working-Joes and Bon Vivants around the edges, enduring and

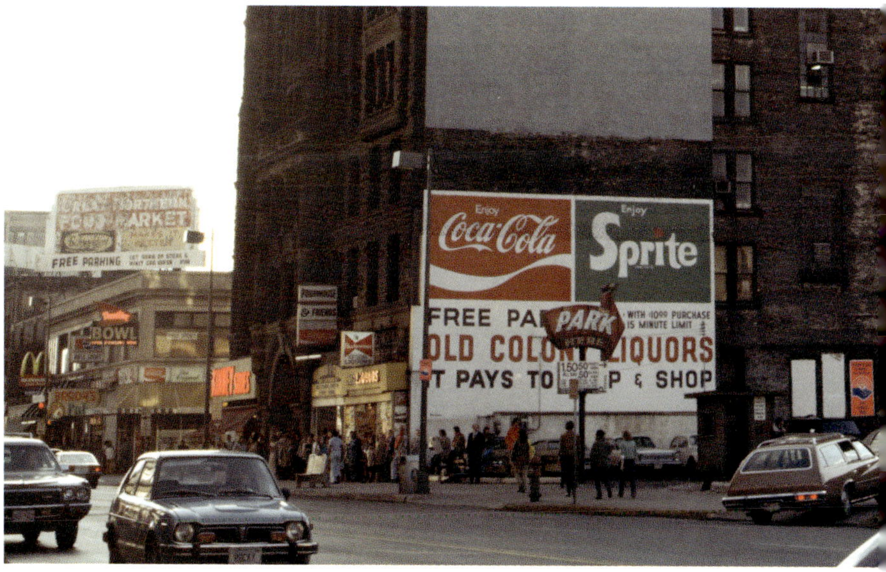

Hennepin Avenue near Sixth Street

thriving in their little corner of the city. Some of them are front and center.

One story about the late poet Frank O'Hara was that he wrote most of his celebrated "Lunch Poems" on a showroom typewriter during his lunch breaks from the Museum of Modern Art in New York City. O'Hara recounted this anecdote himself, writing (in third person) that "this poet, strolling through the noisy splintered glare of a Manhattan noon, has paused at a sample Olivetti to type thirty or forty lines," before eating lunch and then returning to the office.

Employer-mandated limitations, in other words, can go a long way in helping an artist develop his work.

Mike's photos were made under such an employer-mandated limitation for at least two years—a period of some of his best work. Between the time he got off the bus and when he started his shift at the post office, he

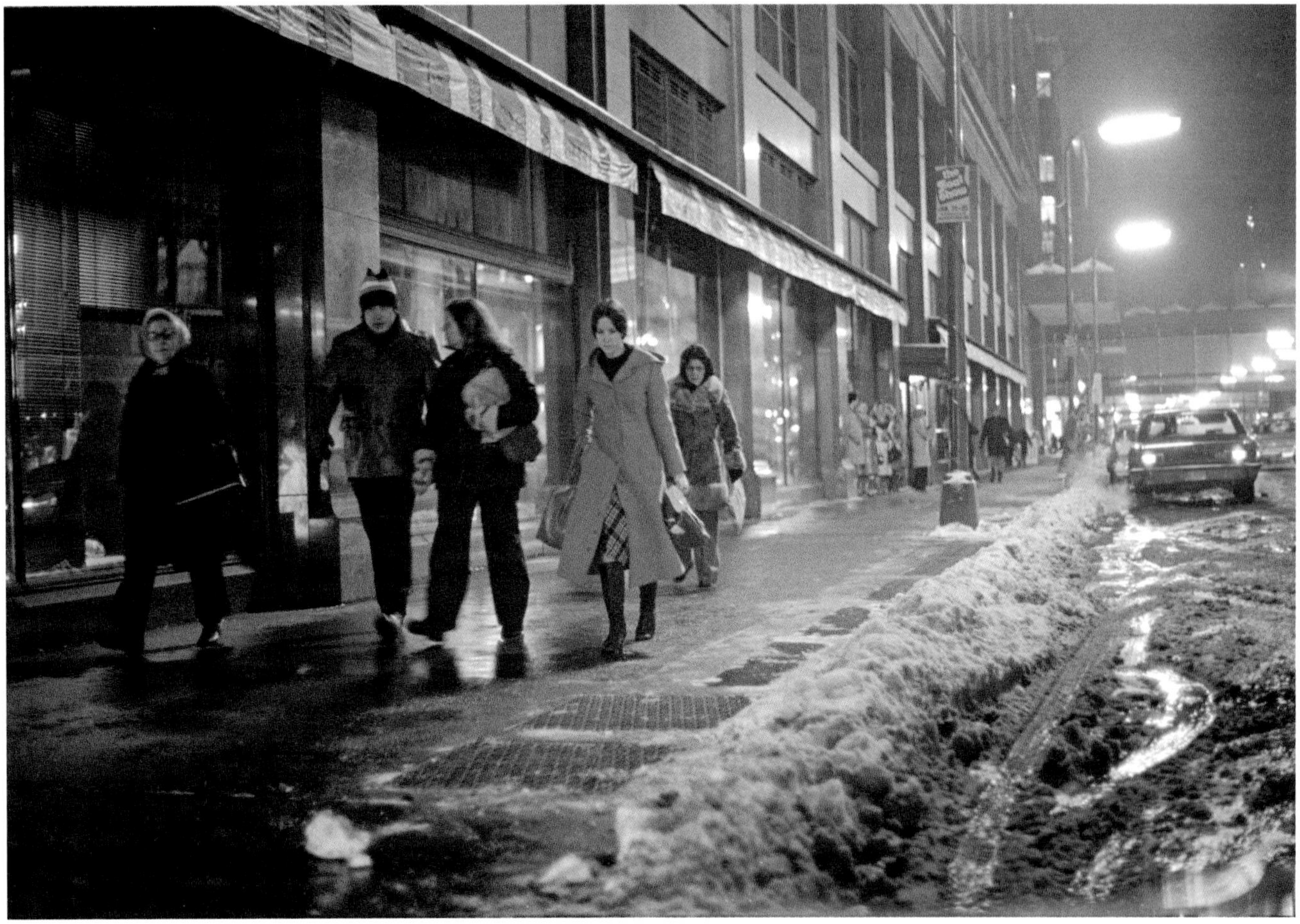

Wintry scene outside Dayton's

had less than two hours to wander through the noisy, splintered glare of downtown Minneapolis to shoot as much film as he could afford to. This schedule, Mike recalls, "gave me some time to kill nearly every afternoon and thrust me and my cameras into the heart of a vibrant city, teeming with excitement. I grew up in a sleepy suburb, so everything was new and fascinating and beautiful." This concentration of time and space may partially explain why Mike stuck to such a limited geographic range. Some of the images stretch as far as Northeast Minneapolis, but most stay in that "interesting rectangle" bounded by Nicollet, Hennepin, Ninth, and Washington. It made his walking beat all the more new and fascinating and beautiful. It concentrated the energy and the experience.

To be sure, there was plenty to see in that time and space. And sight is only one aspect of the sensory perception: "If you can smell the street by looking at the photo," photographer Bruce Gilden once told a reporter, "it's a street photograph." Looking at Mike's photos, you get the sense of not just sights and smells but the full sensory experience—hearing the clomps of heavy boots on pavement and the honks of automobiles, feeling the snow against your face or the smoothness of the store windowpanes under your fingers, tasting the metallic fumes from the buses.

Nicollet, Hennepin, and the blocks in between were full of people on weekday afternoons, a cross-section of the socioeconomic strata of the Twin Cities. Though the city of that period seems startlingly white and Scandinavian (African Americans constituted a little more than four percent of the city's population in 1970), a wide diversity of types of characters is evident in terms of age and social standing. The excitement that Mike must have felt as a teenager—and the excitement we associate with that time—is intoxicating. The girls in short skirts and halter tops and the guys with their long hair and sideburns look loose and free, conforming closely to our image of the era's youth culture.

While a wide array of youth movements were active in the city at the time—a host of antiwar, feminist, indigenous rights, ecological, and food co-op movements—Minneapolis was not in the grips of a youth explosion. Despite its progressive reputation both then and now, this Minneapolis was, in many respects, a homogenous, graying, conservative midwestern city. Its mayor was a former police detective named Charlie Stenvig, whose rise to power on a platform of law and order was largely thanks to an aging constituency embracing Nixonian reactionary politics and an increasingly disillusioned younger constituency checking out of the electoral process.

And so, of all the characters we encounter, it's the older people in Mike's shots who look the most of another world. As far as the young men and women—in their oversized plastic-frame glasses and knit caps and tight pants—are concerned, we feel like we could run into them at the CC Club or a Northeast Minneapolis loft party this upcoming Saturday night. But the elderly men and women, outfitted with babushkas, Coke-bottle glasses, and Brylcreemed hair, look nothing like anyone we might see on the streets now; from the perspective of a person born after 1970, they seem like something from the far distant past. This Minneapolis seems to be a city split in two: one portion inhabited by an older generation and another by the younger one, with very different views on personal expression, style, politics, and social mores. Nonetheless, they all share the same public space. The people in these photos are, for the most part, not focused on one another but rather on simply moving through the city at their own pace, in their own way.

As Mike himself has noted on several occasions, he had a teenage boy's enduring interest in the women of downtown Minneapolis ("bear in mind I was seventeen years old at the time," he explained years later). Of course, in that time and place, he wasn't the only one: the aforementioned *Star* critic Don Morrison devotes an entire page to the subject of springtime girl-watching in a 1966 book he wrote with photographer Jerome Liebling entitled *The Face of Minneapolis*. "Oh, yes,

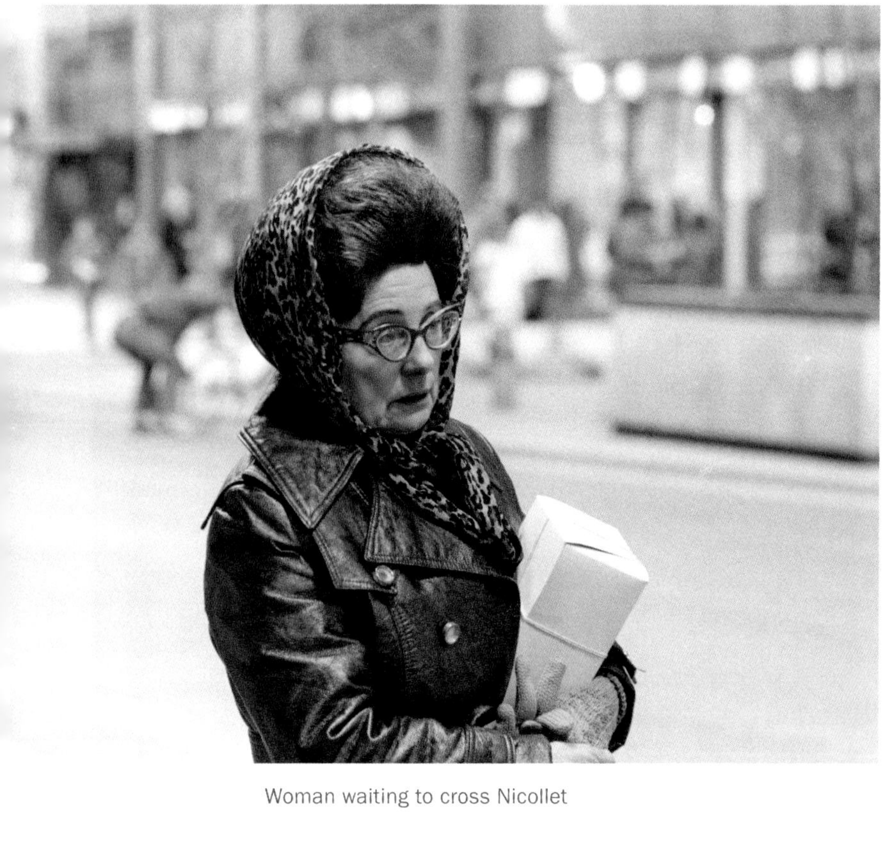

Woman waiting to cross Nicollet

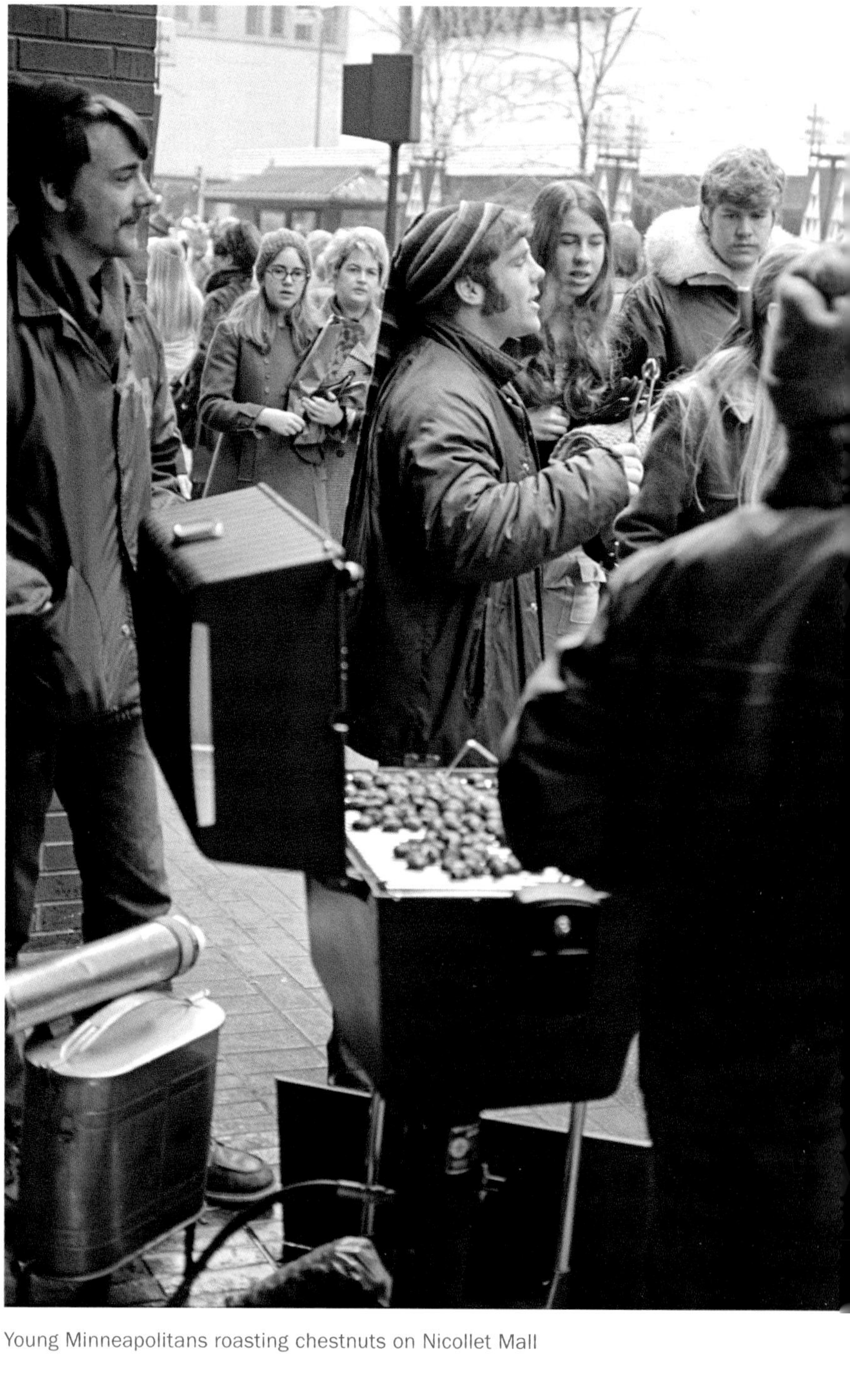

Young Minneapolitans roasting chestnuts on Nicollet Mall

the girls," Morrison writes. "Every street corner, every 20 feet of thoroughfare provides distraction to the eye. Clutches and gaggles and coveys and bevies of pretty girls suddenly seem to spring out of the earth and command attention."

As a shoot-from-the-gut photographer working fast and loose, Mike has an innate empathic eye for all the characters he finds—men, women, children, young people, old people. Nearly all are shot at a distance, and the majority of subjects are unaware, lost in their thoughts or focused on the street ahead of them. Occasionally, Mike will be confronted with a friendly peace sign or a withering glare, but for the most part, his subjects aren't posing for us or even aware of us. They're just getting along. Some of the best are of individuals in some state of repose—sitting on one of the Nicollet Mall benches Barbara Flanagan mentions, or leaning against a wall waiting for a ride.

"For me, cities are enormous bodies of people's desires and I search for my own desires within them, I slice into time, seeing the moment," says Japanese street photographer Daido Moriyama about his work.

For Mike, "my cameras functioned as something of a shield or personal force field, protecting my introverted self, while I put myself out there in the crowd. I could be a little more forward and a little bolder than I would on my own. Snapping a picture of a beautiful girl, for example, might lead to an actual conversation. And somehow it seemed less threatening (or dangerous) to grab a shot of a panhandler or the crazy guy shouting on the sidewalk than to talk to them."

Susan Sontag famously wrote—in fairly dramatic terms—of this in her 1977 book, *On Photography:* "The Photographer is an armed version of the solitary walker, reconnoitering, stalking, cruising in the urban inferno, the voyeuristic stroller who discovers the city as a landscape of voluptuous extremes." Equipped with a camera, photographers can be both of the worlds they move through and apart from them, uniquely empowered to stop time and to capture moments that would otherwise slip away unmarked and unremembered.

Perhaps it's best summarized by Tom Arndt, who's been making street photography in and around the Twin Cities for more than forty years. In his collection *Home*,

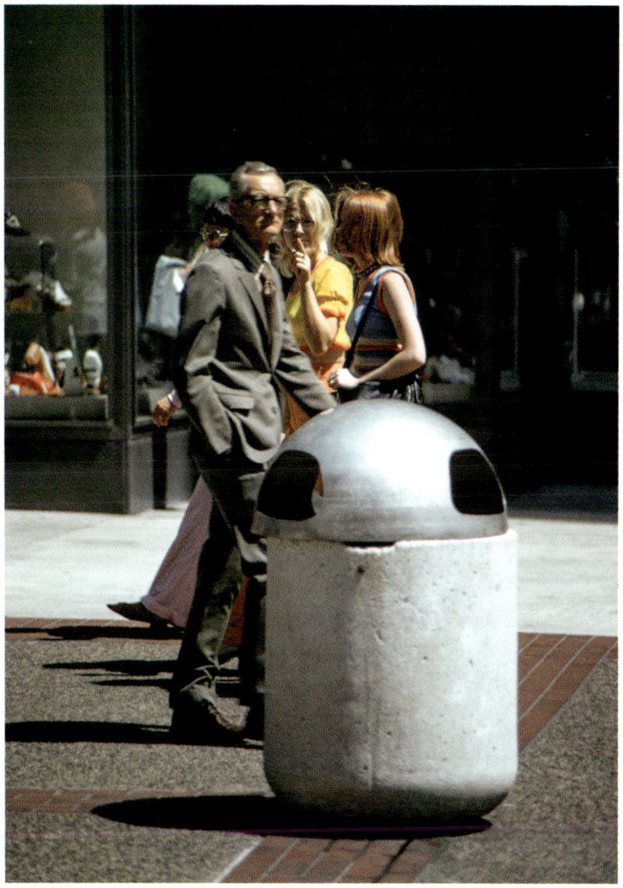

Pedestrians on Nicollet Mall spot the rogue photographer

Arndt writes accompanying commentary to a photo of a woman he's snapped, walking past him on a St. Paul street. It summarizes perfectly not only the experience of a brief street encounter but the time-bending qualities of the best photography: "This is just a snapshot, but it holds my attention. I shared 1/250th of a second with this woman, and she is always right there in that time. Thirty-five years later, but it's still then."

If you live in Minneapolis and use Facebook regularly, there's a decent chance you follow the "Old Minneapolis" page. It's a wildly popular repository for images and video of Minneapolis as it appeared prior to October 18, 1988, the day Block E was demolished, as good a marker as any for the day "the old Minneapolis" came to an end. Started up a few years ago by a local resident named Jesse Jamison, the page has almost 57,000 followers as of early 2015, or about 14 percent of the city's current population. Most of the users are highly engaged.

Any image that goes up—whether it's of an old bar, a long-gone restaurant, a candid family Polaroid, a menu, a business card, a storefront—is followed by a thread of dozens and sometimes hundreds of comments. Most are of the simple "hey, I remember that" variety, but people also tell personal anecdotes, crowd-source questions, and converse back and forth.

Spending a little time on the page is a strangely moving experience. At first, it can seem like simple civic nostalgia for civic nostalgia's sake, but looking further, you're confronted with a sense of yearning that's very powerful. There's this almost overwhelming outpouring of desire from users to remember, preserve, and dissect the past of a city that, traditionally, has always assiduously dismissed its own past for the newer, more modern thing—the dark flip side of being a city that is, as we heard earlier, *willing to take big risks.*

The material you come across on Old Minneapolis is wide ranging. A few are popular historical images you've seen in books or elsewhere, but many are unique objects, fished out of people's closets, file drawers, and old trunks, scanned and uploaded, and seen again for the first time in decades.

I joined the page a few years ago, and one of the things I'd see regularly was street photographs taken in the early seventies by the same person. They were images of people and places, mostly around downtown Minneapolis. Each one had a small credit watermarked on the bottom left-hand side of the photo: © Mike Evangelist.

Mike had started uploading the photos to Flickr a few years earlier. When he discovered the Old Minneapolis Facebook page in about 2012, he realized it was a good fit for his images. Since then, Mike's photos have become perhaps the most popular feature of the page, typically attracting the largest number of comments. Looking at them imparts the quality of being let in on a secret, being granted access to a body of work that you'd stumbled upon by accident. They're not postcard images, or family snapshots, or photojournalistic assignments clipped from glossy magazines of the era. All of these types of images have their own value as artifacts or as works of art, but Mike's photos resonate by standing in the middle of a Venn diagram of two slightly overlapping circles: *interesting, little-seen subject matter* and *quality photographs.* Mass-produced postcard images might put you in the latter, and family snapshots in the former. But not much gets to stand in the middle.

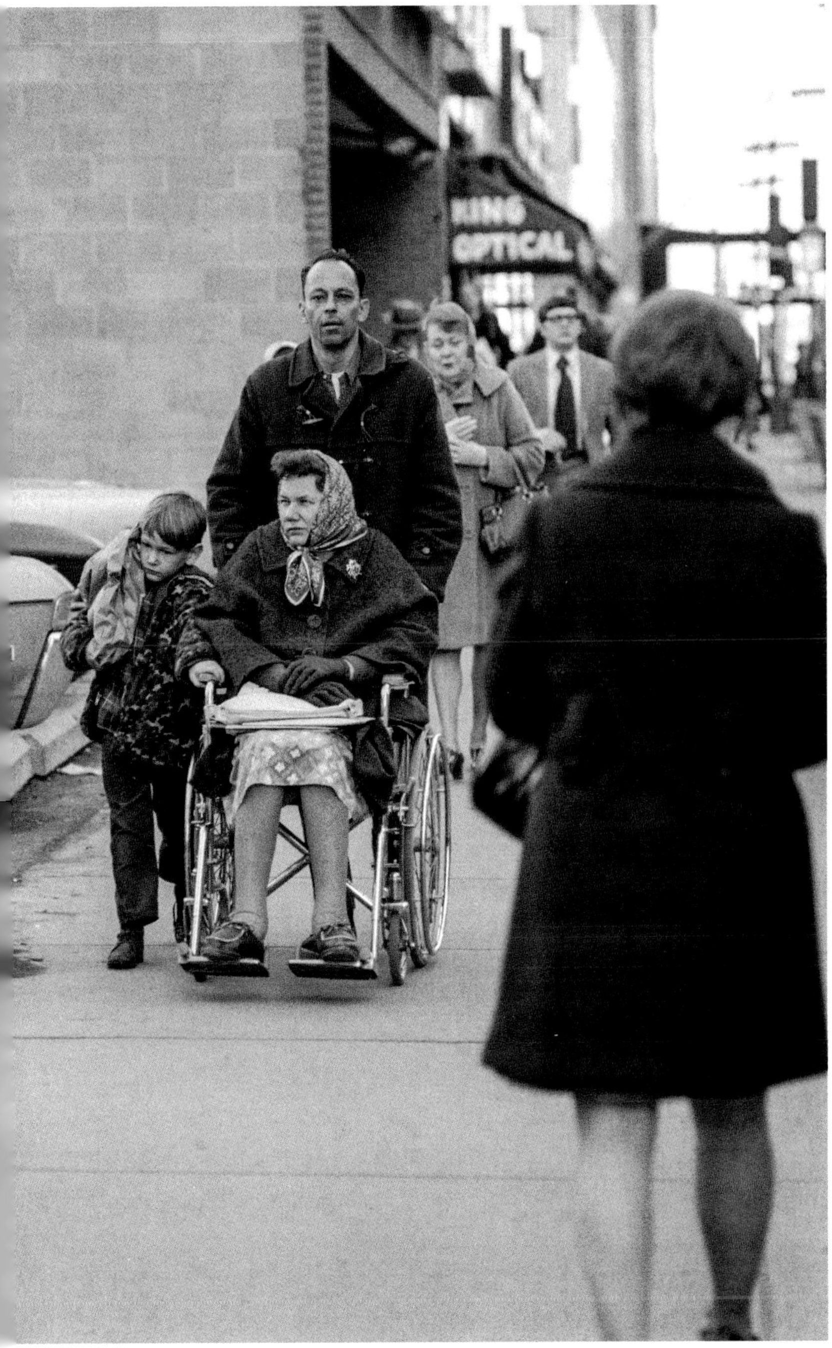

The Bremer family on Hennepin, heading to the bank after work

Aside from the fact that they're excellent images, it's that unfamiliar-but-not-alien quality I noted earlier which is part of what makes these images resonate. If the images were from twenty years earlier, wide swaths of the city they depict would be as unrecognizable to us as they were to Bob Murphy, that *Star* columnist we found wandering through the ruins of the Gateway District looking for disappeared landmarks. If they were twenty years later, it'd be tough to get too excited. The 1990s just aren't distant enough past yet.

But forty years is the sweet spot. Those who were teenagers or young adults at the time Mike snapped these photos have by now firmly entered, or passed, middle age, many of them parents of a new generation of teenagers and young adults reminiscent of those featured in Mike's images and in whom they, perhaps, see their past selves. But even for those who are far younger than these images—and many of the members of the Old Minneapolis group fall in that range—seeing them imparts a thrill of considering what the city looked like in the almost immediate past, before childhood memories of downtown in the 1980s or '90s, just out of reach of their own consciousness.

There's also the matter of these images enjoying a strange and fascinating reincarnation on the Internet. One of my favorite stories relating to this is when Mike received an e-mail about one particular photo posted online: *a man pushing a woman in a wheel chair and a little boy holding onto the armrest*, as the correspondent described it. *That little boy is my husband (and the man and woman my in-laws)! I'd love a copy of that picture.*

Mike sent her the image in high resolution. She replied: *Thank you so much. This is wonderful. My husband said this picture brought back a lot of memo-*

ries of being downtown with his parents making their bank run for his dad's printing business. Very cool that you captured that moment in time. It turned out that the man and woman in the photo owned a print shop downtown near Block E. The image itself was snapped on Hennepin Avenue, two blocks from the store.

The correspondent also sent a photograph of her own: *Here's a picture of them 20 years later, in 1993, the day my husband and I were married. (His parents are both deceased now.)*

Looking at the original image, you may tend to imbue it, as I did, with a certain sense of sadness. The family looks somewhat worn down. The woman is in a wheelchair. The boy clings to her side. Where are they going? Isn't this a sort of rough part of town? Are they going to be okay?

The photo of the same family, two decades on, couldn't be more different: dressed in wedding finery, the parents of the groom beam with pride, aged a bit but unmistakably the same people. It's jarring and a little thrilling to see them in such a different context. It lends some additional generosity to the original interpretation. *Of course they looked worn down*, you realize about the older photo. *It was the end of a workday. They were on their way to the bank. They were probably exhausted.* Knowing this backstory doesn't make the image any less powerful as a reflection of three people making their way along a downtown street.

It is, however, a reminder that any piece of street photography comes invariably from a personal perspective. It's never an objective truth, or a piece of infallible reportage. It's a scene viewed through one person's eyes, bringing along his or her own experiences and opinions and attitudes. The best of this type of street photography, though, speaks to some universal quality in the scene. In this shot, we see the best of family life: a small unit, sticking close and getting through the day together. It doesn't always look cheery or fun from the outside. But it doesn't have to.

Of course, Mike was behind the lens for all of these images, and he knows what he was thinking for many of them. There's too many to have distinct memories of each individually, four decades on, but there are some good anecdotes. He hasn't added a lot of commentary online or elsewhere. Especially important in this sort of work is that the images speak for themselves, and Mike lets them.

Regarding the *Clockwork Orange* photo written about at the start of this introduction, though, Mike does add the following: "When the movie let out, I was with my buddy and we were walking with a bunch of other people past the Musicland, just by that trash can you can see in the photo, when a drunk or disturbed guy came out of nowhere brandishing a knife. I think he intended to rob us, but there were a lot of people around, making that somewhat ridiculous. A couple guys picked up the trash can and used it as a shield so they could subdue the guy. Then several of us held him and waited until the police arrived."

What happened after?

"I think the police officers in the attached photo were the ones who responded. But I'm not sure, so I probably don't want to be that specific."

The photo of the following scene is labeled "Officer Ken Smith."

Wait, how do you know the cop's name?

"He reached out to me on Facebook." His message: "Mike, the cop on the corner of 7th and Hennepin in 1972 is me. Can I get a copy of that picture? It is great. My grandkids love it. Ken."

By the end of the first week of March 1972, the weather had warmed up slightly. There were some dustings of snow, but by the weekend, the high temperature had inched over freezing into the high thirties. Spring weather was still a few weeks off, but jackets and boots came off all over downtown Minneapolis anyway. *A Clockwork Orange* closed at the World in May after a surprisingly long run of twelve weeks. By then, Mike had finished his junior year of high school. *A Clockwork Orange* was replaced at the Downtown World by Woody Allen's *Play it Again, Sam,* which opened the last week of May.

Don Morrison liked it. The gags, he wrote, were "about 65 percent yockable."

Minneapolitans picked up copies of the paper to read on their bus rides home, or while seated under the shadow of the IDS Tower during their lunch break. Life downtown goes on. We look at these images and we feel, if only for a moment, that we're there with them, too.

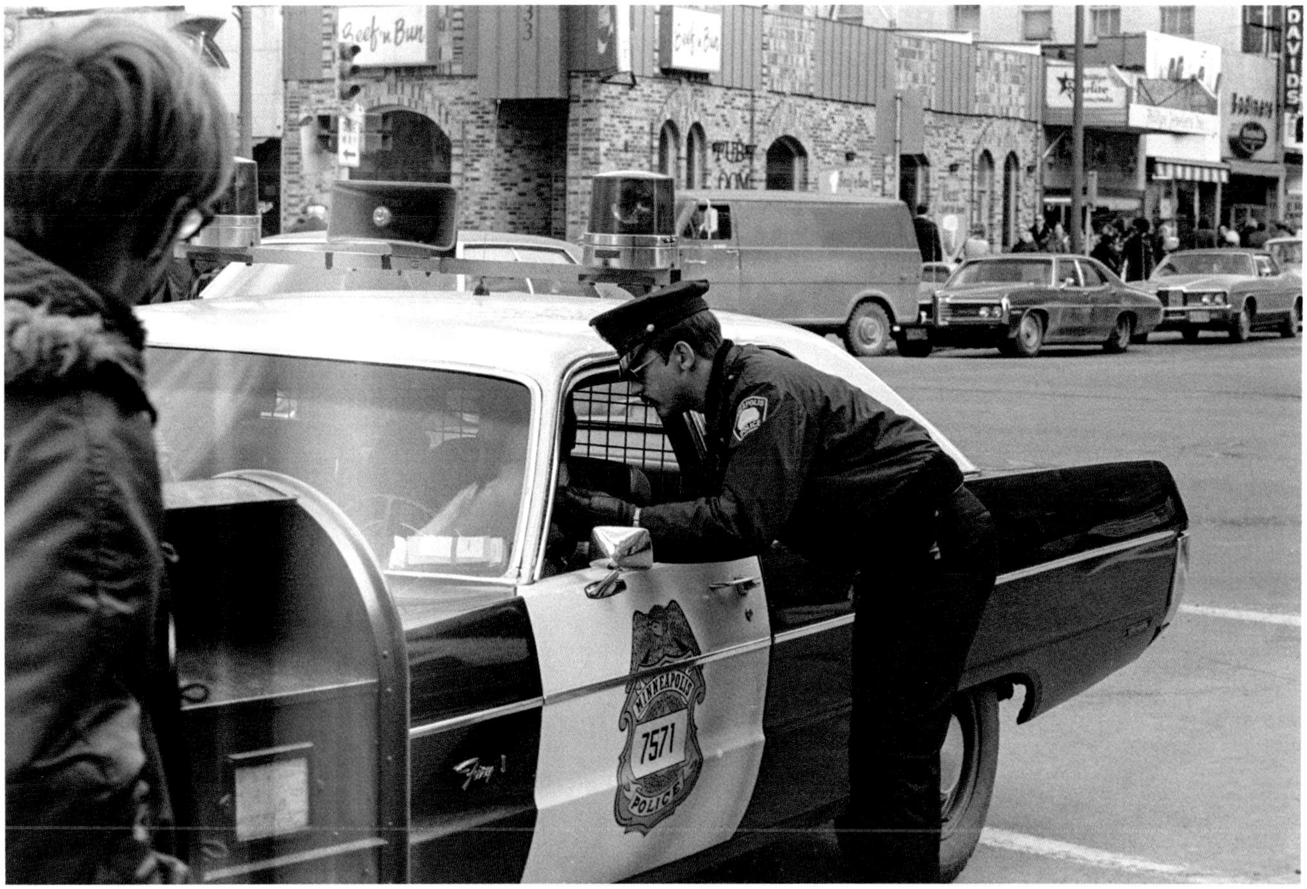

Officer Ken Smith conferring with another officer on Hennepin Avenue

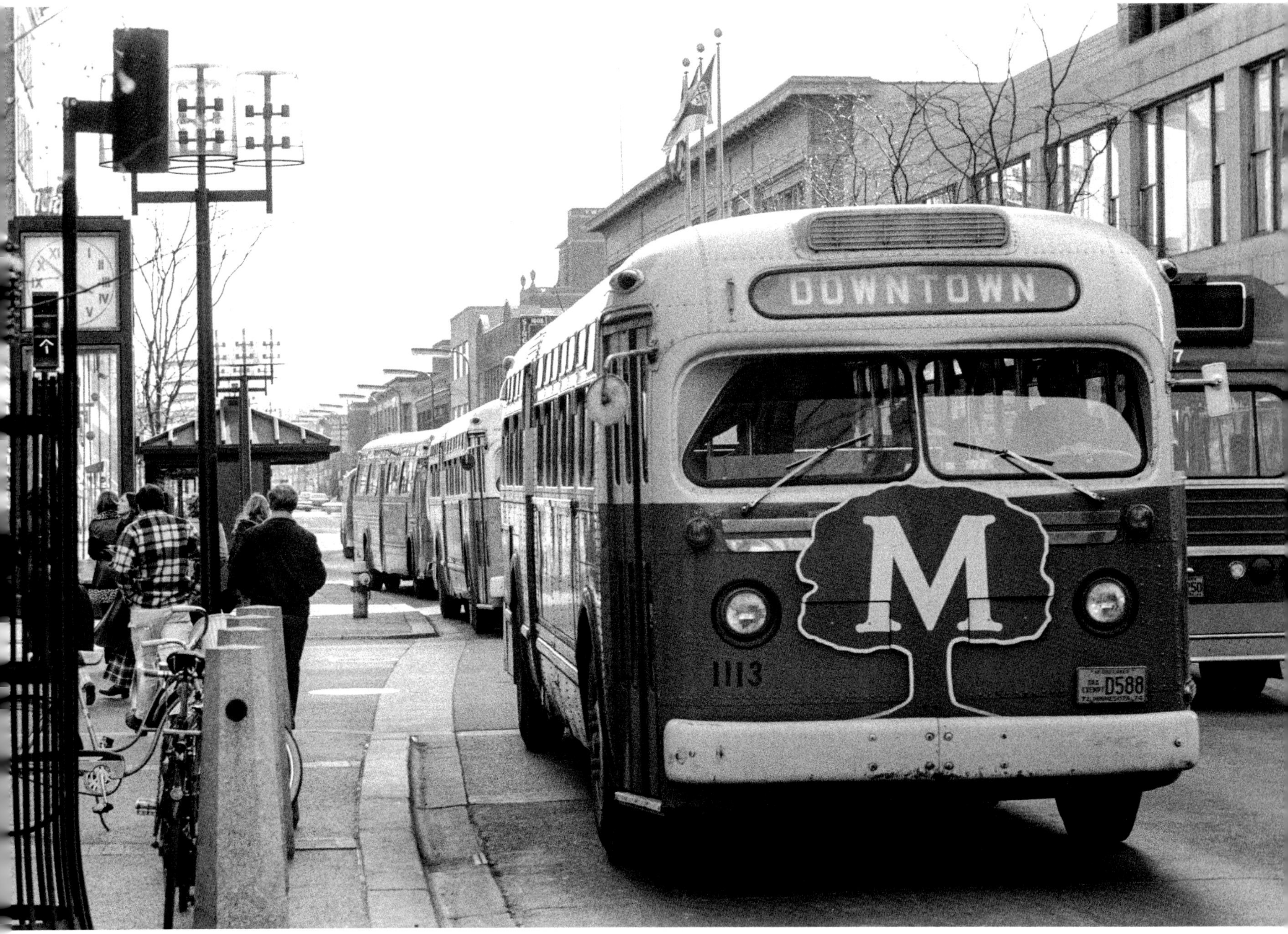

A caravan of buses on Nicollet Mall

PHOTO GALLERY

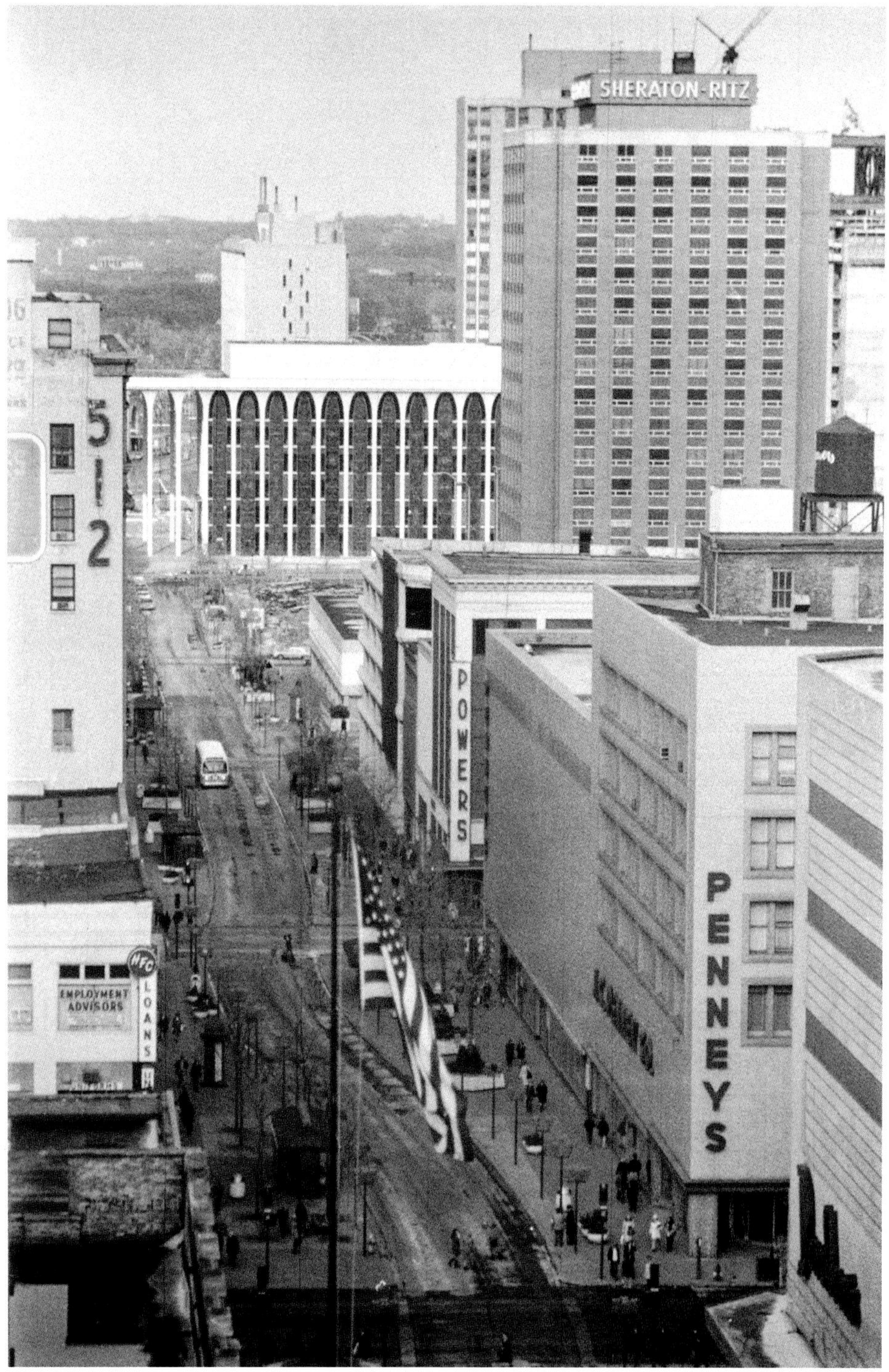

Nicollet Mall viewed from the twelfth floor of Dayton's department store

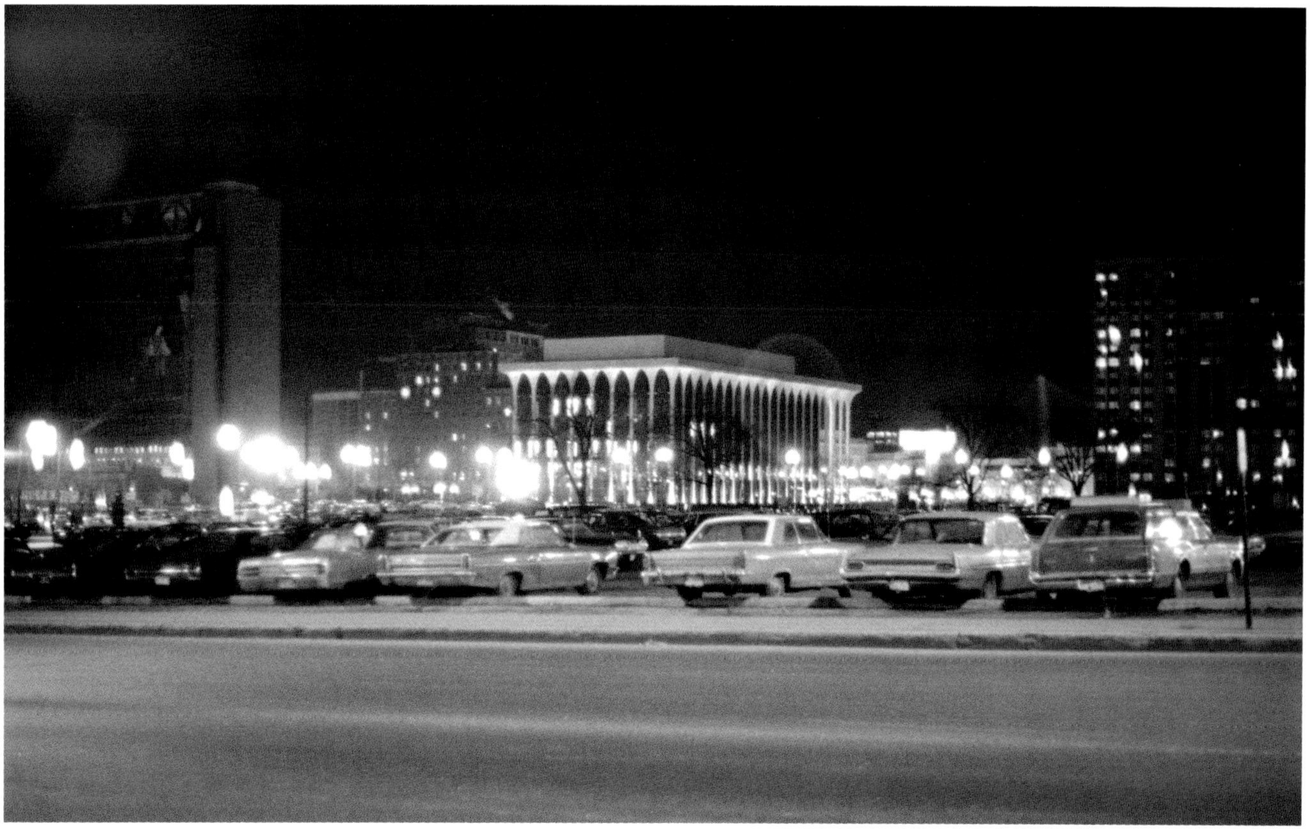

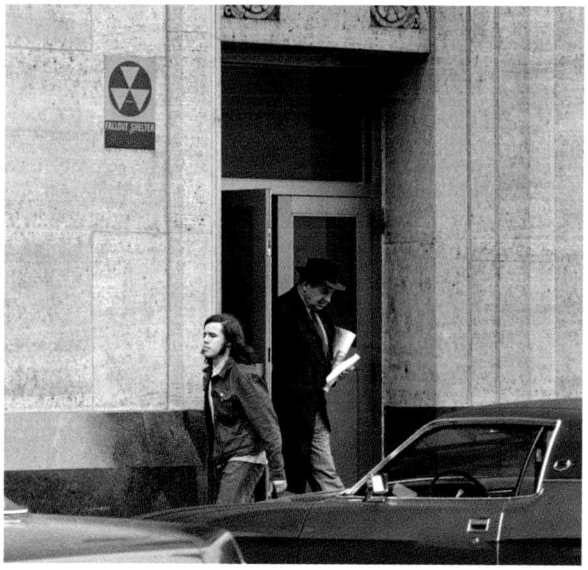

Above: Parking lot at night, near First Street South

Right: Old and young employees leaving the post office

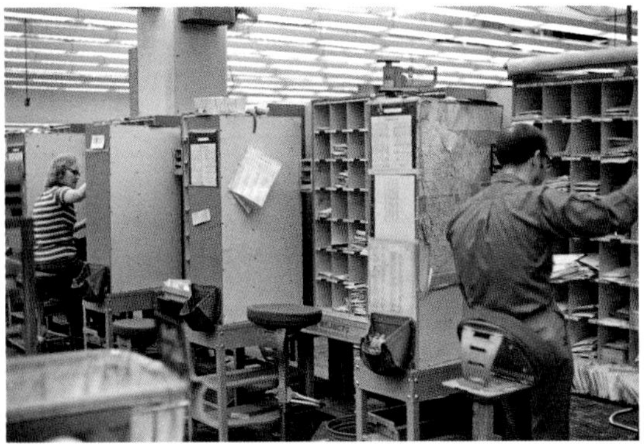
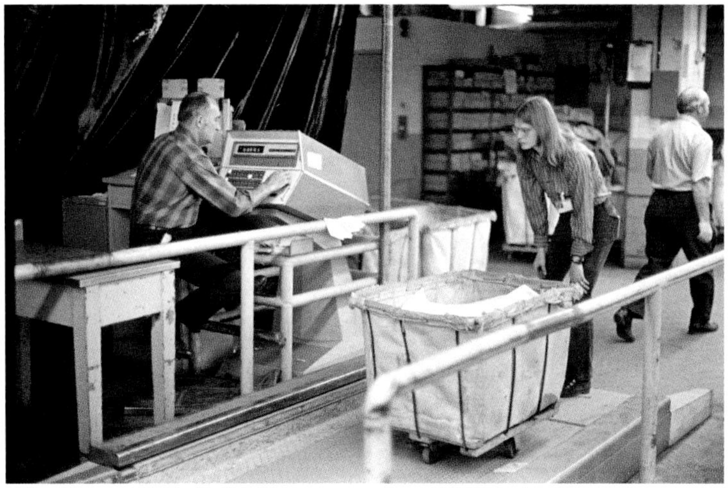
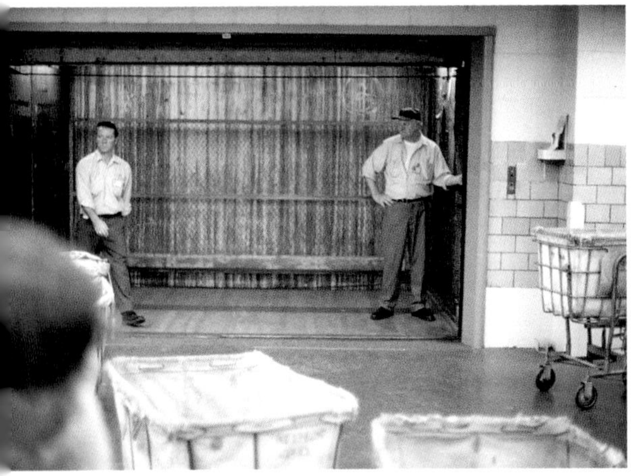
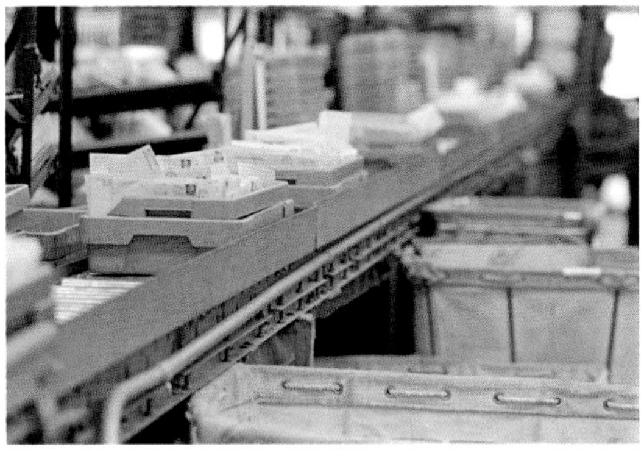
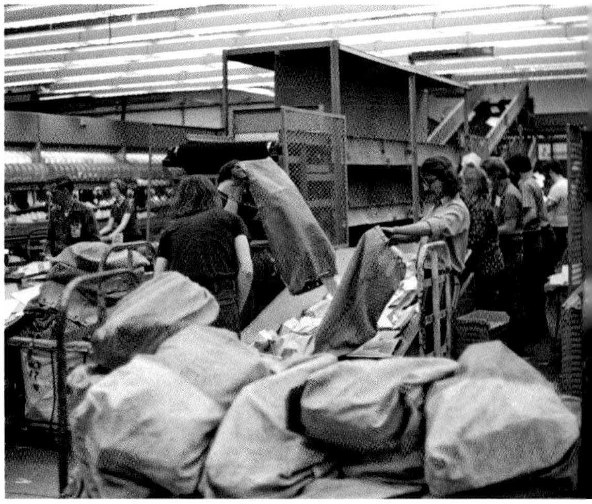
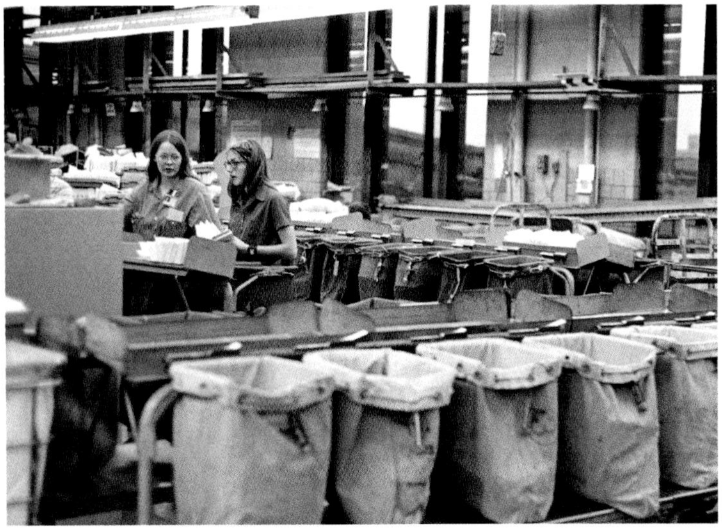
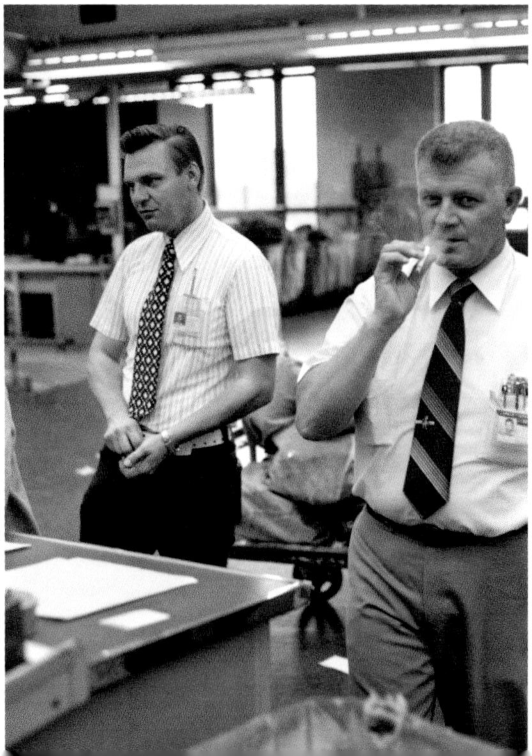
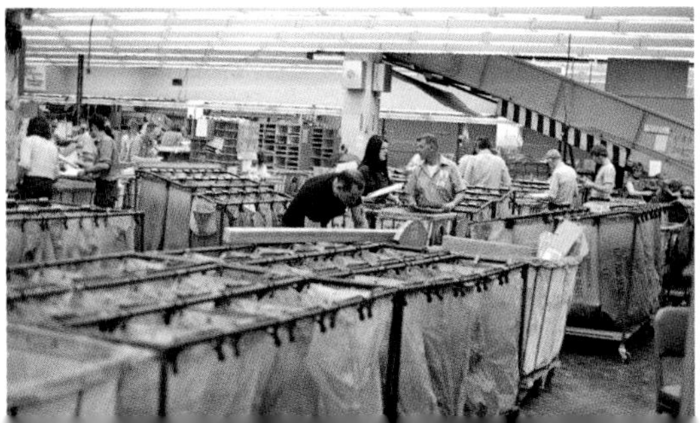

"My job as postal assistant at the main Minneapolis post office brought me downtown nearly every day for two years—the period when most of the photos in this book were shot. Typically I spent my shift working the 'culling belt.' This was where all the mail picked up from mailboxes around the city was dumped onto a big conveyor belt and then sorted, by hand, onto three other conveyor belts: one for packages, one for 'flats,' and one for normal letters. From there they moved on to other people and machines for further sorting. It was hard, dusty work, but it paid pretty well and certainly beat my previous job at Burger Chef. Today it would be unthinkable that someone could wander around a government facility with a camera and shoot these sorts of behind-the-scenes photos. But back then, no one gave me a second thought."

MIKE EVANGELIST

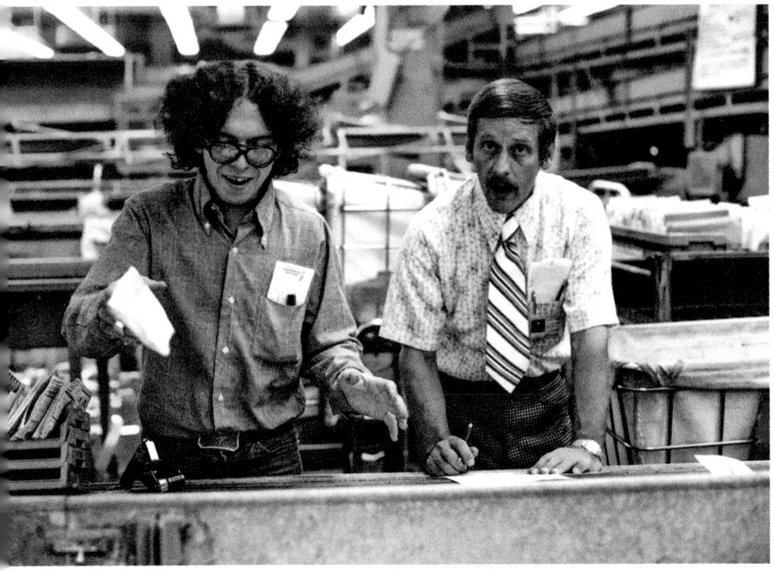

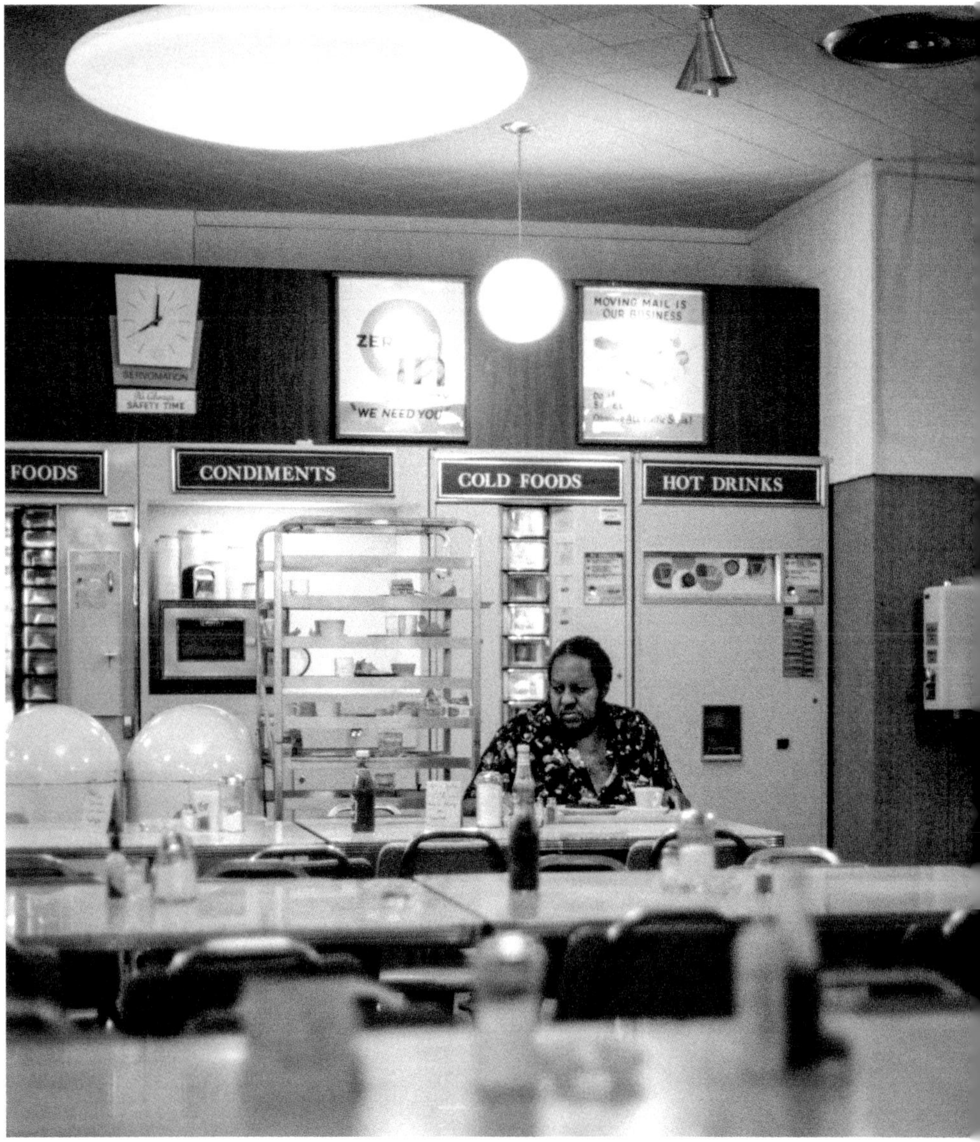

Above: The post office break room, featuring "Servomation"

Opposite: Various scenes from inside the downtown post office

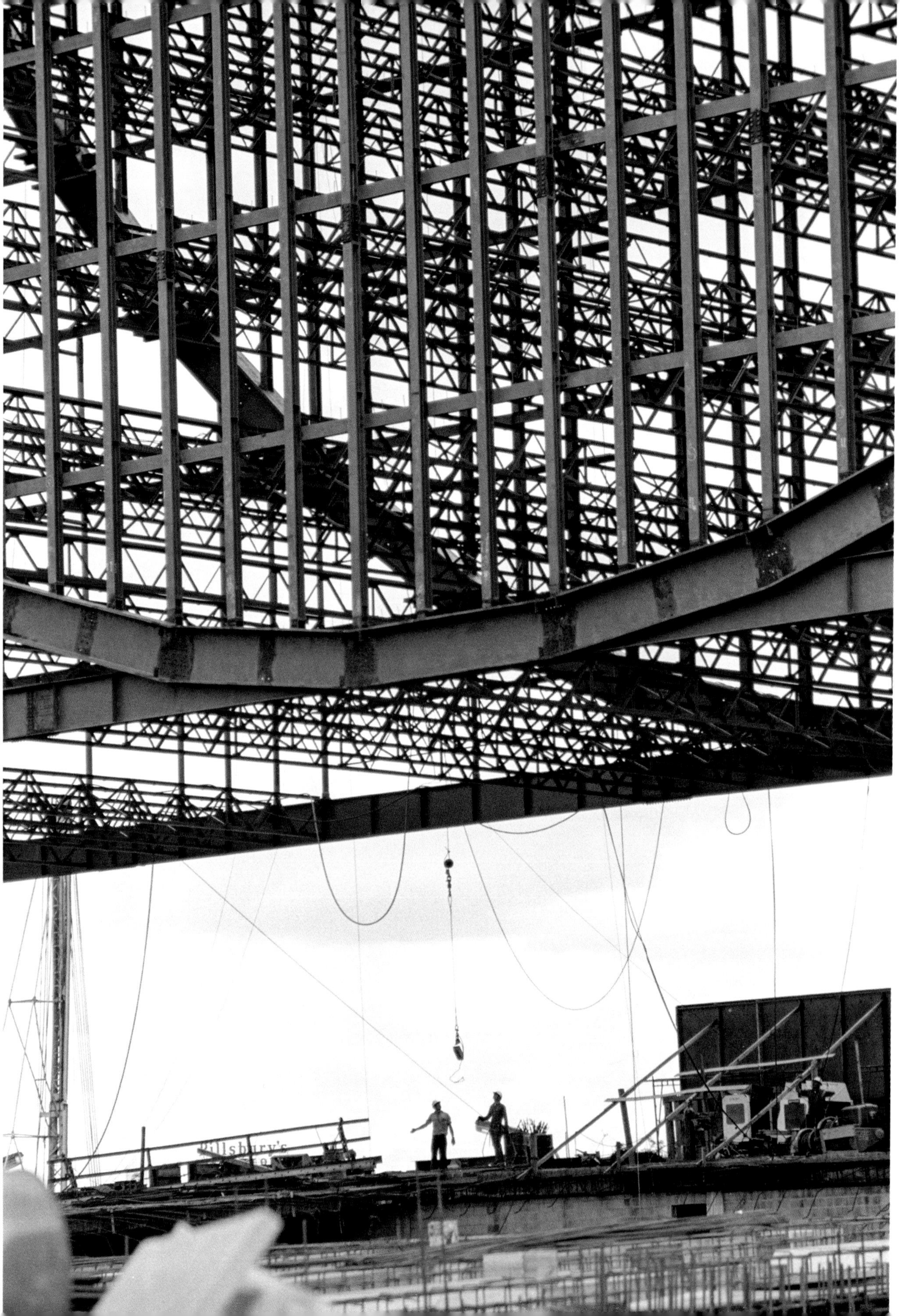

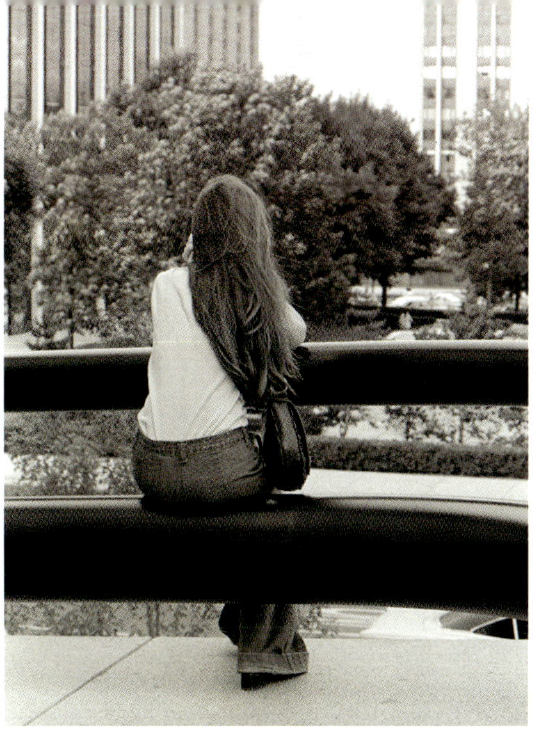

Left: Relaxing on Federal Reserve plaza

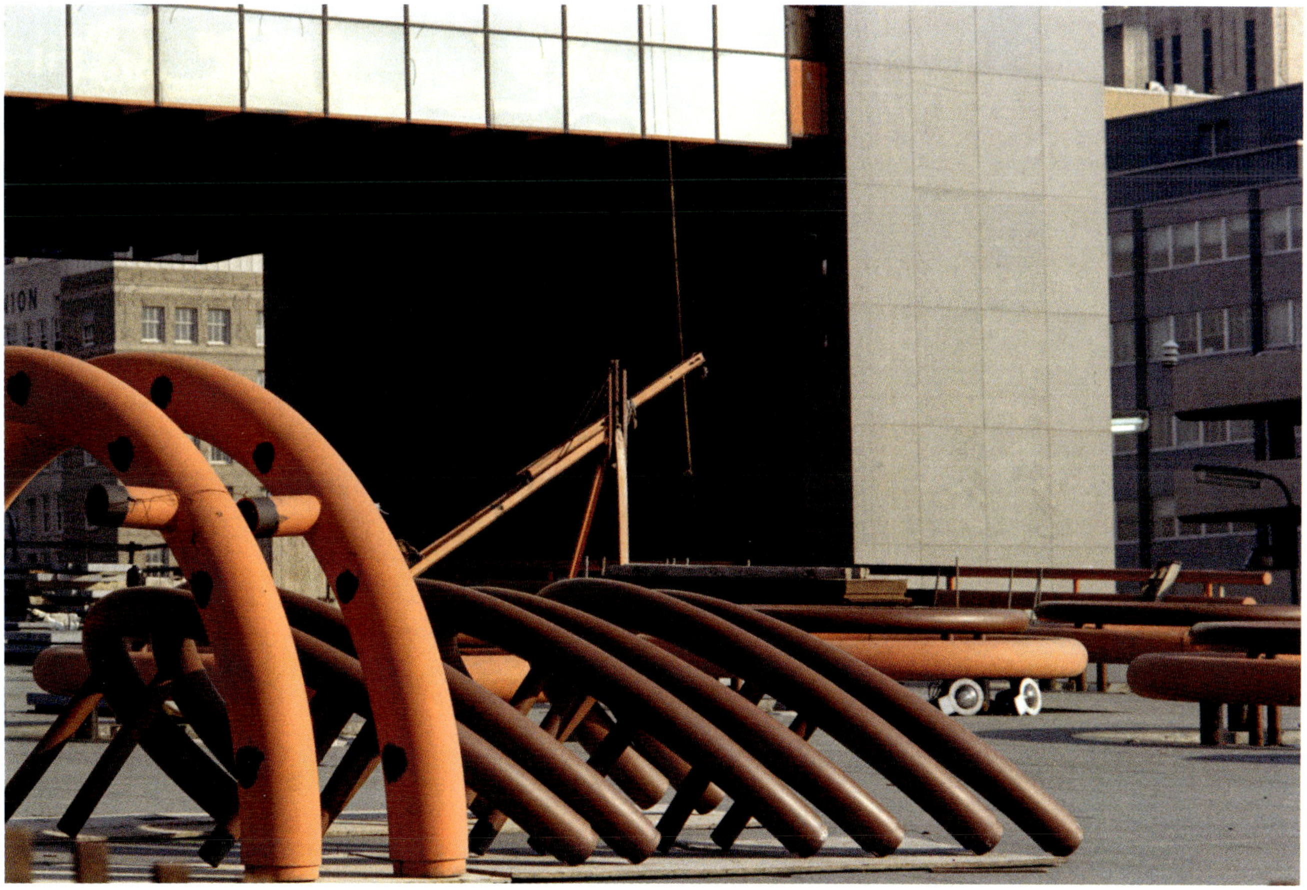

Above: Future bench materials for Federal Reserve plaza

Opposite: The Federal Reserve building under construction

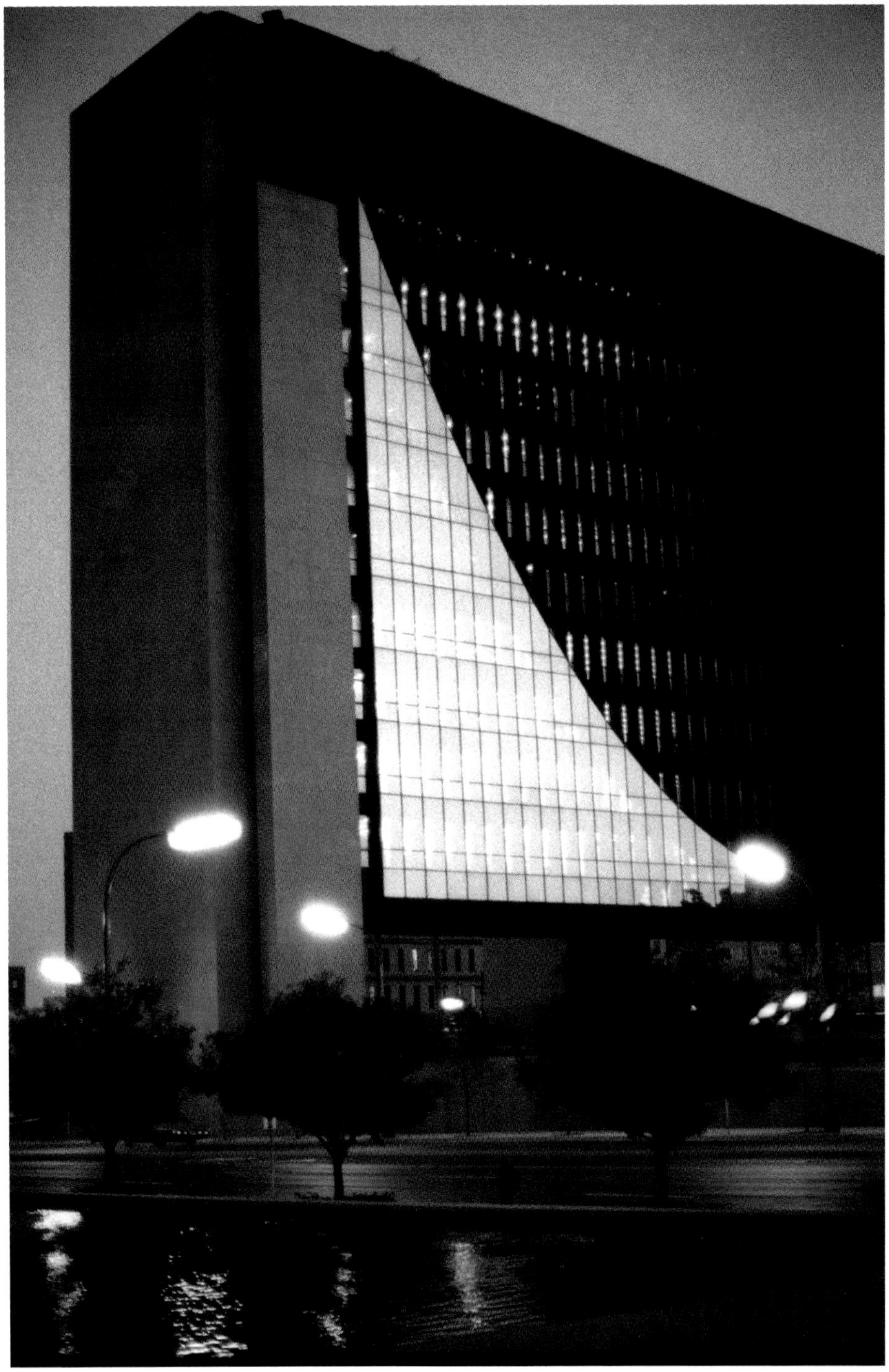

Left: The Federal Reserve at twilight

Opposite: New trees on Fed plaza

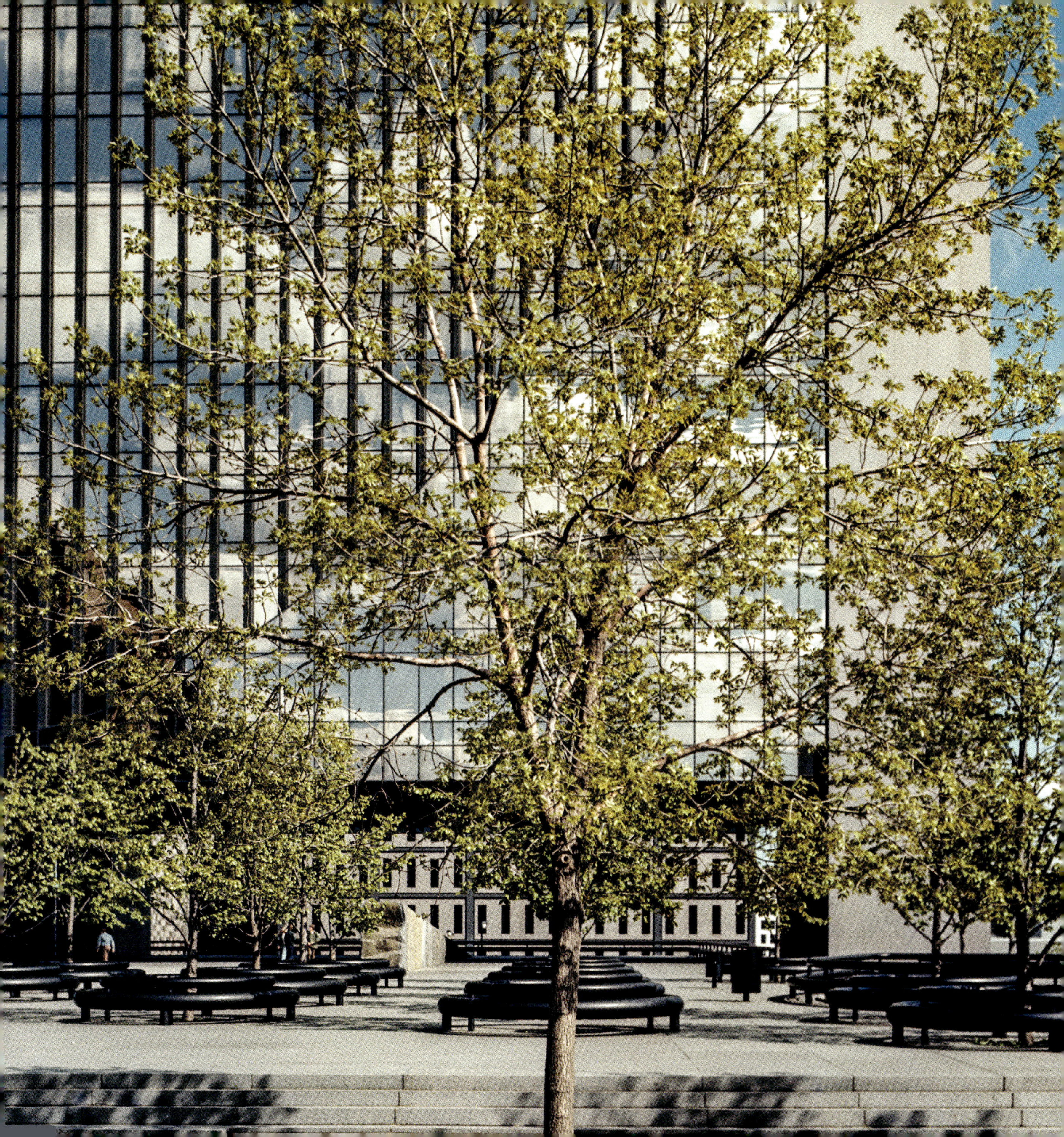

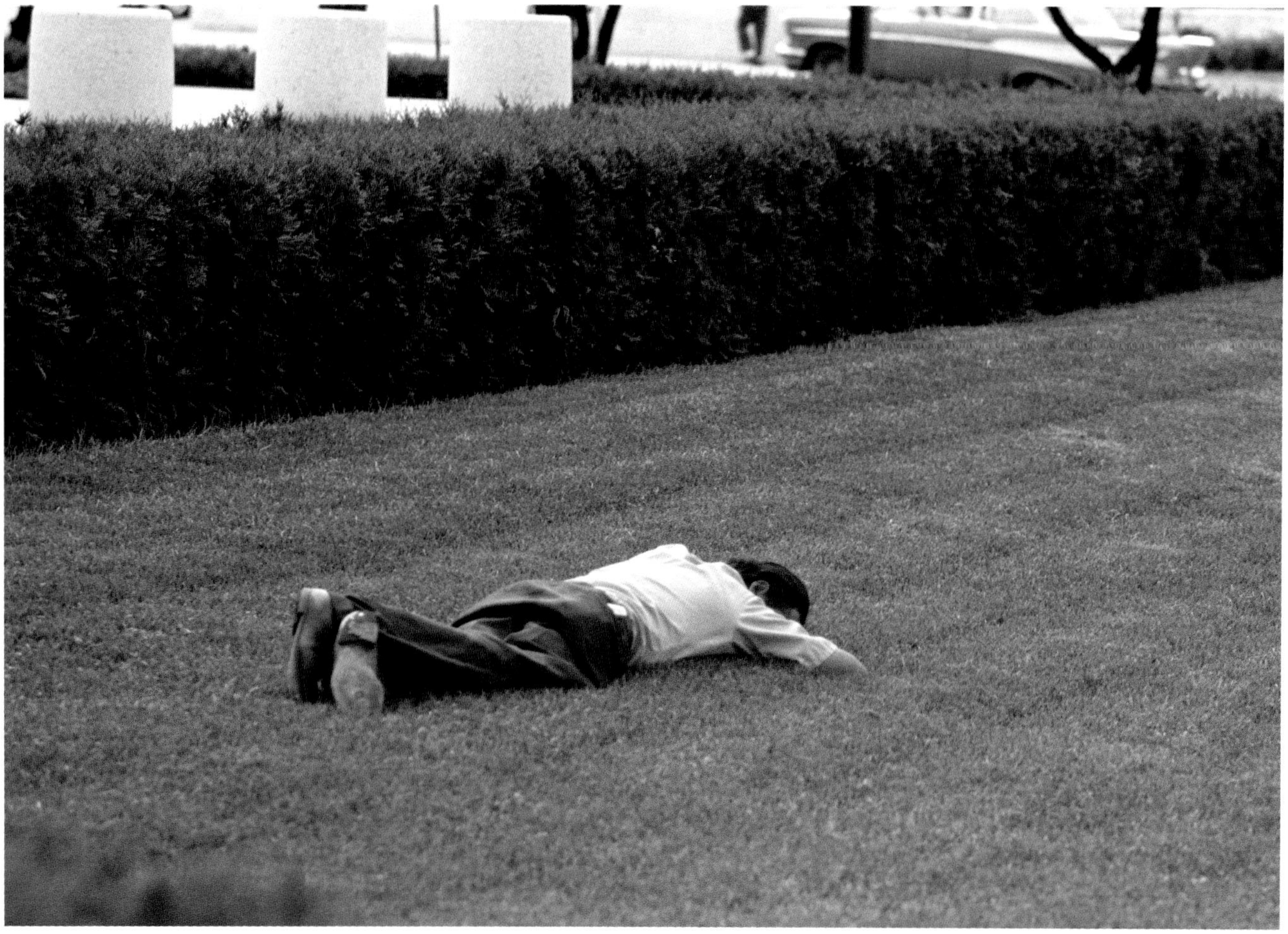

Snoozing on a downtown green space near the public library

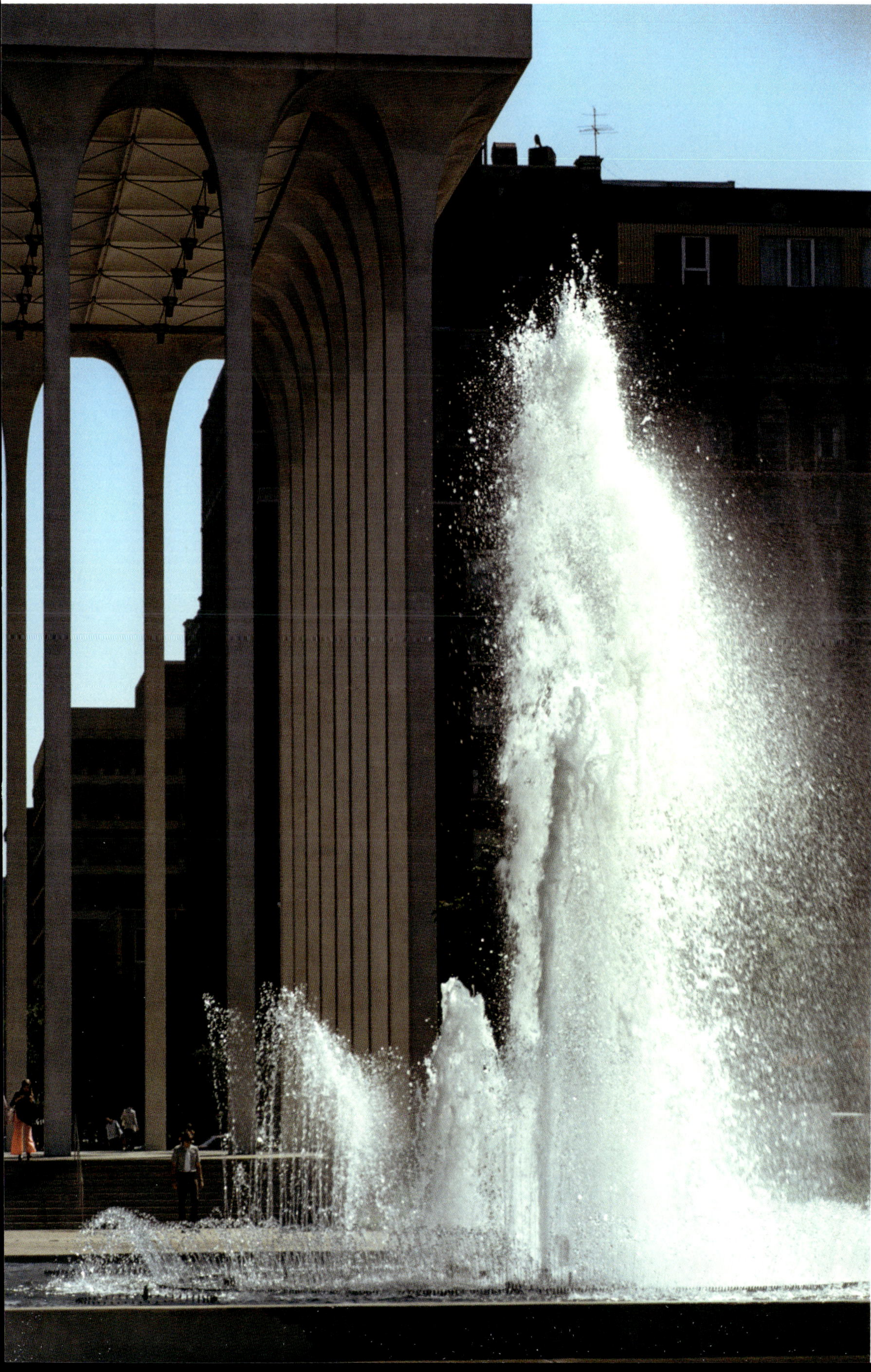

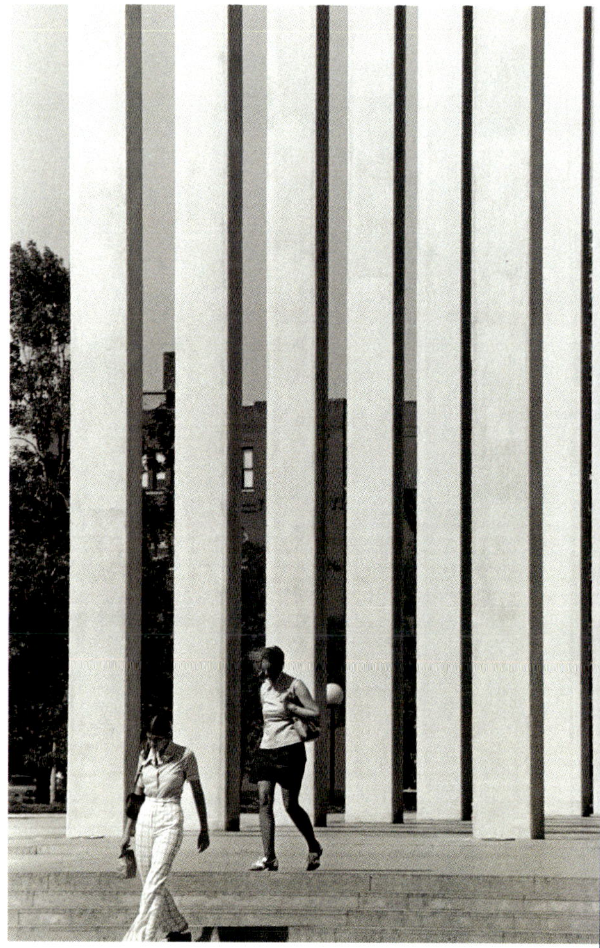

The Northwestern National Life building

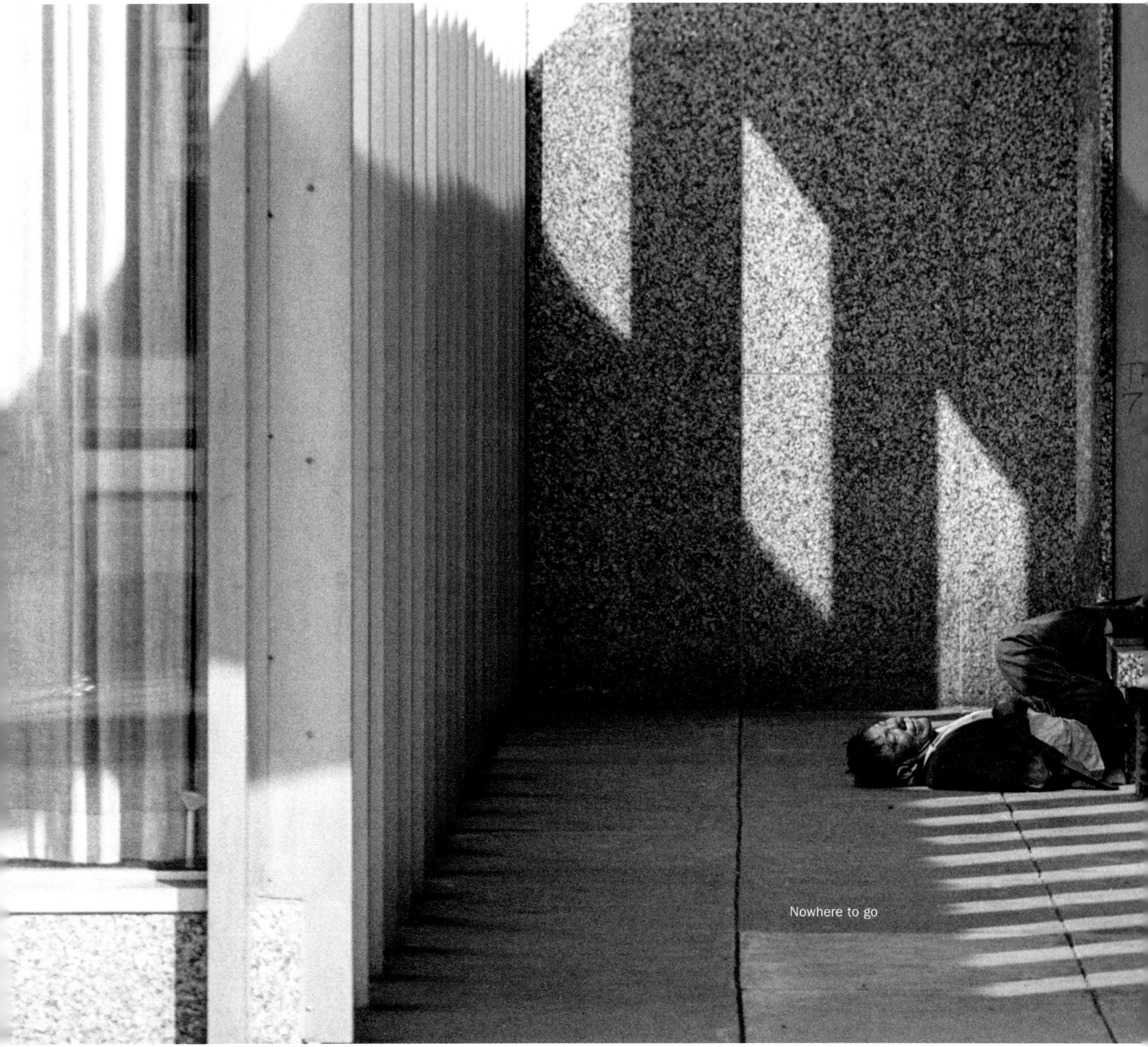

Nowhere to go

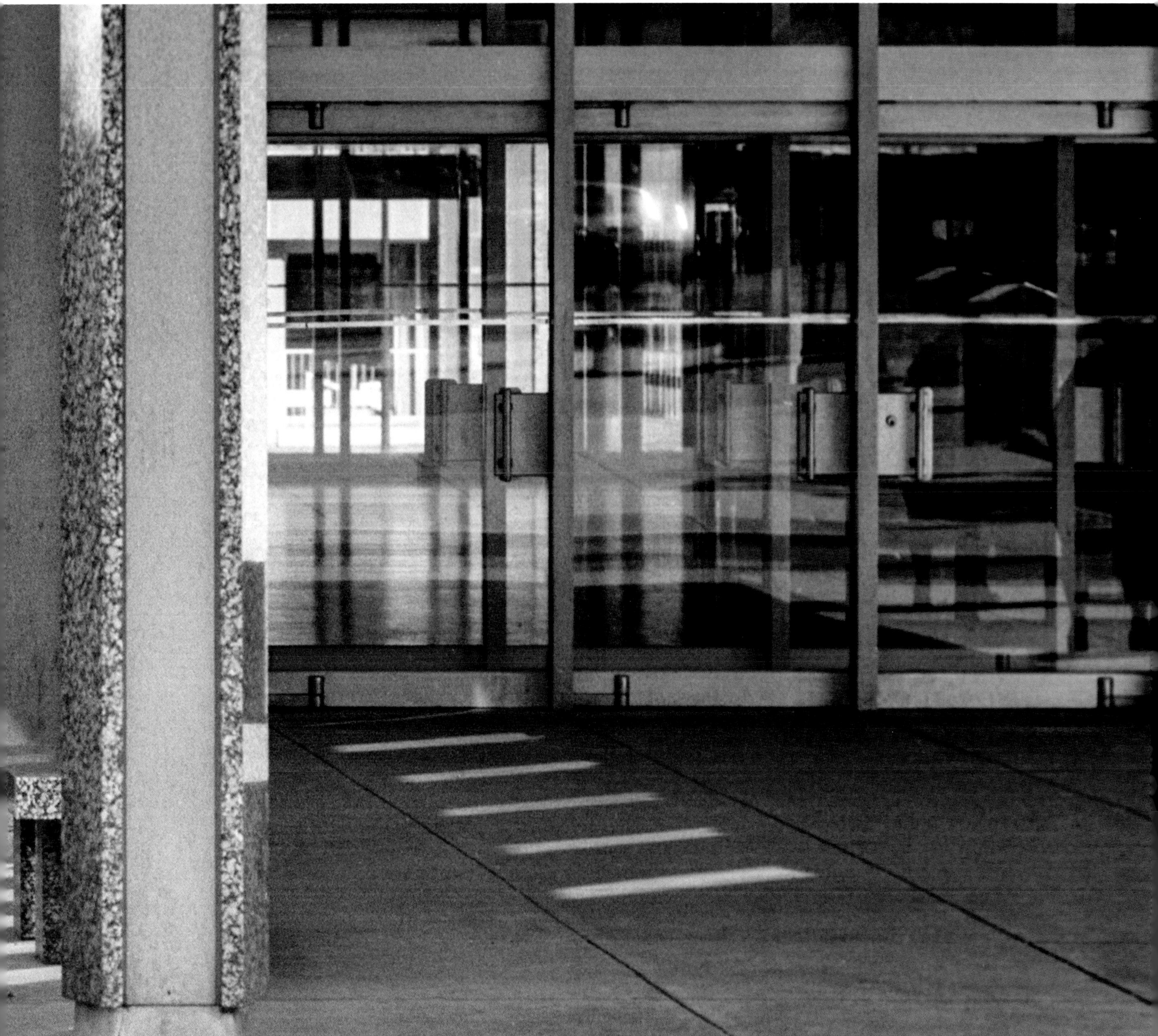

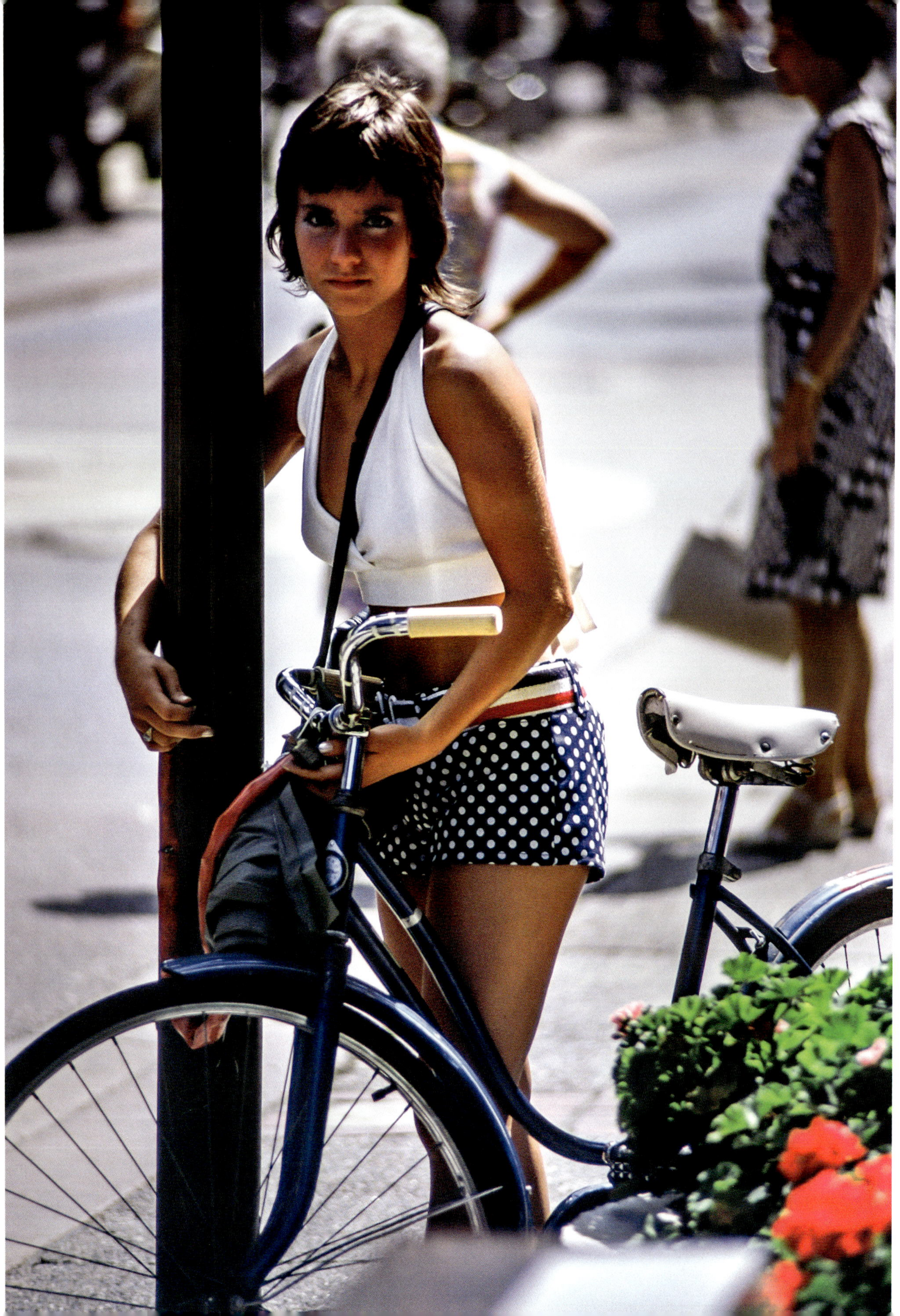

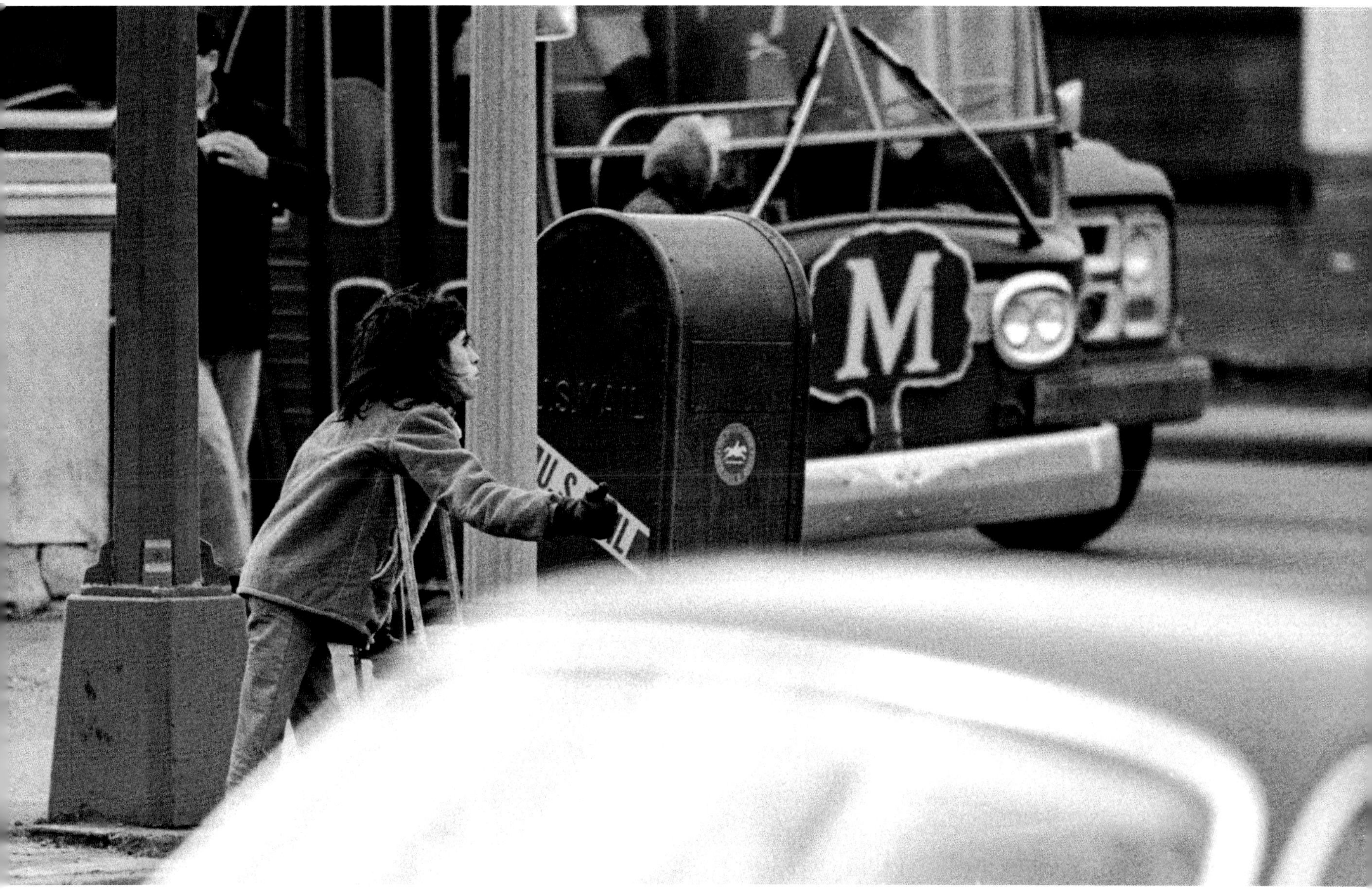

Above: A young man hitching a ride downtown

Opposite: A young woman locking up her bike on Nicollet Mall

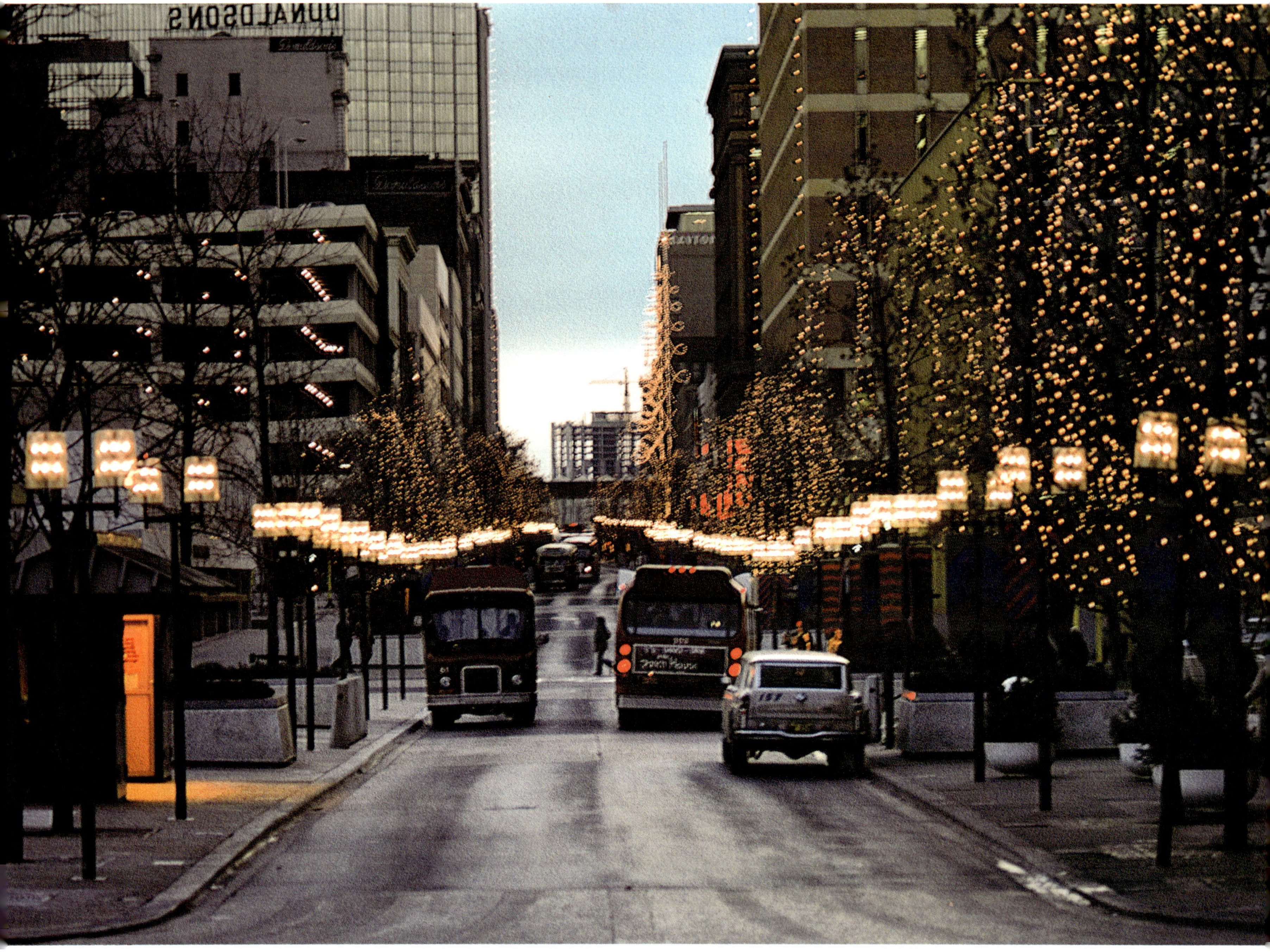

Christmas lights adorn Nicollet Mall in December 1972

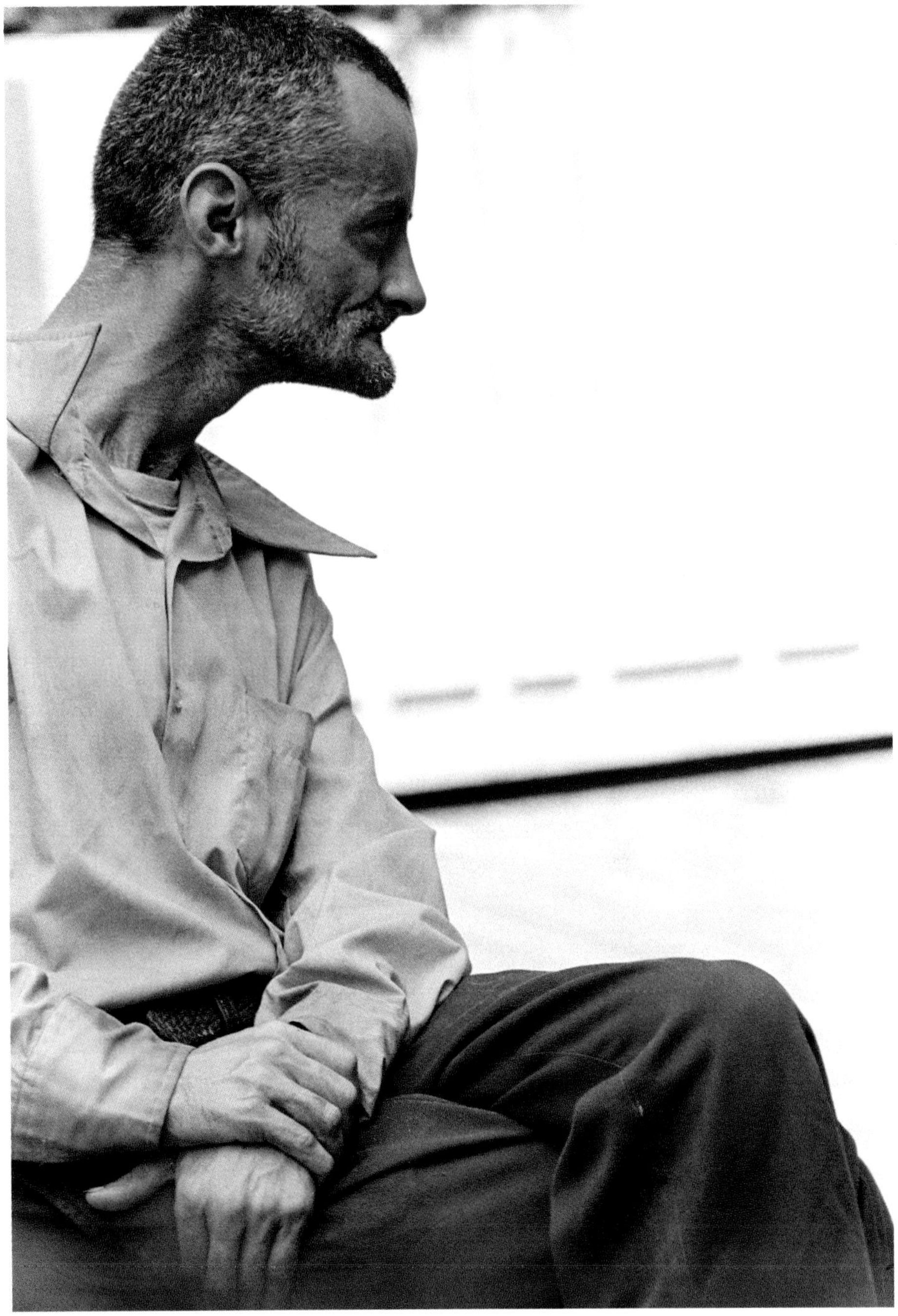

Man waiting on the mall

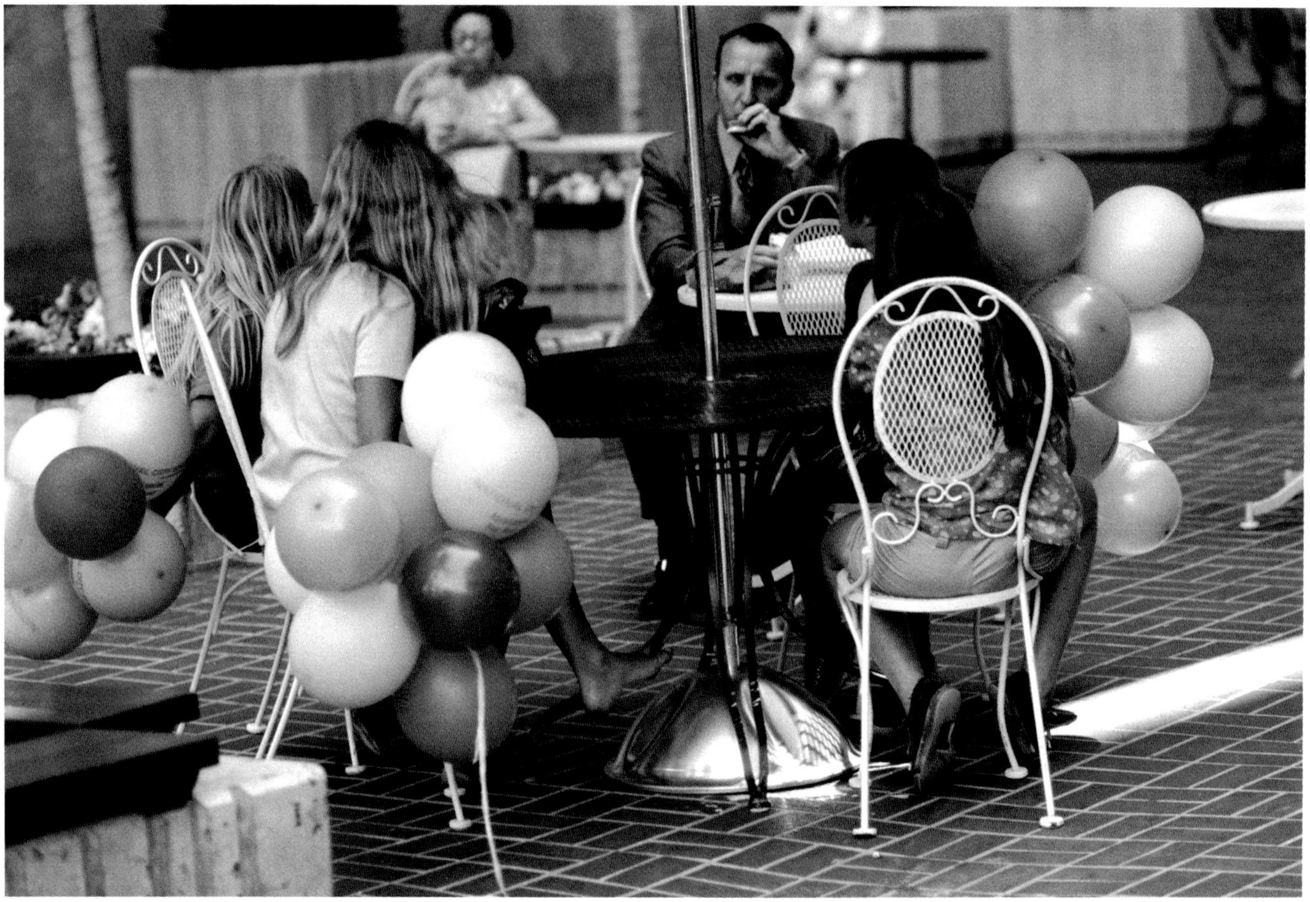

Kids with balloons at a sidewalk table on Nicollet Mall

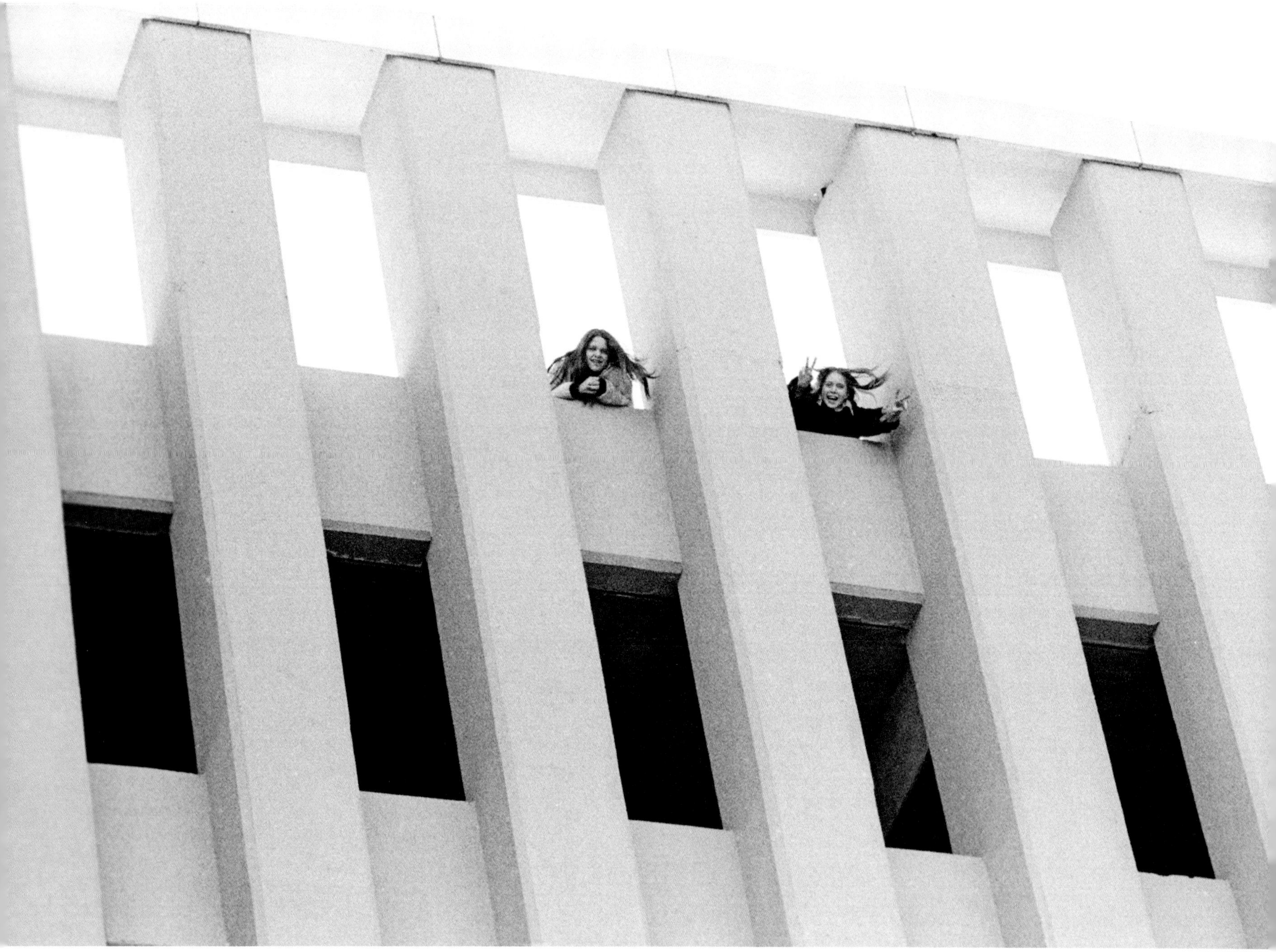

Young girls waving and flashing peace signs from the top of a parking ramp

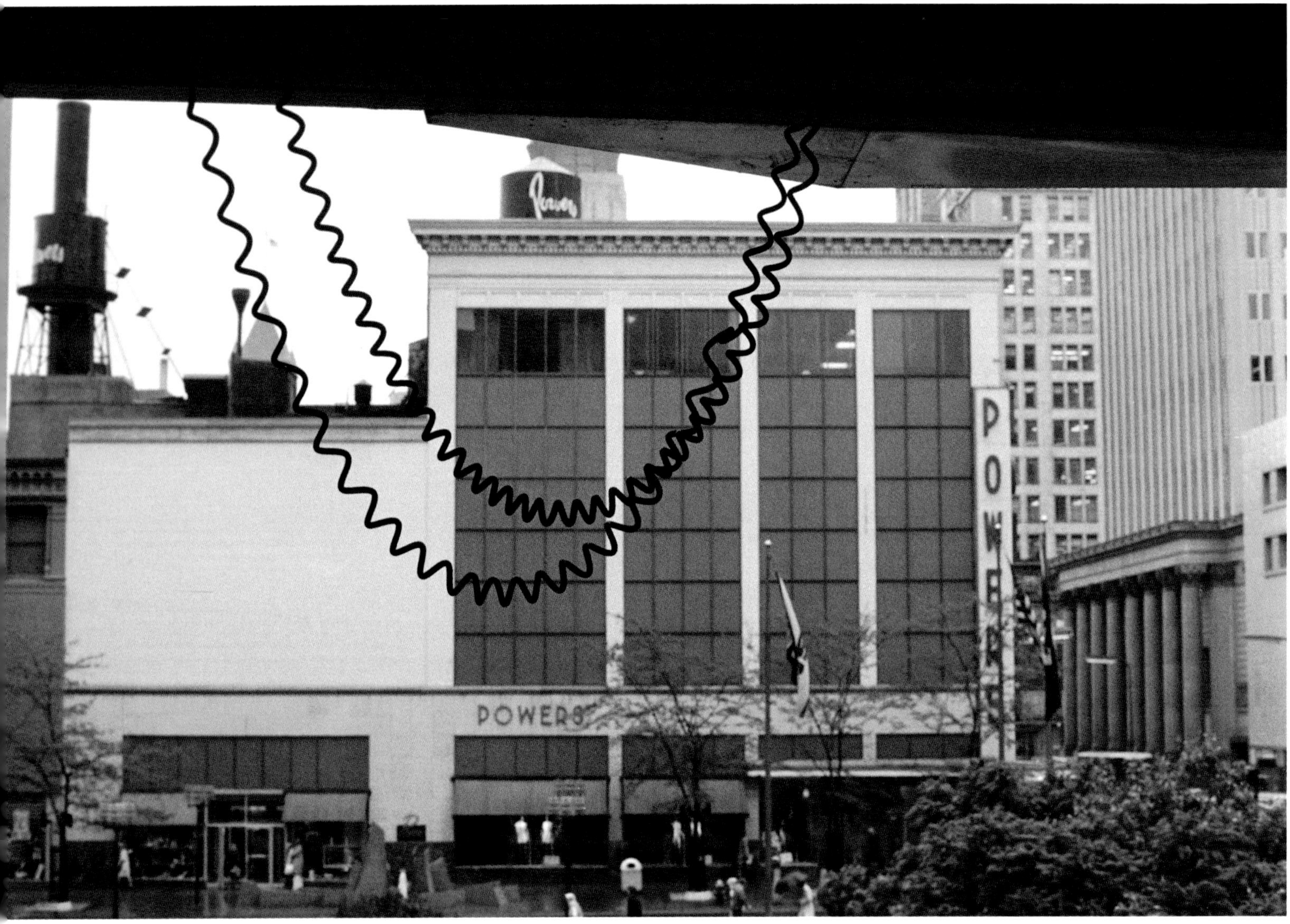

Powers department store on Nicollet and Fifth Street, viewed from the Northern States Power parking ramp

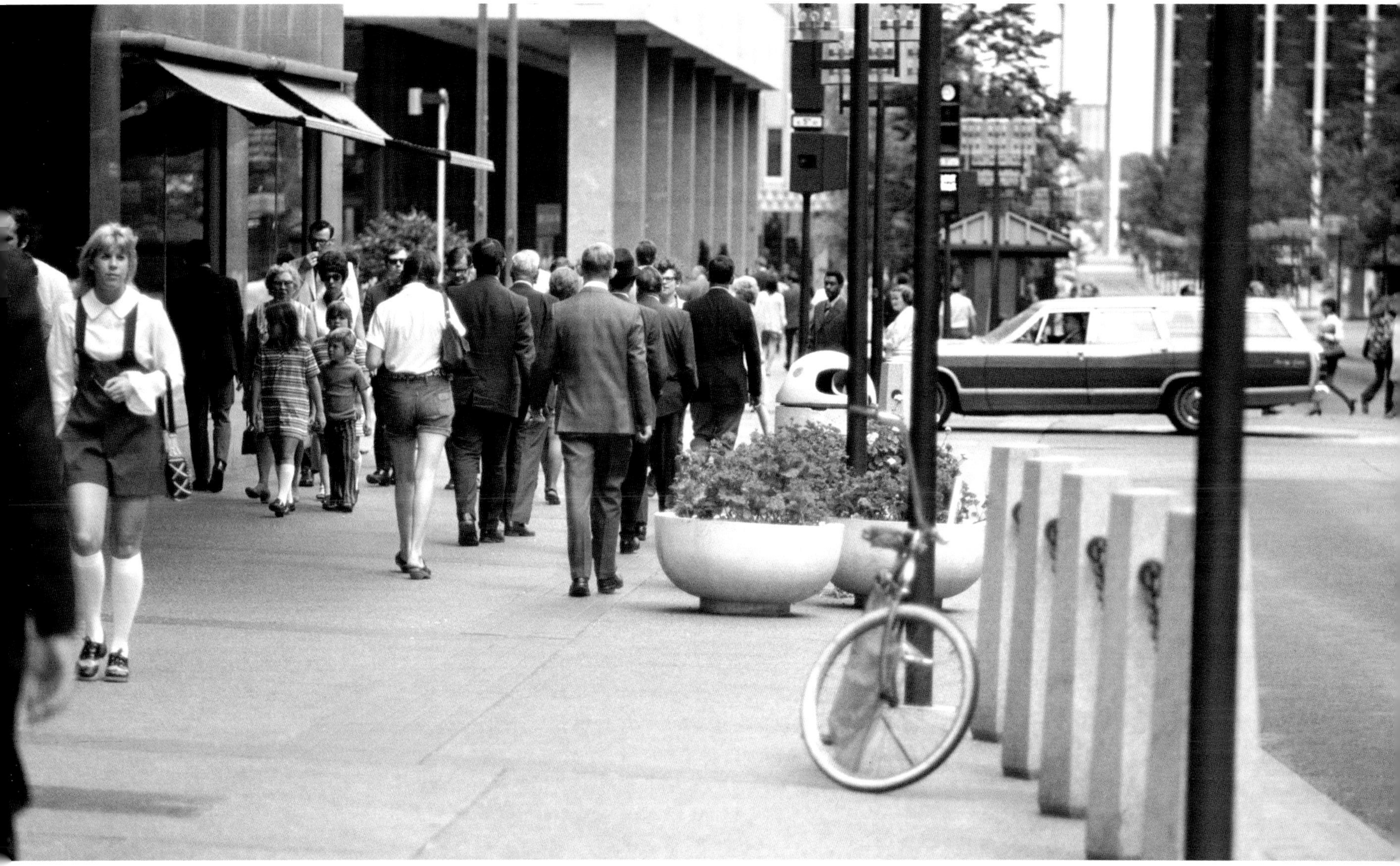

Nicollet Mall bustling with pedestrians, professionals, and families

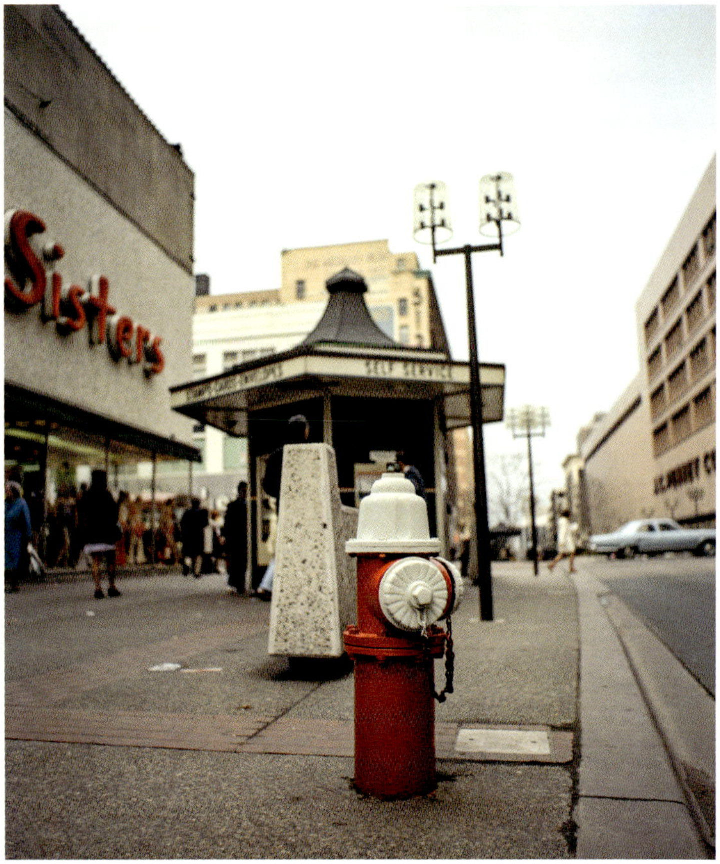

Above: The first-ever self-service stamp vending machine, in front of the Three Sisters clothing boutique on Nicollet, where Tammy Faye Bakker worked briefly as a salesgirl in the early 1960s

Opposite: A winter scene on Nicollet Mall, with the Powers Christmas tree

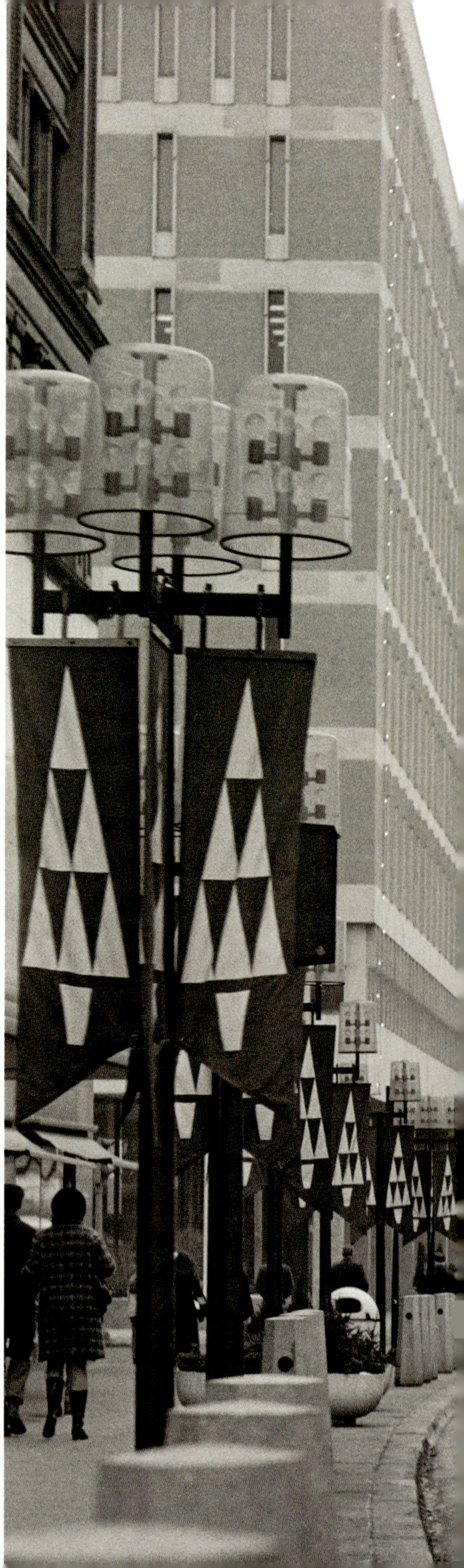

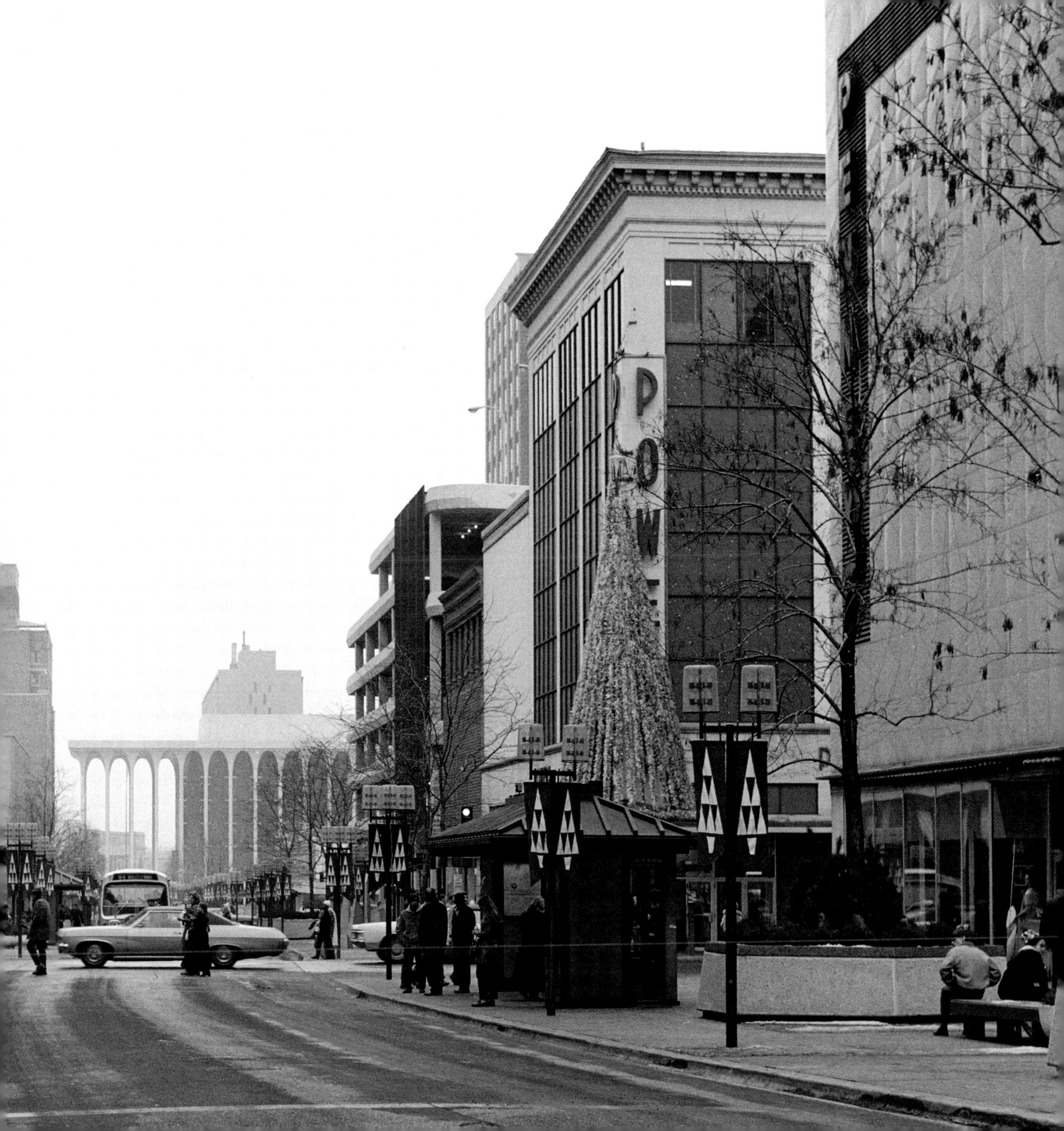

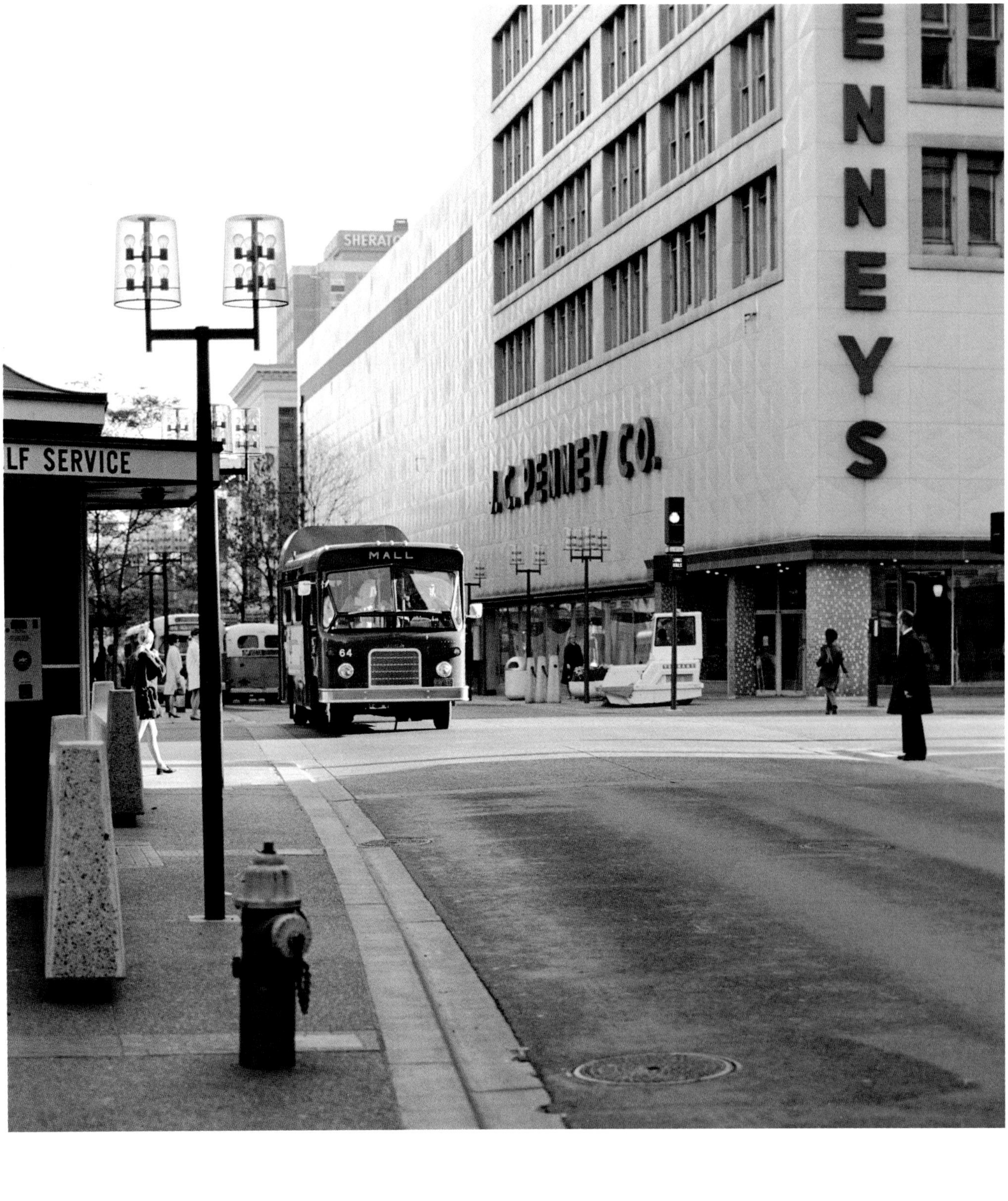
LF SERVICE
SHERATO
J.C. PENNEY CO.
ENNEYS
MALL
64

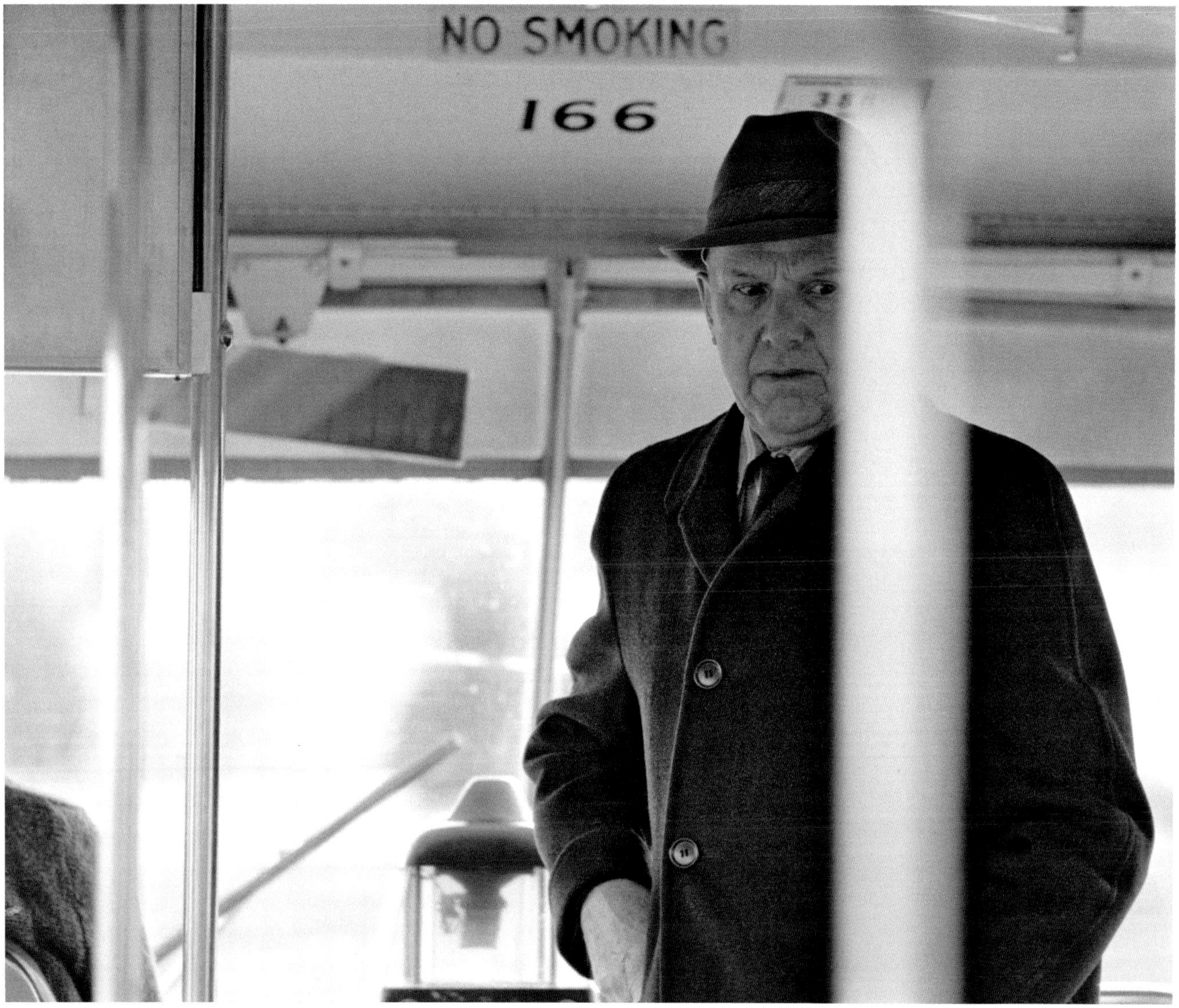

Above: Man on a bus

Opposite: A free shuttle bus passing in front of J. C. Penney at Sixth and Nicollet

JAY'S CAMERAS

Among the various camera shops located in downtown Minneapolis during the 1970s, Jay's Cameras, at Fifth and Nicollet, was where the professionals went for their photo equipment needs—"everything fine in the photographic line," the store boasted. Located in the heart of Minneapolis's upscale retail district and with a huge plate-glass window showing off the latest and greatest in photographic technology, it was also the best for window-shopping. By the late 1960s, there was a large enough contingent of professional photographers in the region to support a high-end shop like Jay's.

Jay's was an authorized dealer for Leica, the West German manufacturer whose gorgeous black and satin chrome cameras were reliable, intuitive, fast, and—most importantly for photojournalists and street photographers—nearly silent. In fact, Jay's had a German-born salesman named Heinz on staff whose specialty was selling and demonstrating the Leicas. The cameras may have required the extra salesmanship, as Leicas weren't a cheap investment. A brand-new, state-of-the-art Leica M5 in 1971 retailed for $627 for the body alone. Adjusted for inflation, that's over $3,600 in 2014 dollars; with a good lens, you're looking at something closer to $5,000 in present-day dollars. Even the less expensive models started at around $300, a price still out of reach for a part-time teenage postal employee like Mike Evangelist.

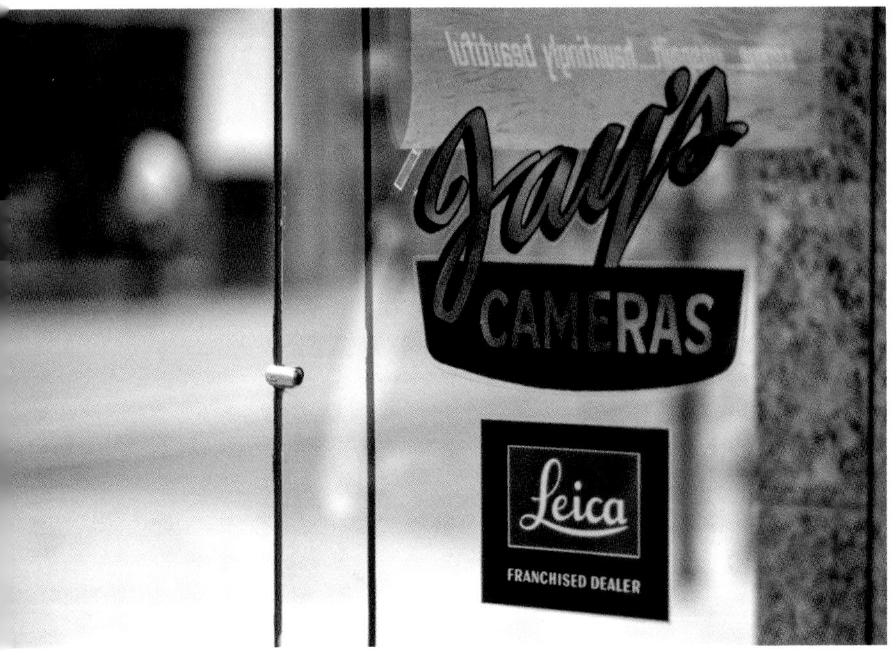

Jay's Cameras on Nicollet Mall

Browsing, of course, was free. The front window at Jay's was a popular stop for aspiring photographers in the Twin Cities—more than a few photographers were born peering in at the goodies inside. Paul Shambroom, whose photographic career began as a college student in Minneapolis in the mid-1970s, remembers lingering at Jay's window, looking at the offerings with what he wryly terms "male gear lust." Mike shoots this very window, containing an enticing panoply of new, high-end cameras. "The store was a bit cramped and cluttered," he recalls fondly, years later, "but they always knew what they were talking about. It was my favorite store."

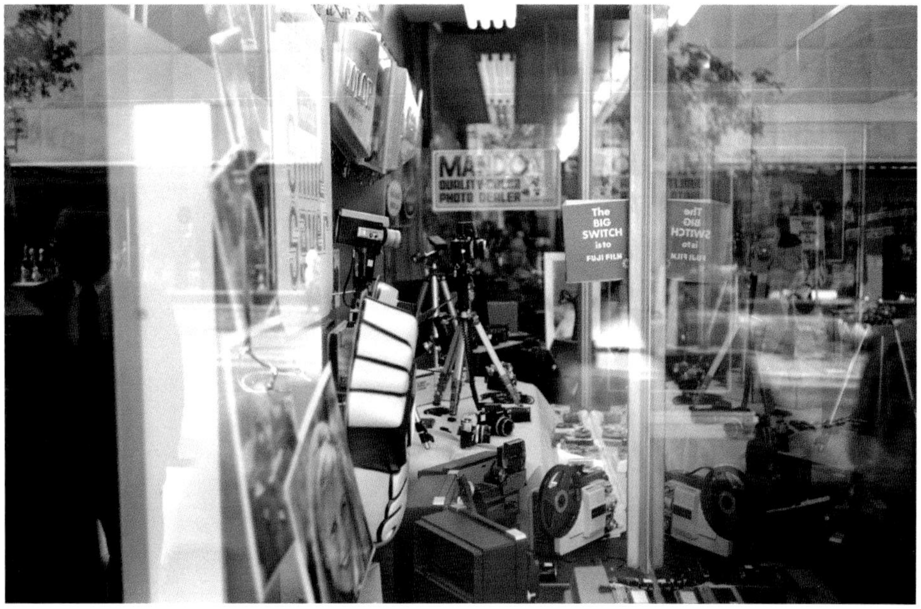

Left: Equipment on display in the Jay's Cameras window

Below: Jay's Cameras interior

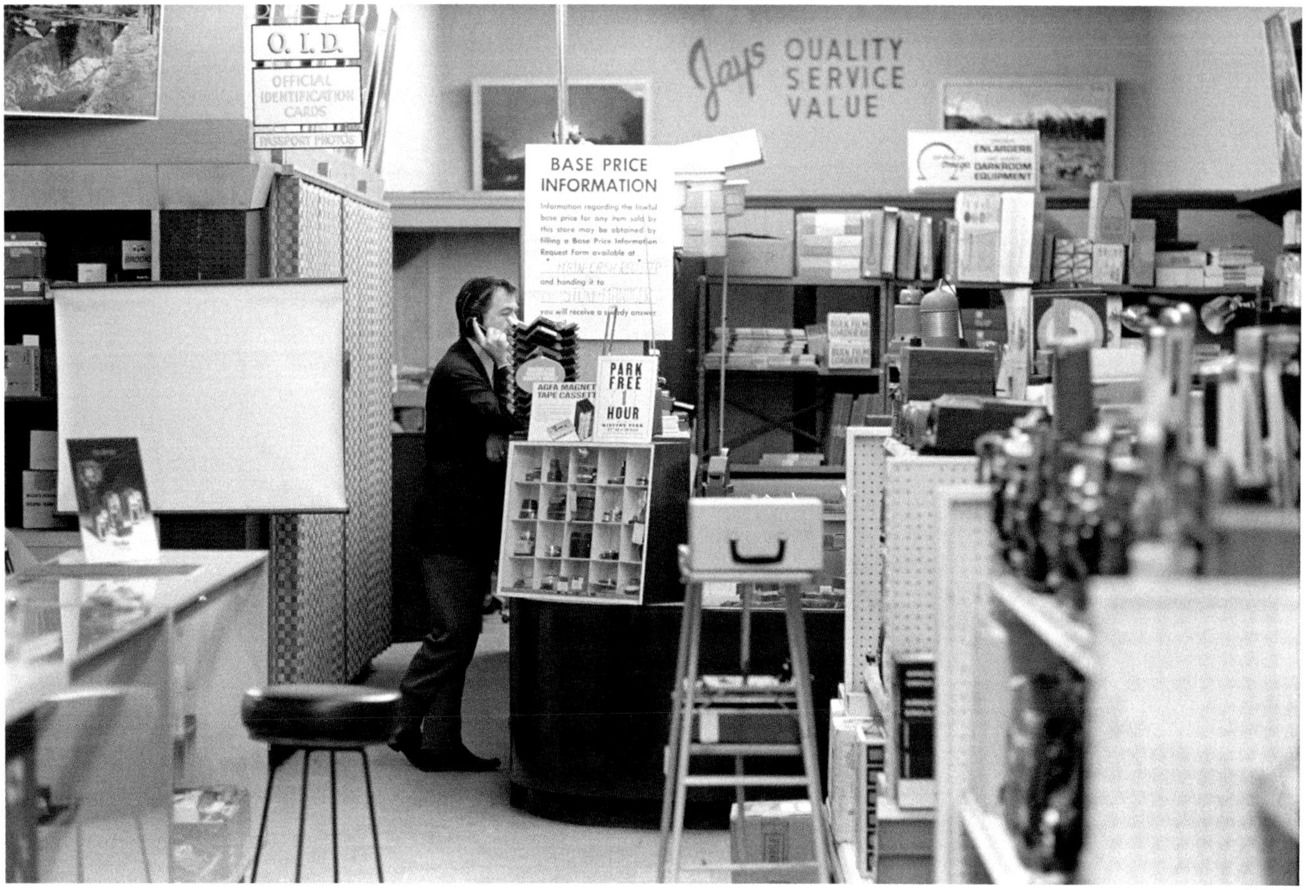

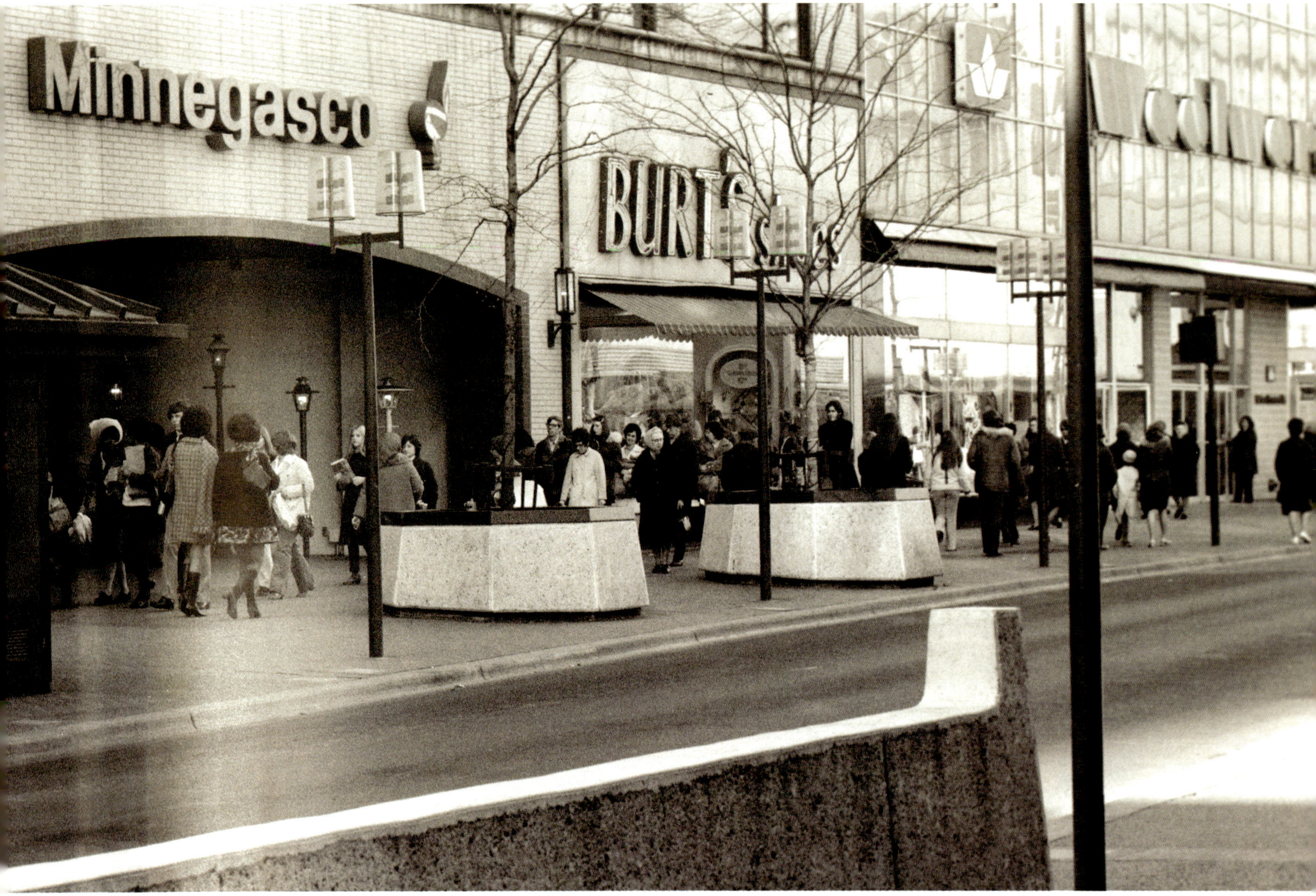

Nicollet Mall between Fifth and Sixth Streets

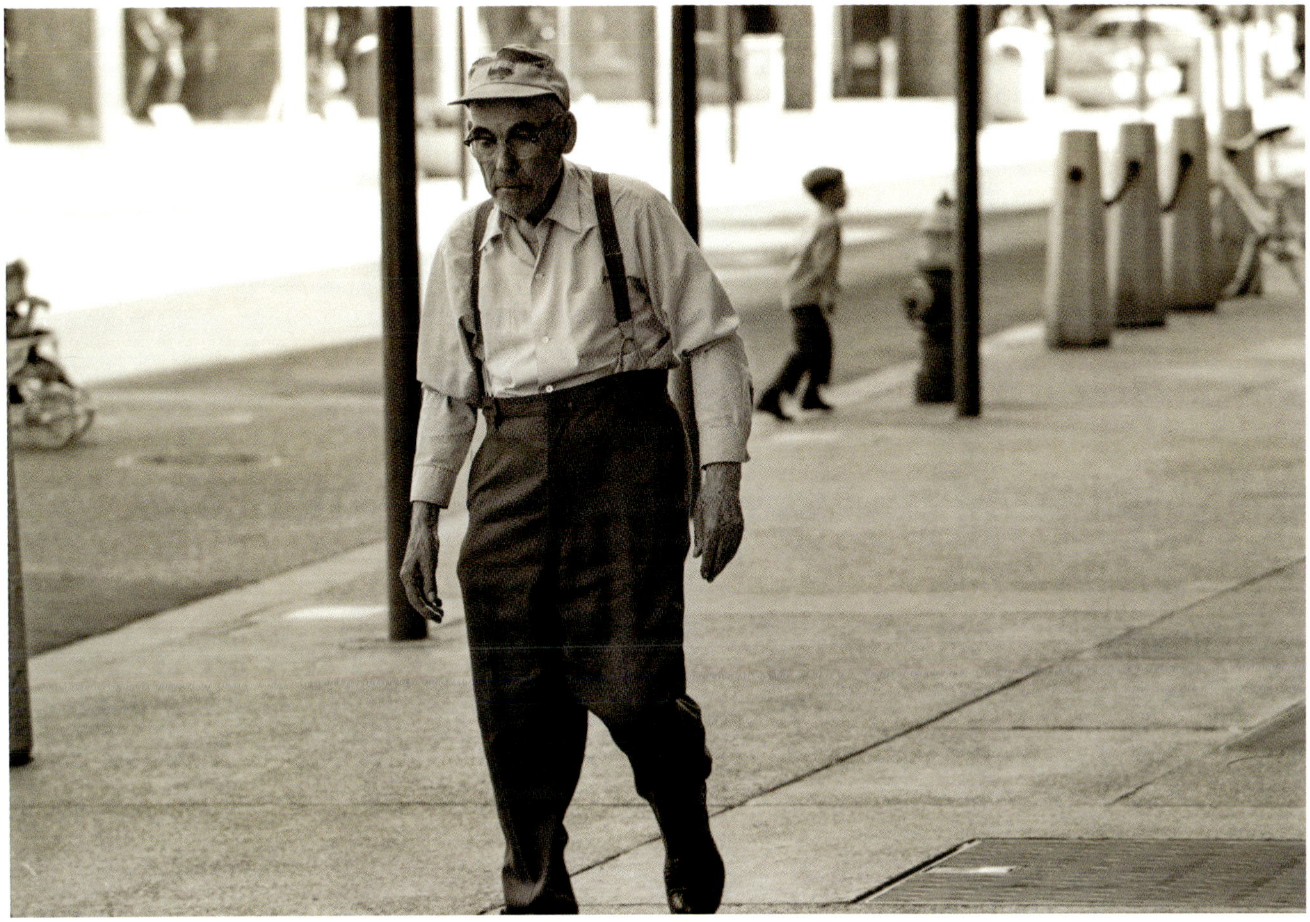

An elderly man walking along the mall

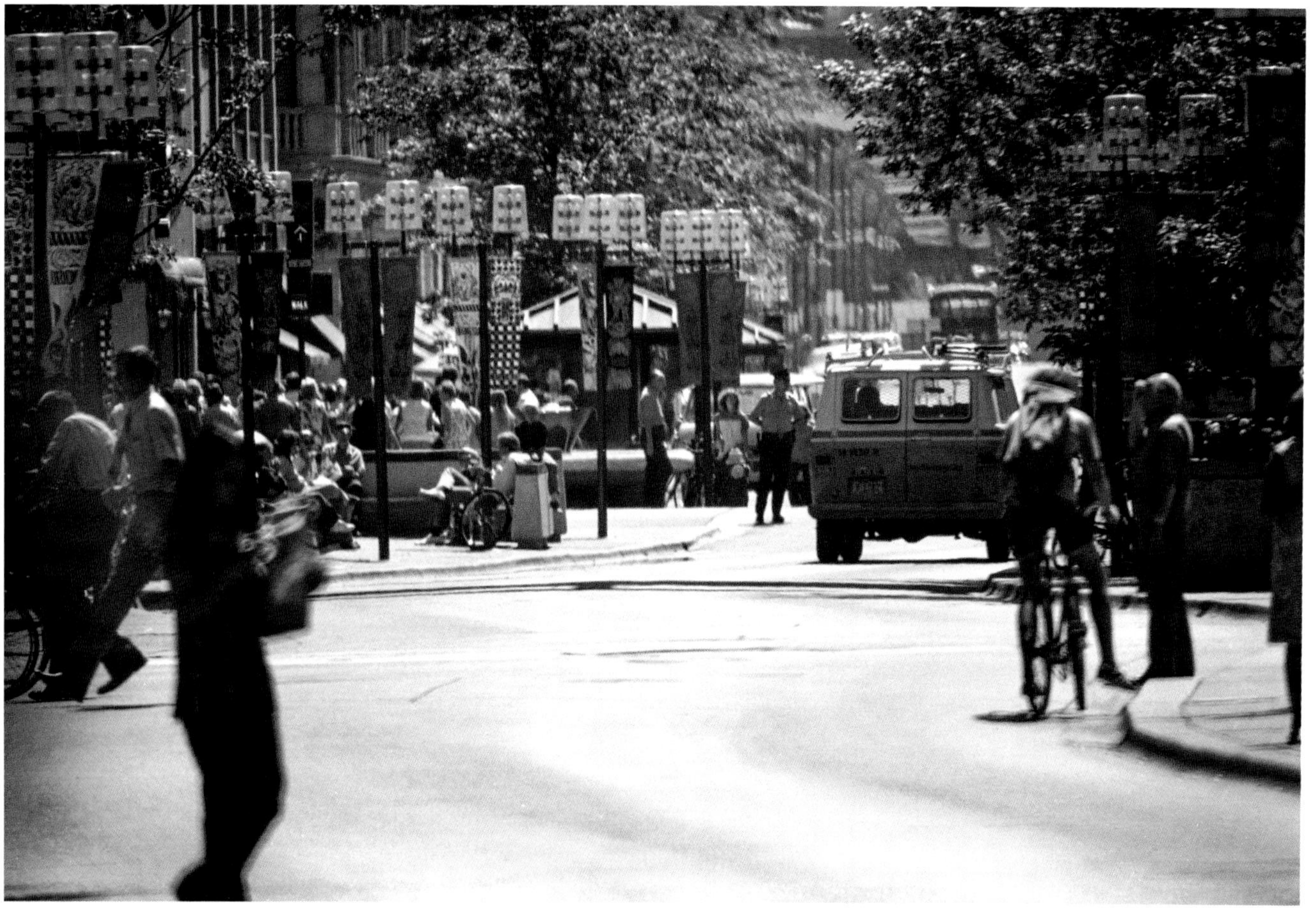

Nicollet Mall alive with activity in summer

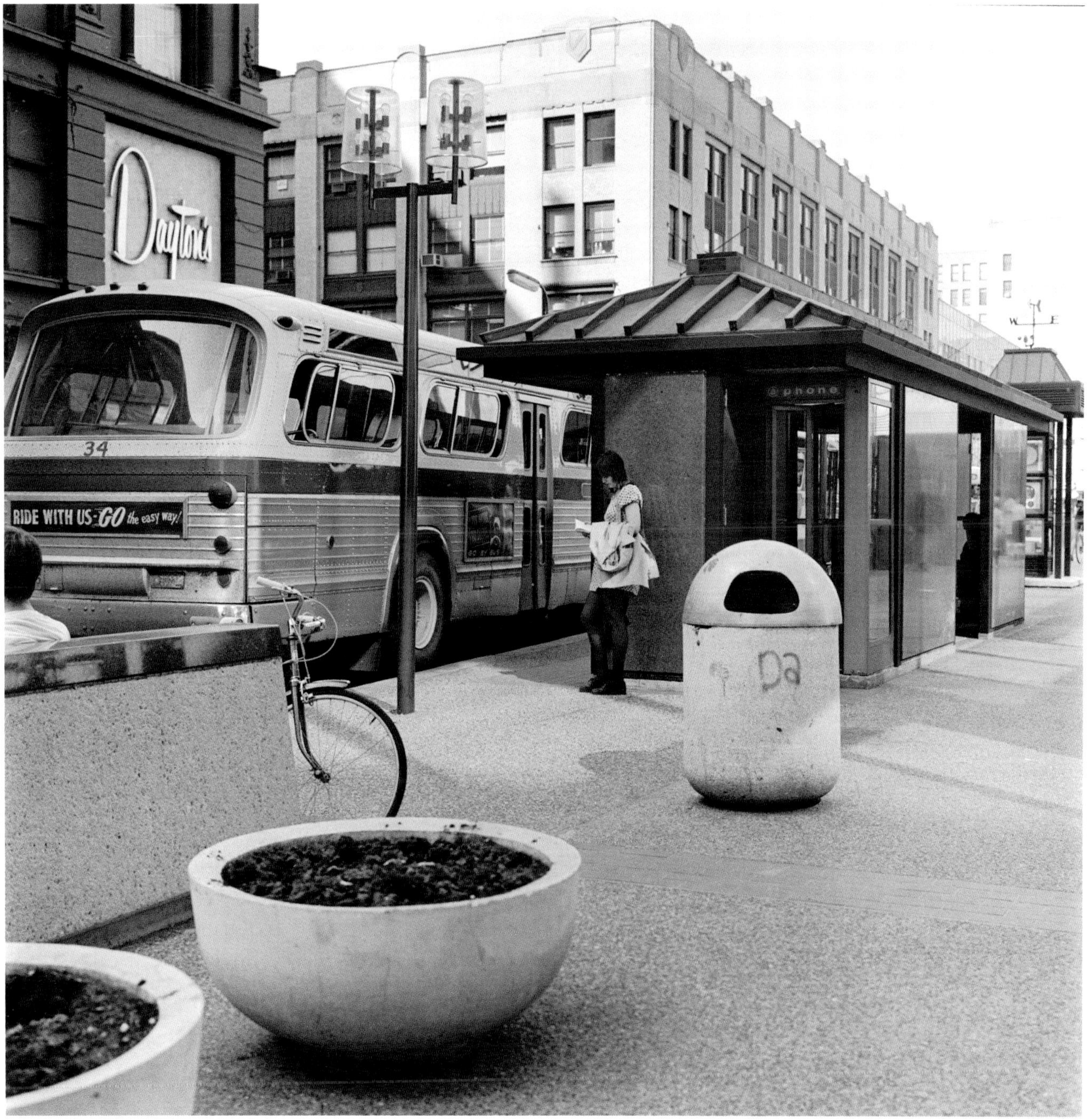

Bus stop across from Dayton's

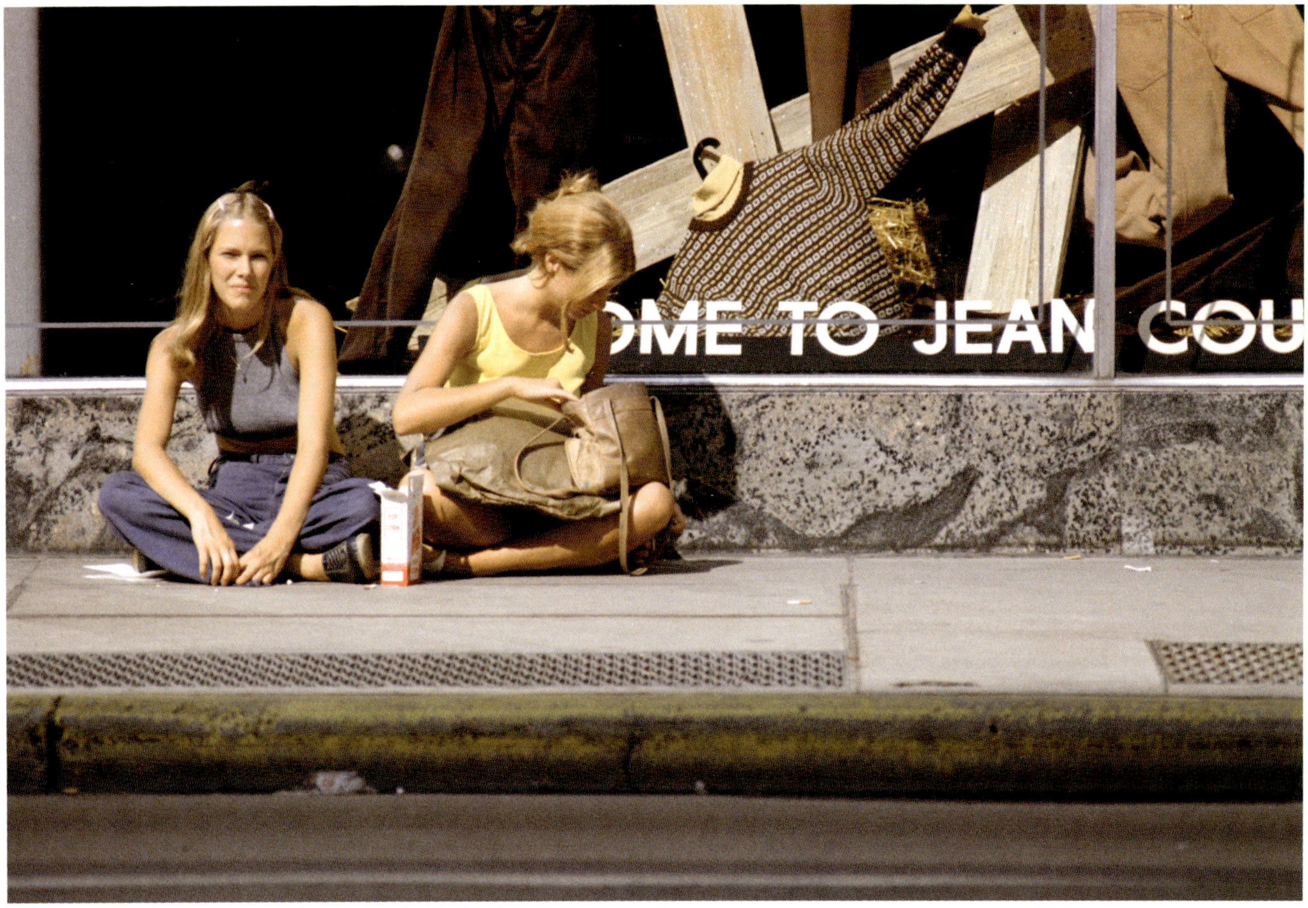

Two girls waiting for a bus on Nicollet

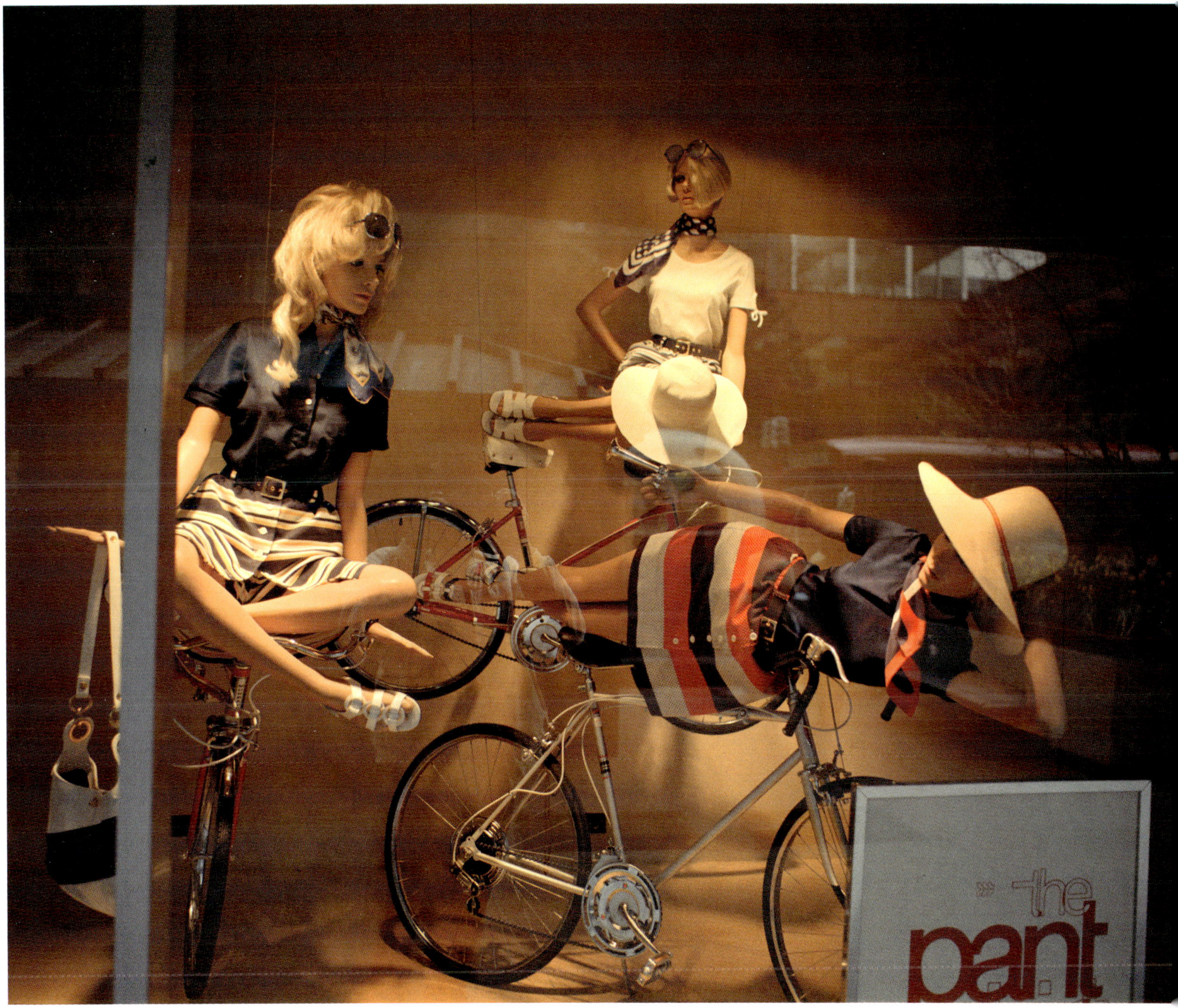

A Dayton's window display

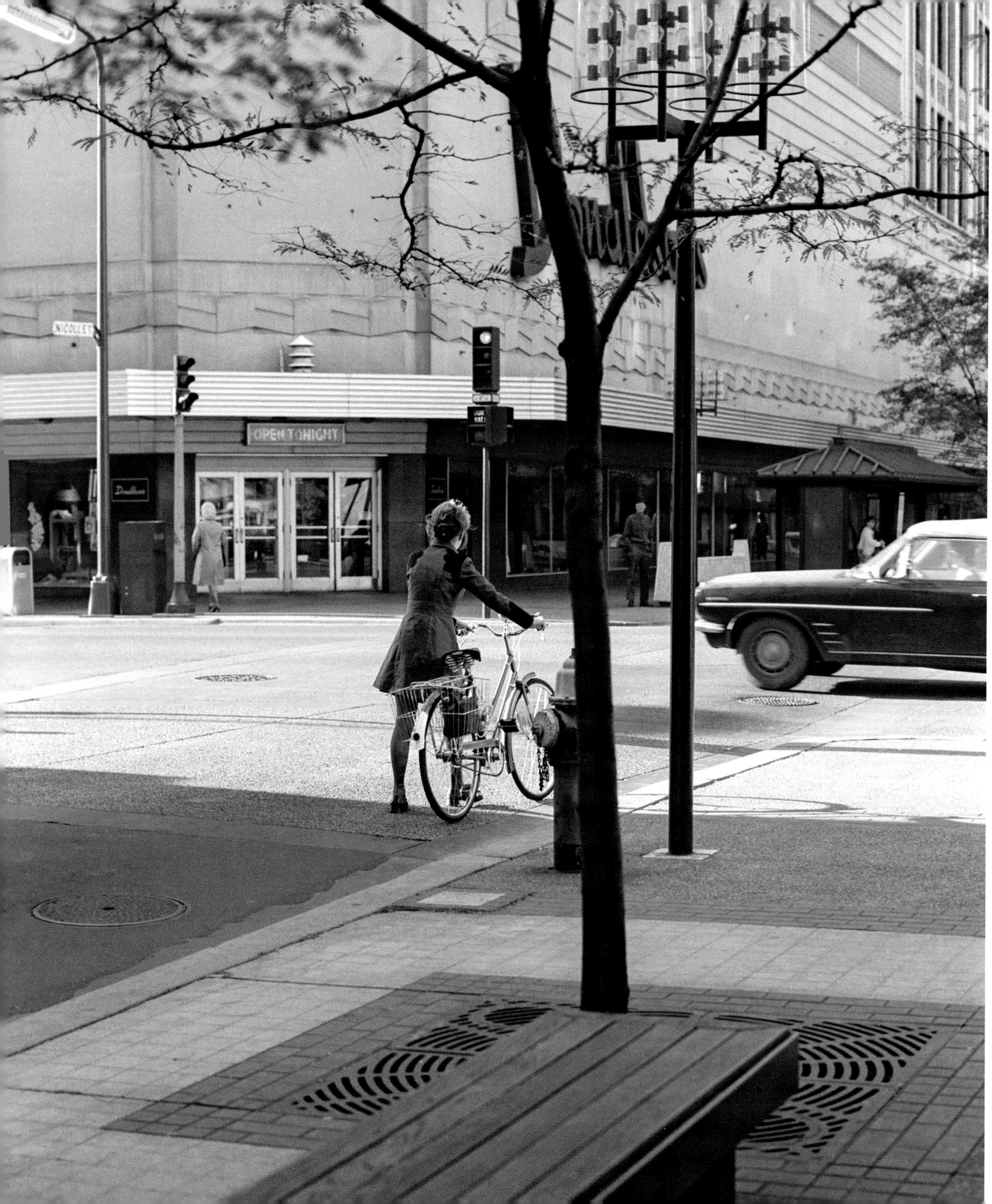
NICOLLET
OPEN TONIGHT

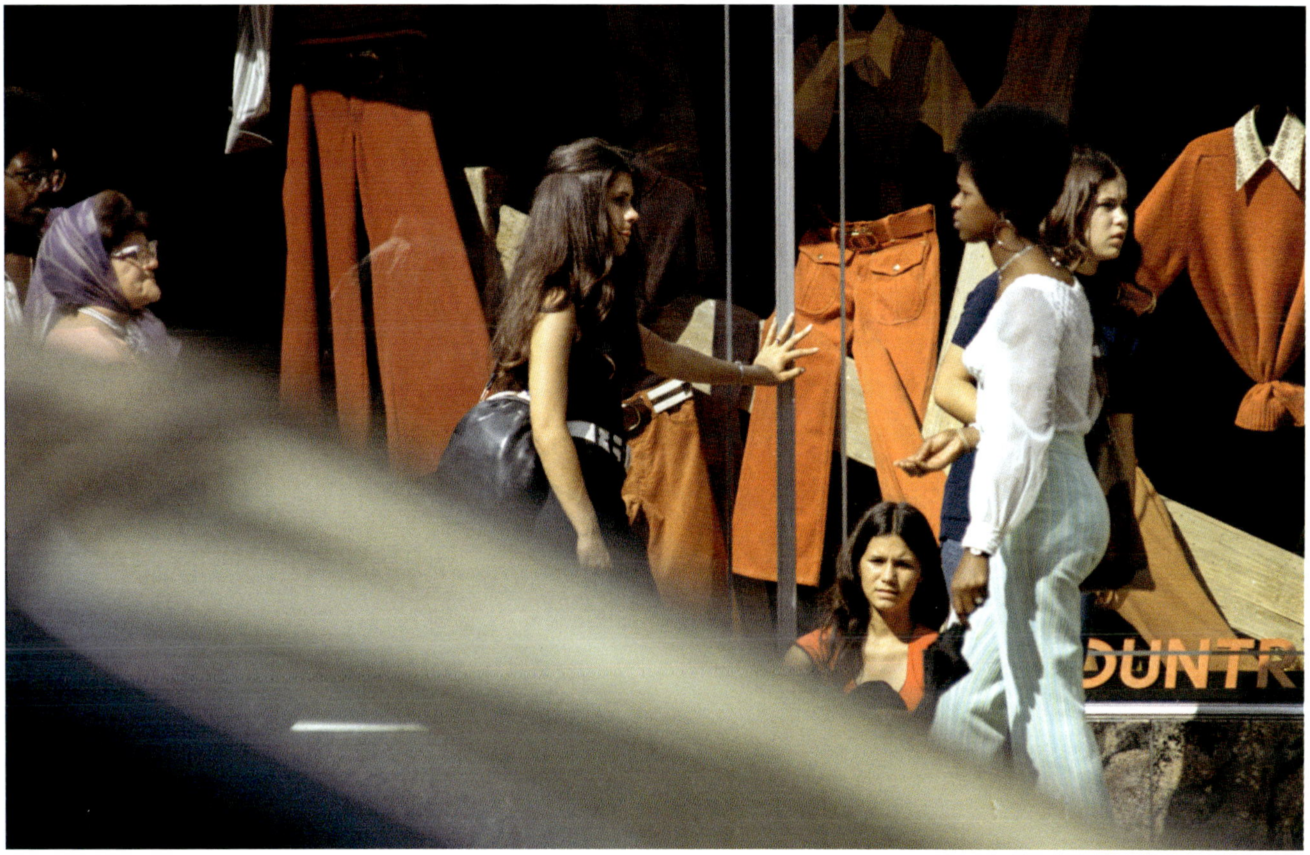

Above: Fall colors in the Powers department store window display

Opposite: Biker at Sixth and Nicollet

THE LOOK

Street photography, as a discipline, has split off into a few different branches since it was first developed in the early to mid-twentieth century. There are photographers out there in the Garry Winogrand or Lee Friedlander mode, prowling the streets, looking for the poignant scenes or interesting juxtapositions that play out in the public realm. But there's also the kind of street photography practiced by someone like the *New York Times*' Bill Cunningham, where the emphasis is documenting the incredible range of fashions that people display while out in the world. Mike's photos have an aspect of that. His eye is drawn toward the interesting, the outrageous, the playful. As much as he loved taking photos of quiet, unexceptional figures in repose, he's most energized by bold displays of fashion and personal style. Many of these are of women, of course, but not all of them.

Nicollet Mall in the early 1970s was not only a place to see and be seen, as the old cliché goes, but also where you'd go to buy clothes. The suburban shopping malls had siphoned off some business, but they hadn't totally stolen away the glamour of the downtown department stores. Opulently attired mannequins on display in the windows of Dayton's and Donaldson's are a big part of the landscape that Mike depicts. Anything a person could imagine wearing, from action slacks to haute couture, is in one of those windows. Anything you see in those windows you also see worn on the streets, and in an in-between state, folded up in the ubiquitous department store bags on the arms of shoppers making their way down the mall—the whole cycle, from window to bag to body.

At Donaldson's, we also encounter the only other photographer we'll come across in these images. Although he's without a camera at the moment, it's Marion "Mundy" Warling, standing with a statuesque model outside the store's front entrance, evidently right before or after a shoot. Warling, born in North Dakota in 1937, was the premier fashion photographer in the Twin Cities throughout the 1970s. A larger-than-life figure—his 2009 obituary reported that in the early 1970s, right around the time of this photo, he tackled a man on Nicollet Mall who was allegedly assaulting a girl at a bus stop—Warling was someone Mike knew a little bit through the photo shops, a figure he "looked up to as someone who actually made a living as a photographer; the first such person I had ever met." Warling's presence in these images reminds us that Minneapolis had a home-grown fashion industry humming along at this time as well. It was an industry supported by a number of talent agencies, the sorts of pro photographers who bought their Leicas from Jay's Cameras, and the downtown department stores who hired them to fill the pages of the *Tribune*, the *Star*, and the several glossy regional magazines with advertisements for their wares (not coincidentally, this work also kept the coffers of those publications full).

Of course, it's not all high fashion on display in the downtown Minneapolis of the early 1970s. There are some eccentrics to be seen, as well as the everyday fashions of young men and women, of business professionals and blue-collar workers, of housewives and retirees. Surprisingly, perhaps, many of these fashions seem remarkably non-dated, or as relatively non-dated as one might expect from forty-year-old photos, anyway. Fashion is cyclical, and some of the looks that defined this era—high waists, shaggy hair, plastic frame glasses—are not too far off from looks that define the current era. In the city's trendier districts of today, the seemingly ubiquitous pair of twenty-somethings slinking down the street with a twinned sense of bored ennui and scuzzy bravado—he with a mustache or beard, she with oversized aviator sunglasses and high-waisted shorts—are conveying a quality, consciously or not, that was developed and perfected in the 1970s.

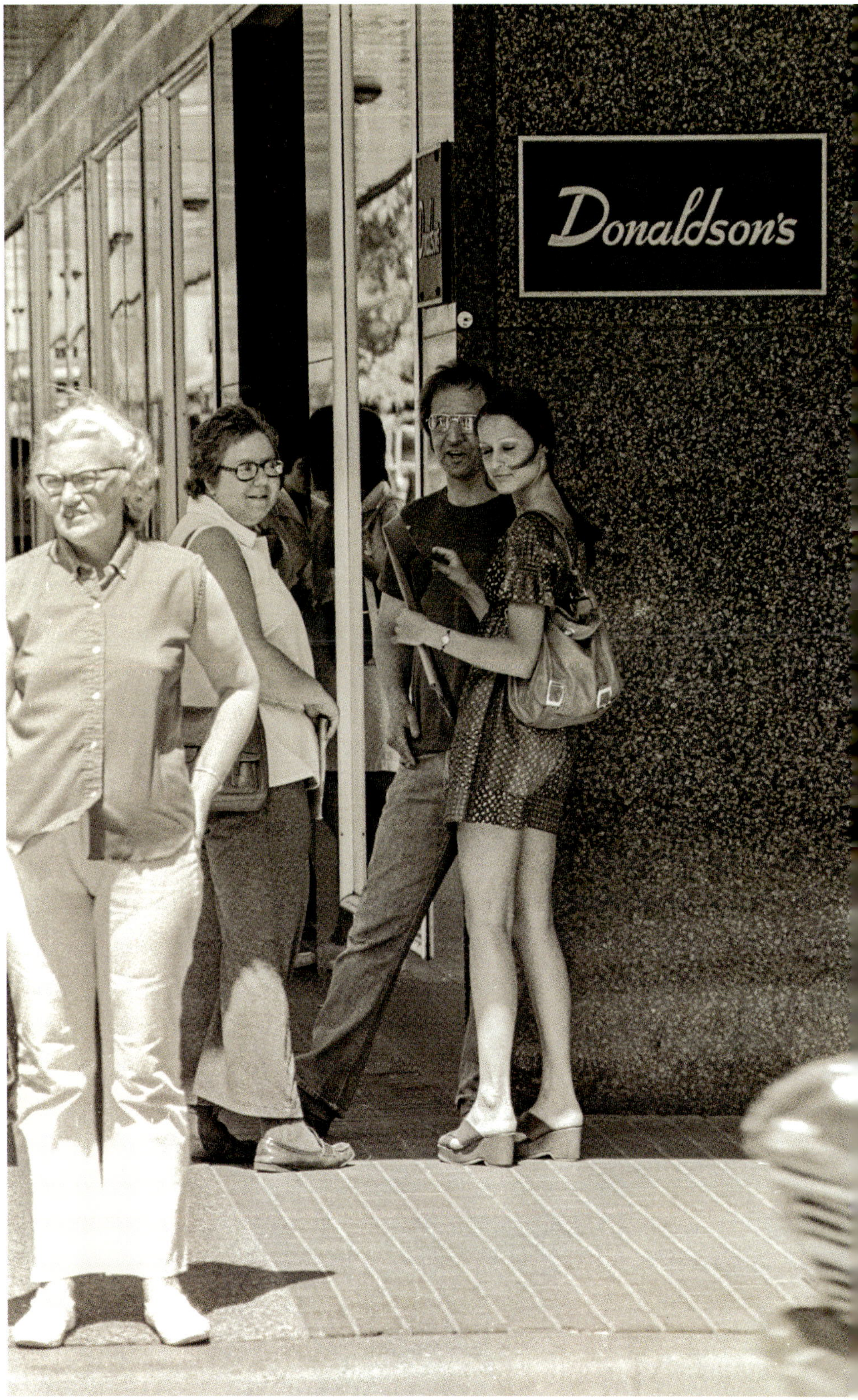

Photographer Marion Warling with a model outside of Donaldson's

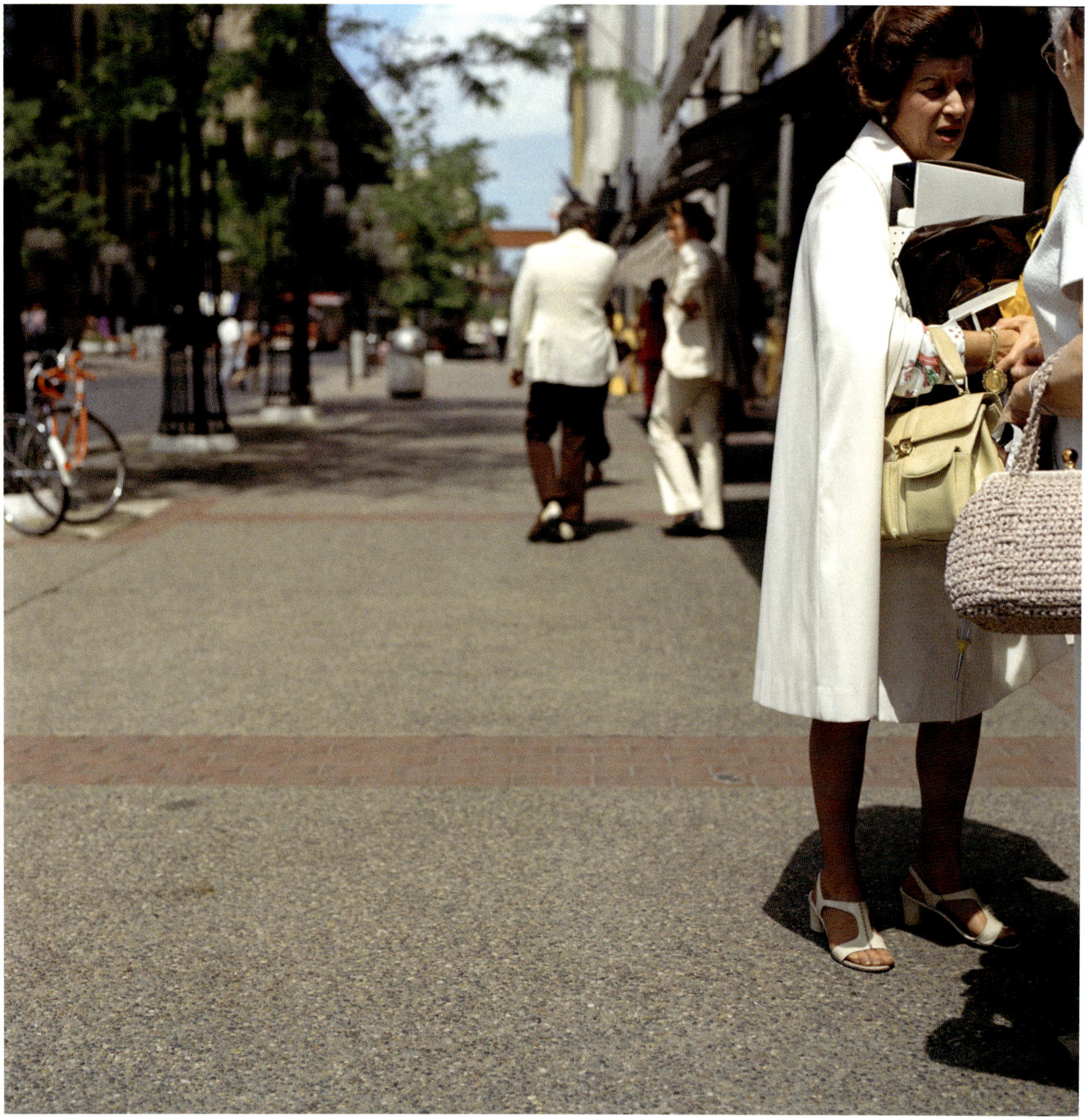

Women chatting on the mall after a day of shopping

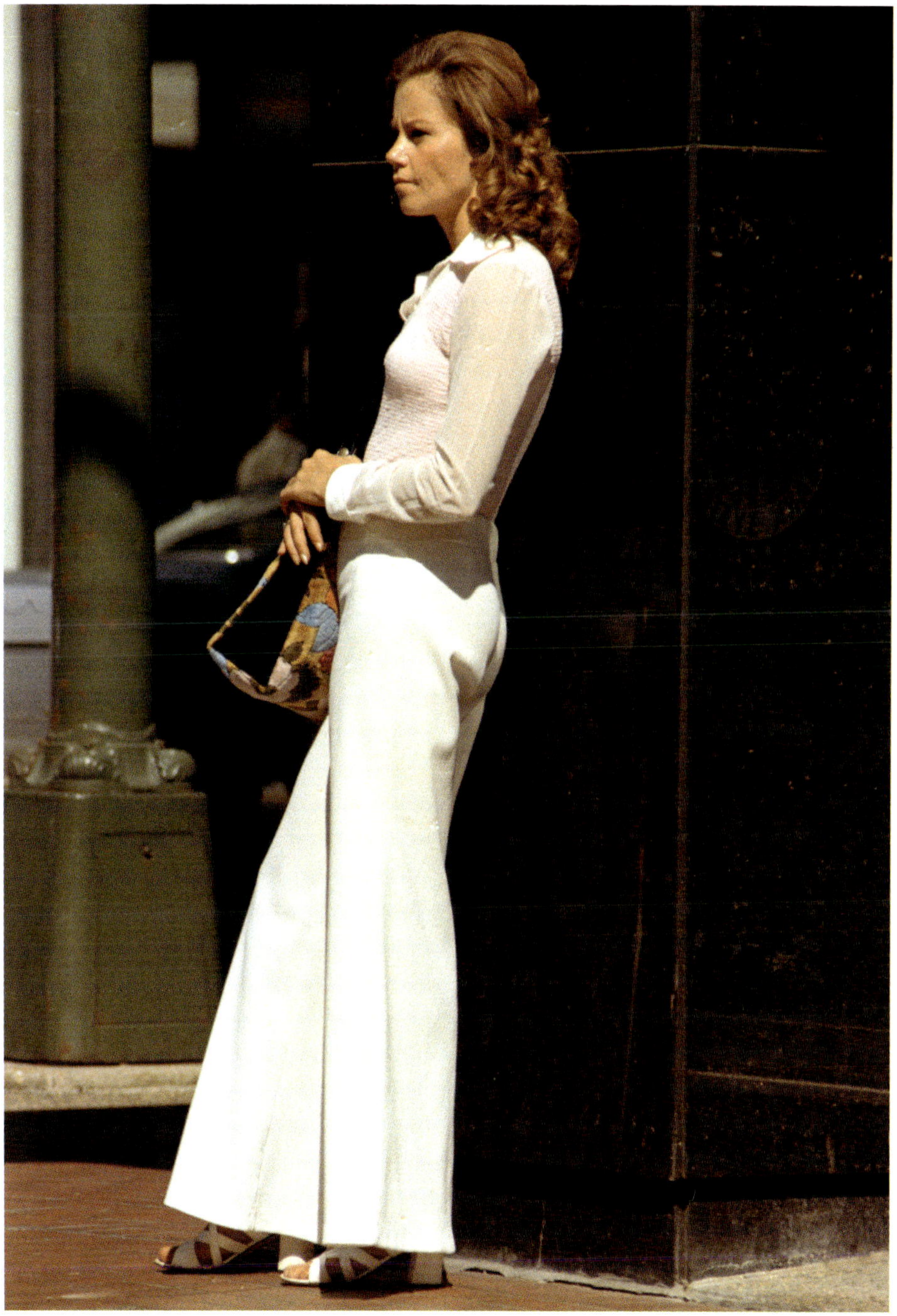

A woman waiting outside a store on Nicollet Mall

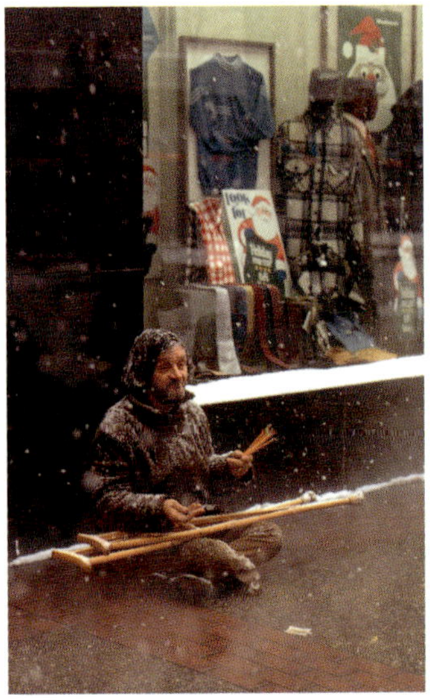

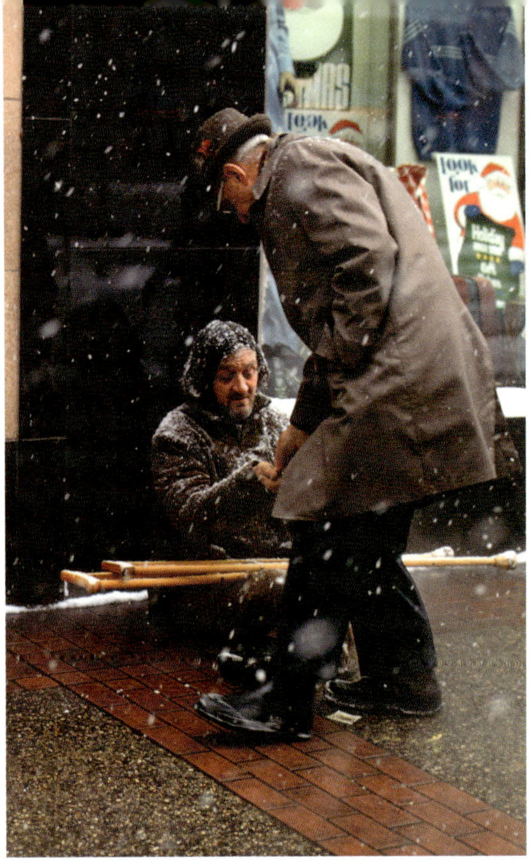

Selling pencils on the mall

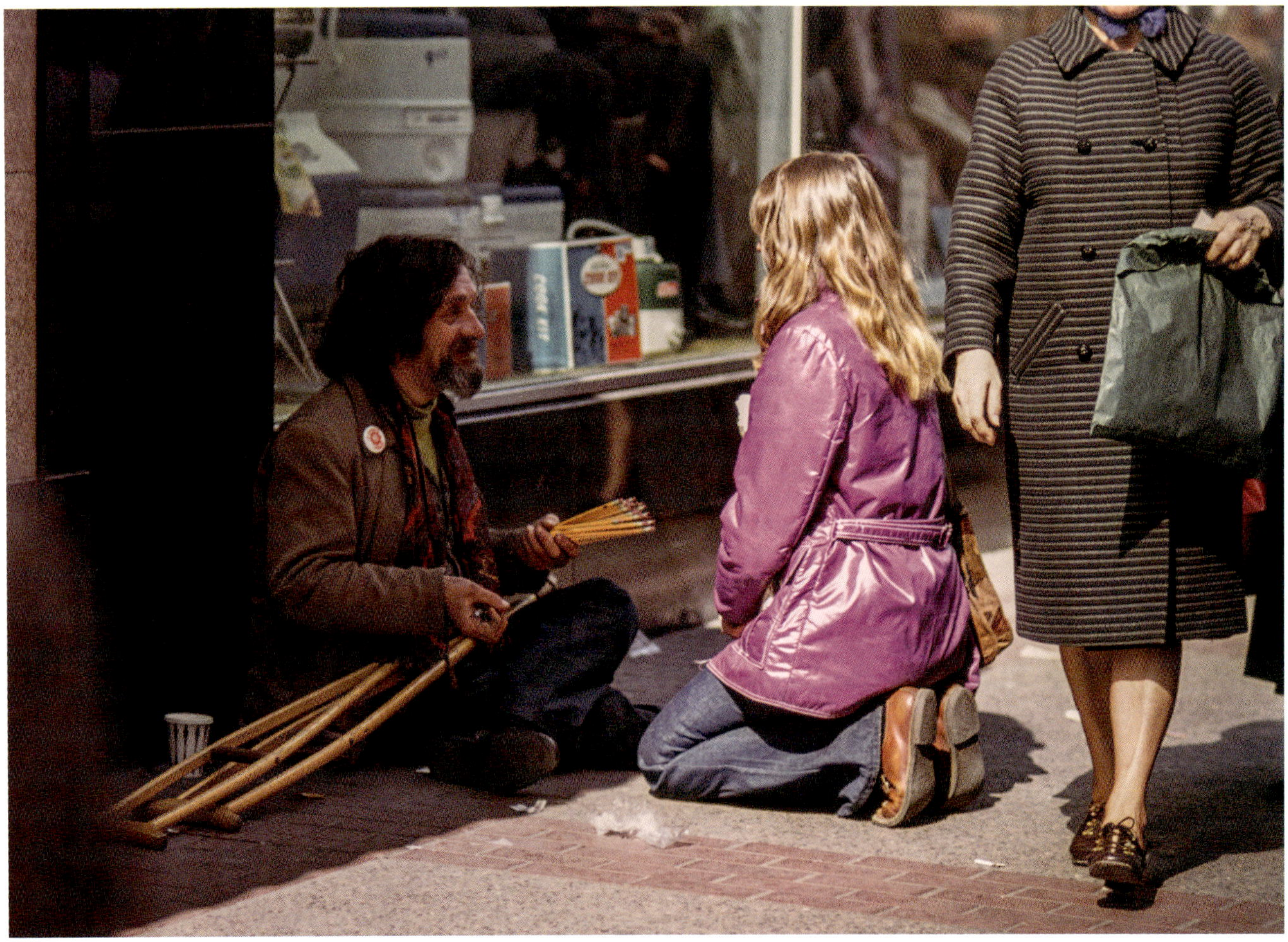

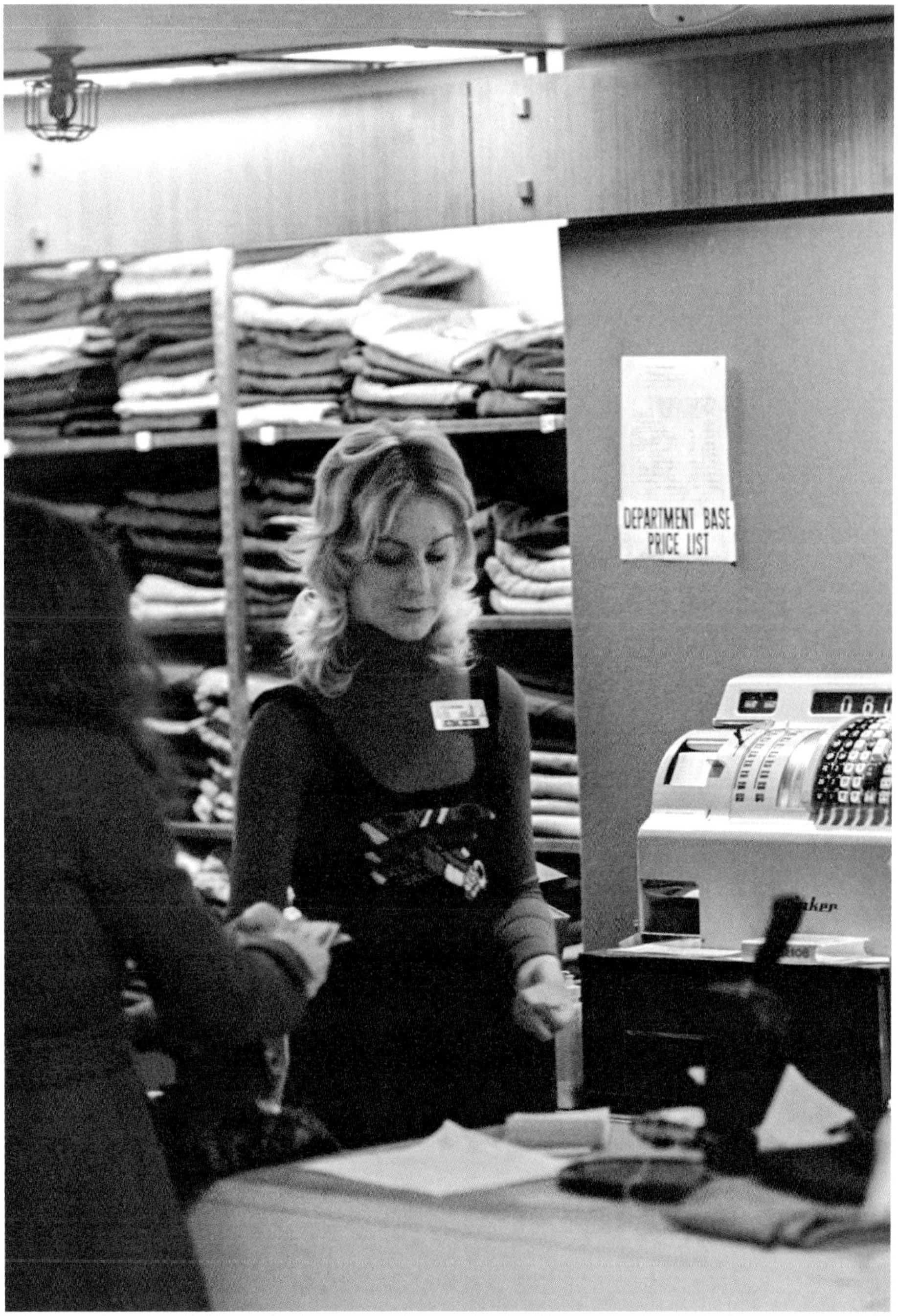

A Donaldson's cashier

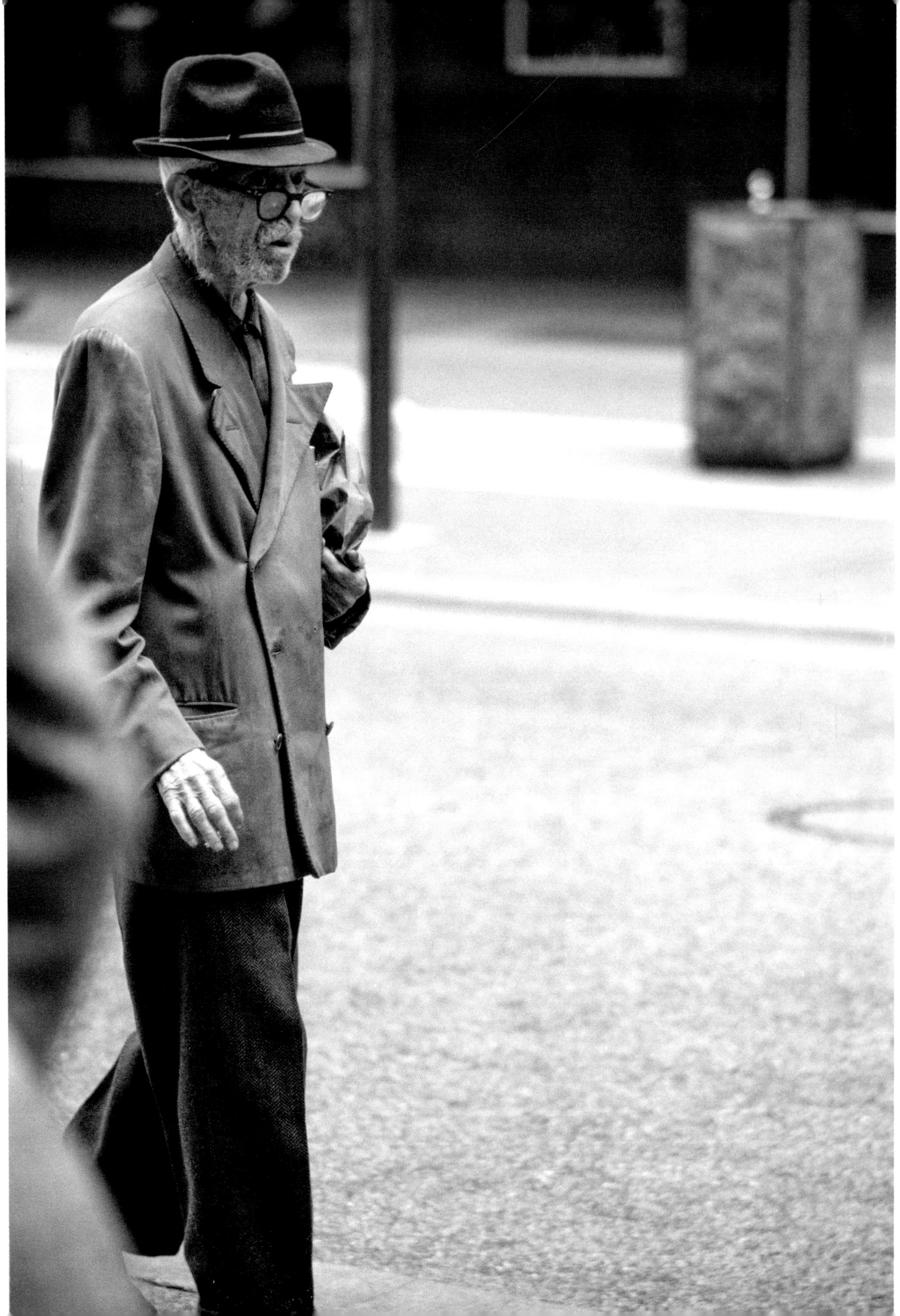

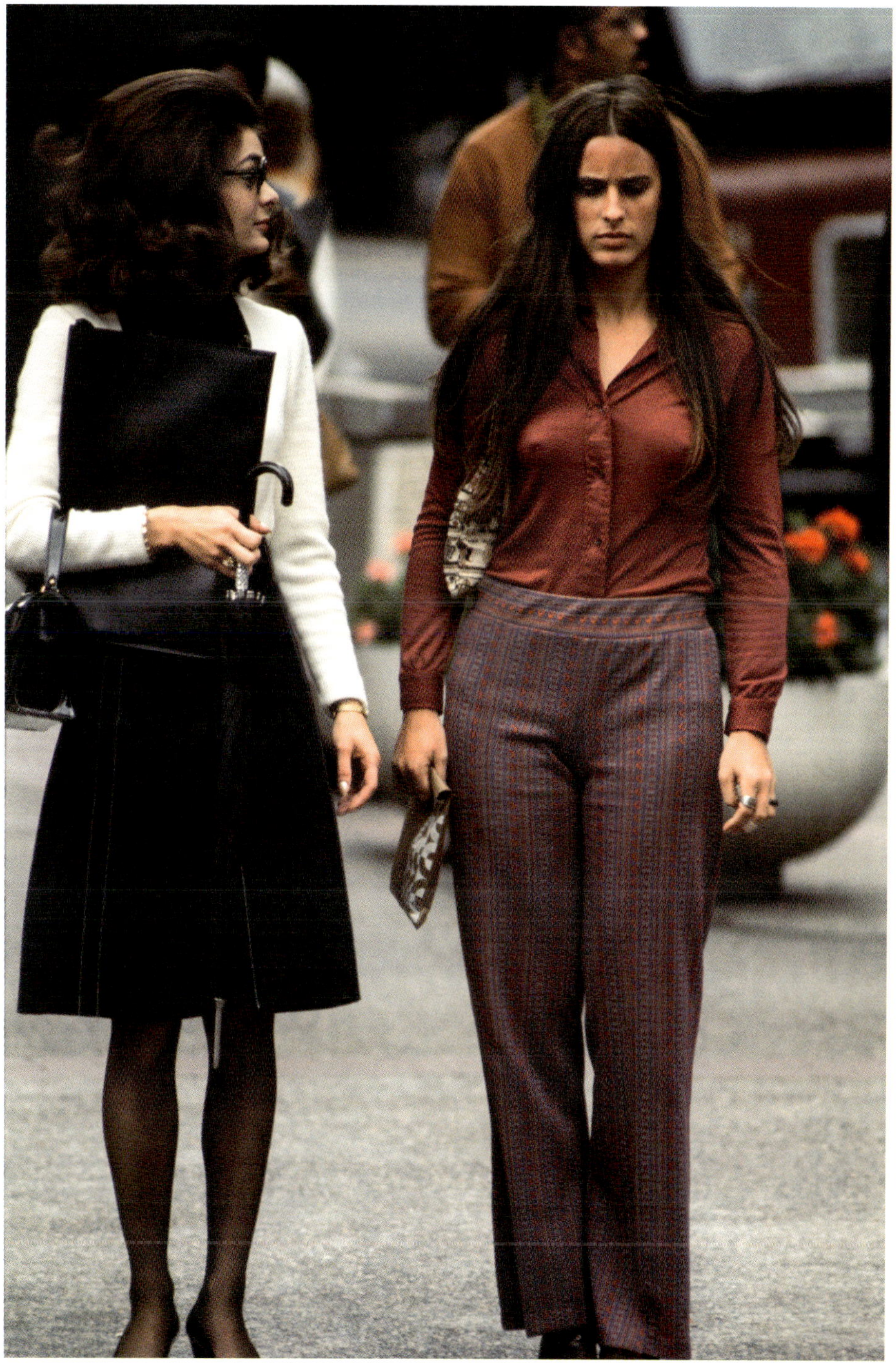

Above: Stylish Dayton's shoppers

Opposite: Out for a stroll on the mall

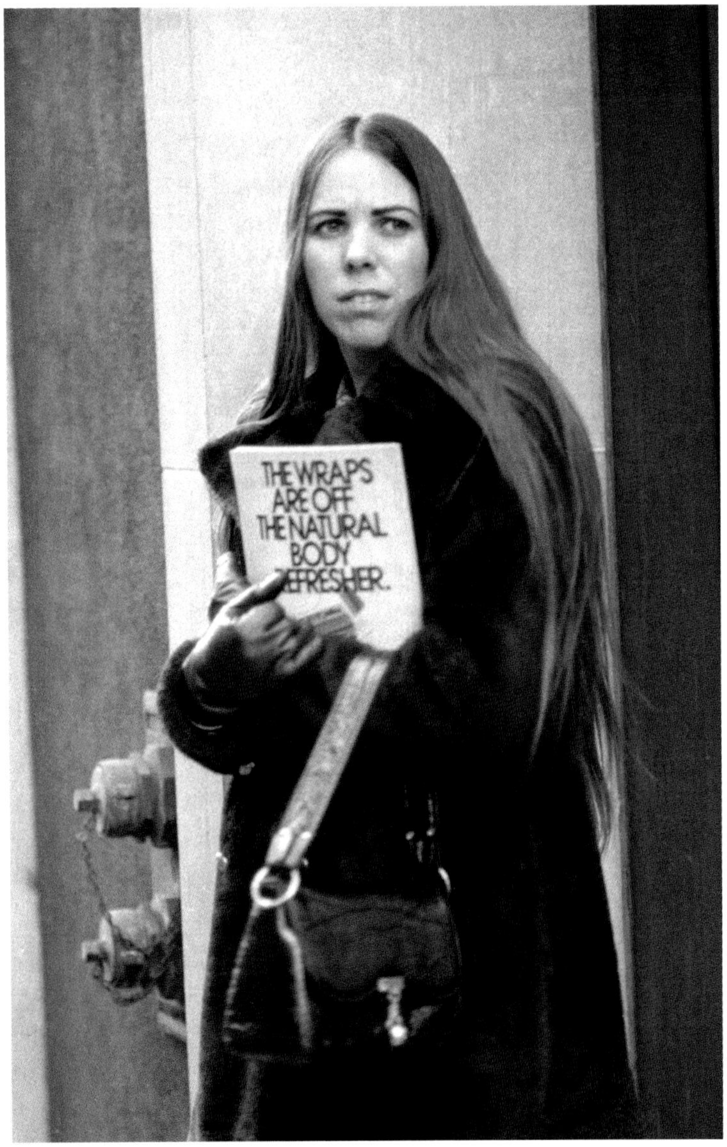

"The Wraps Are Off"

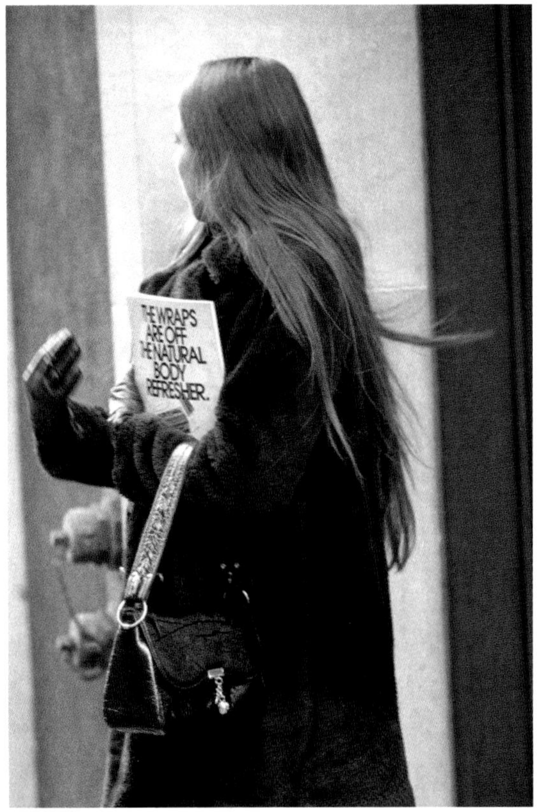

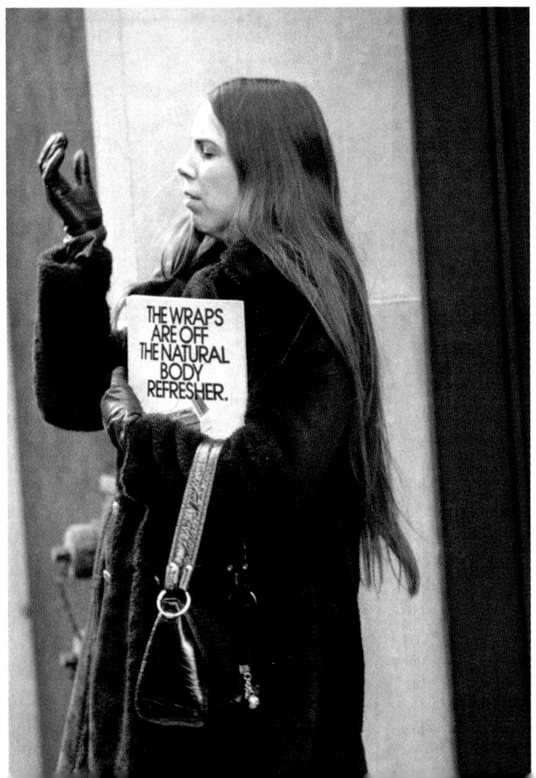

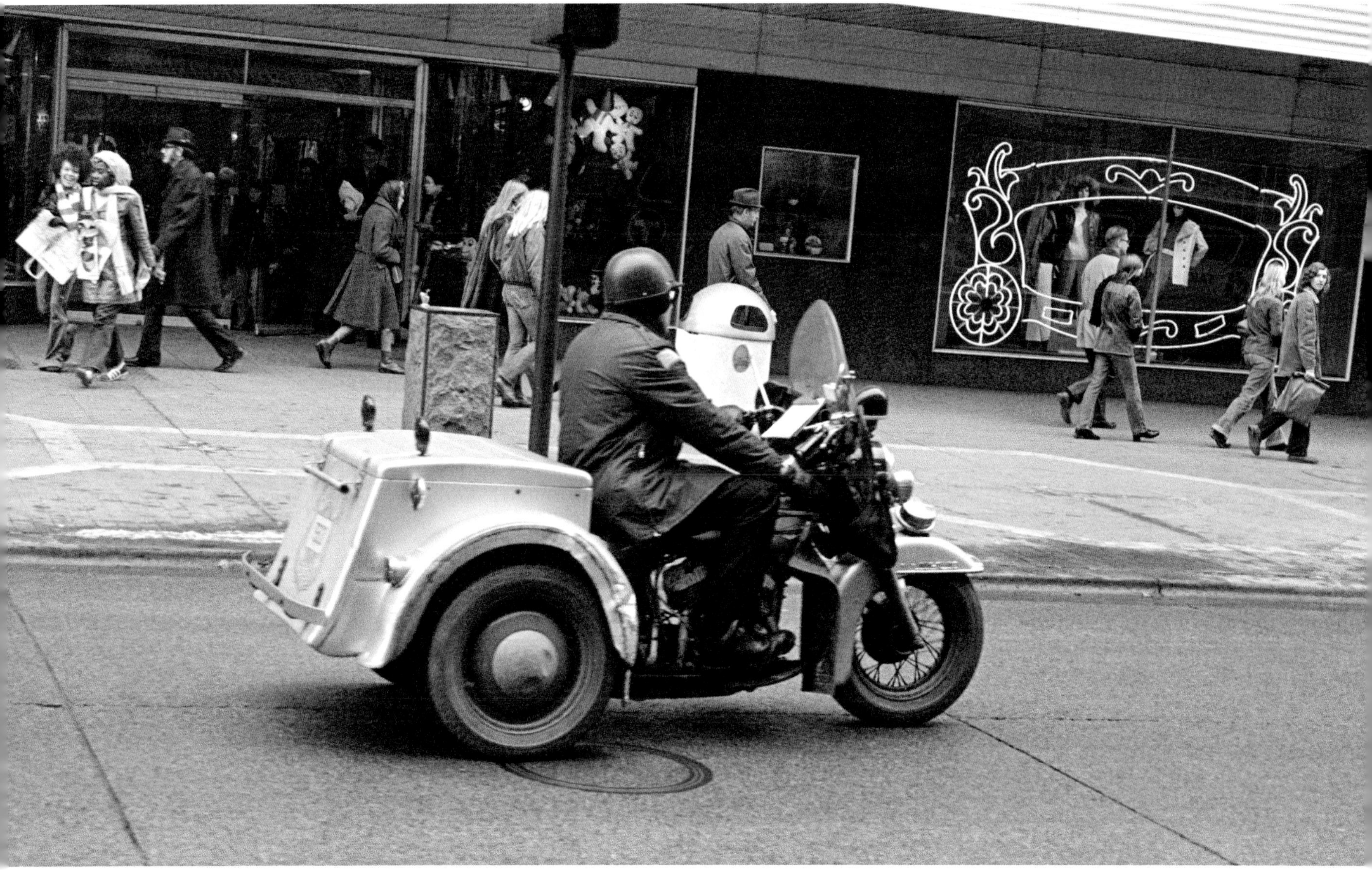

A motorcycle cop patrolling the mall

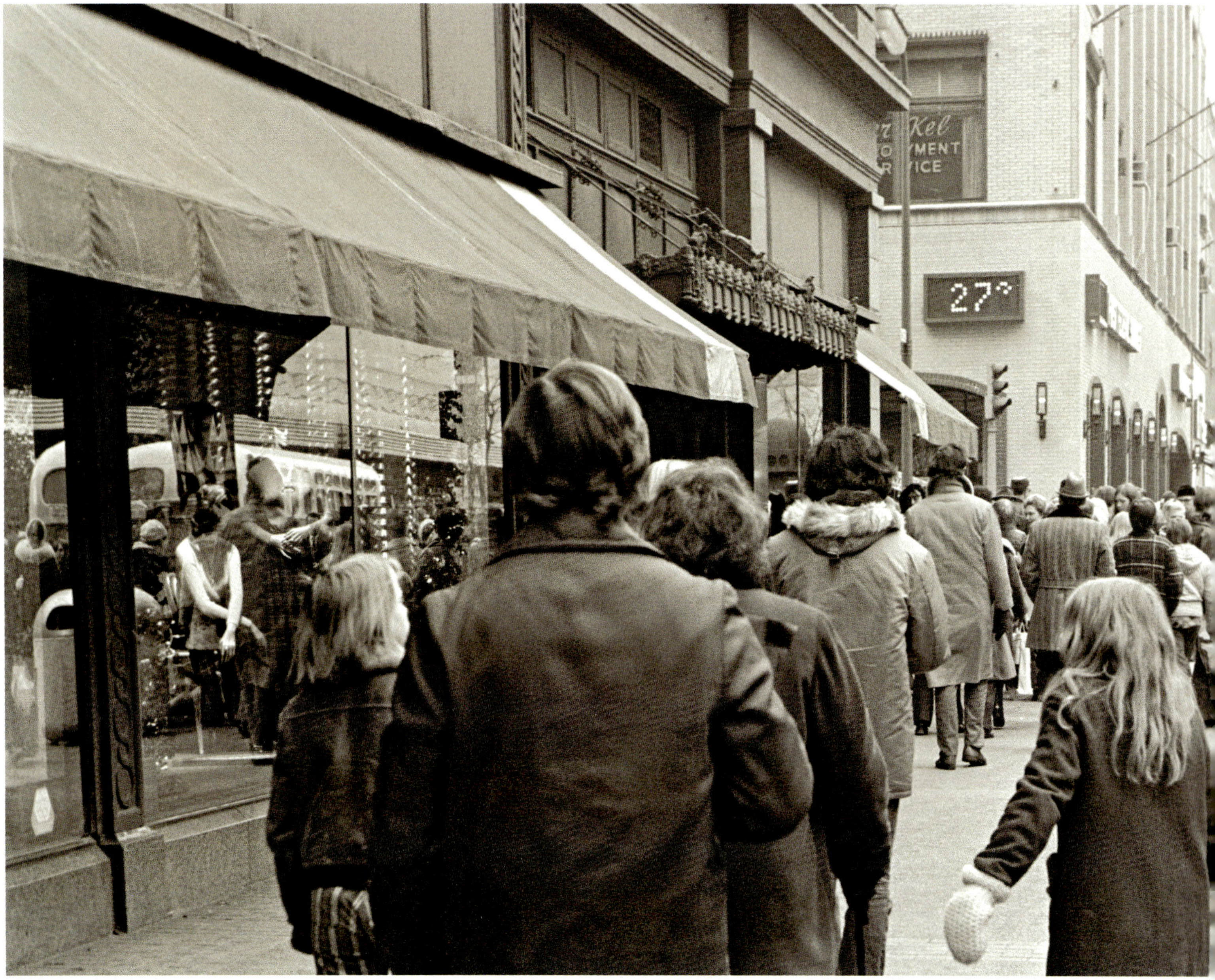

Twenty-seven degrees, and Nicollet Mall is still bustling

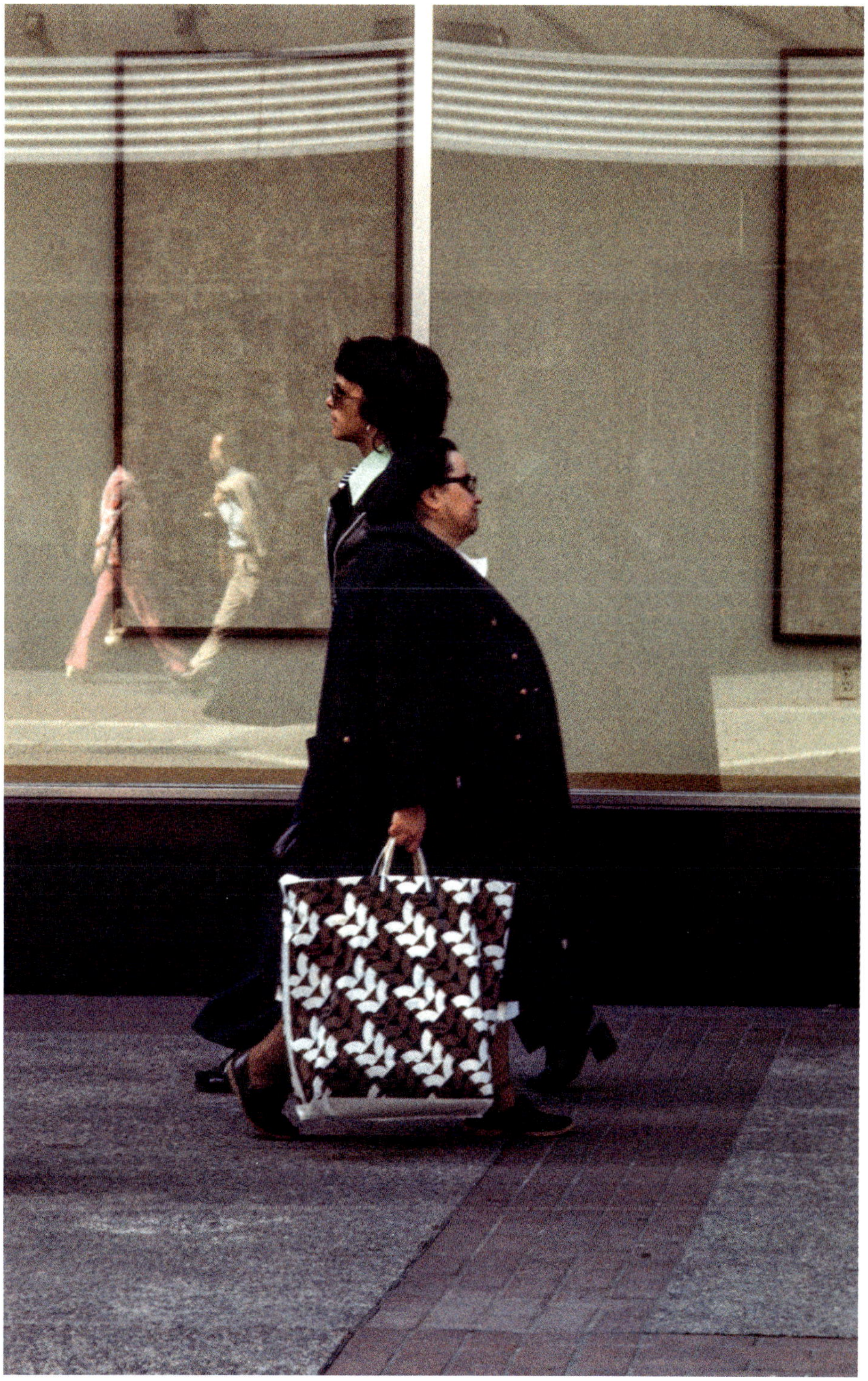

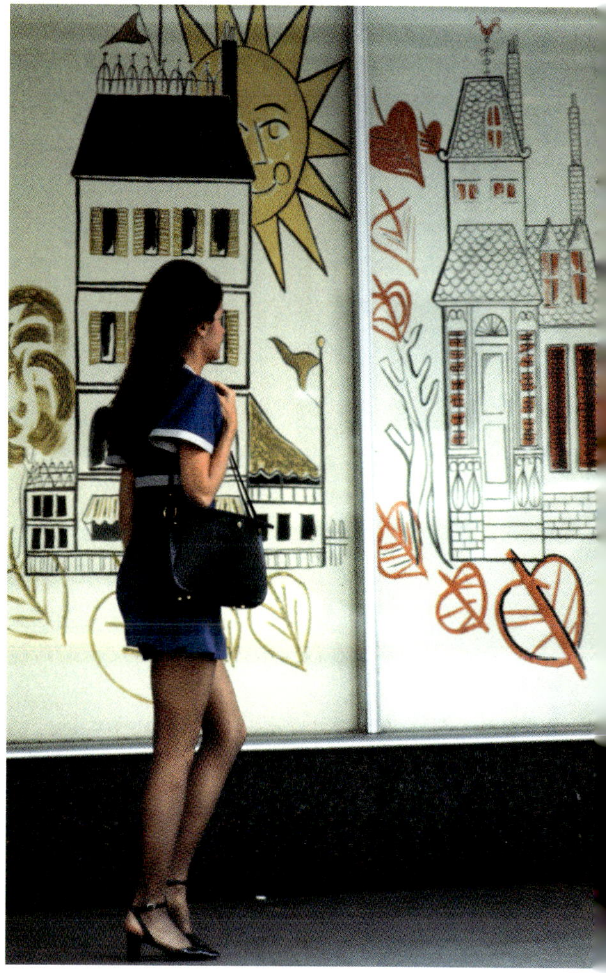

Above: Fashion and art on the mall

Left: More Dayton's shoppers

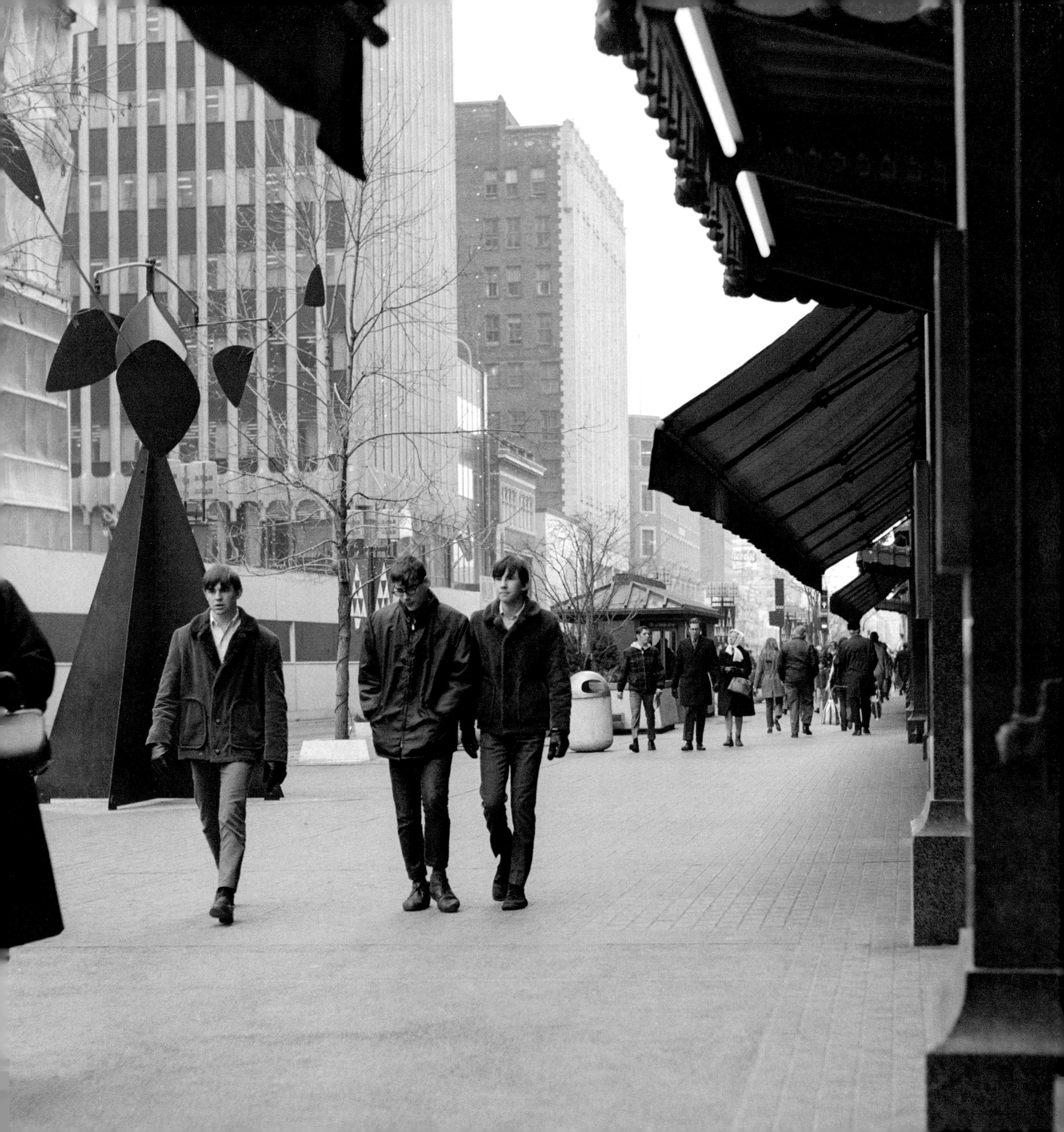

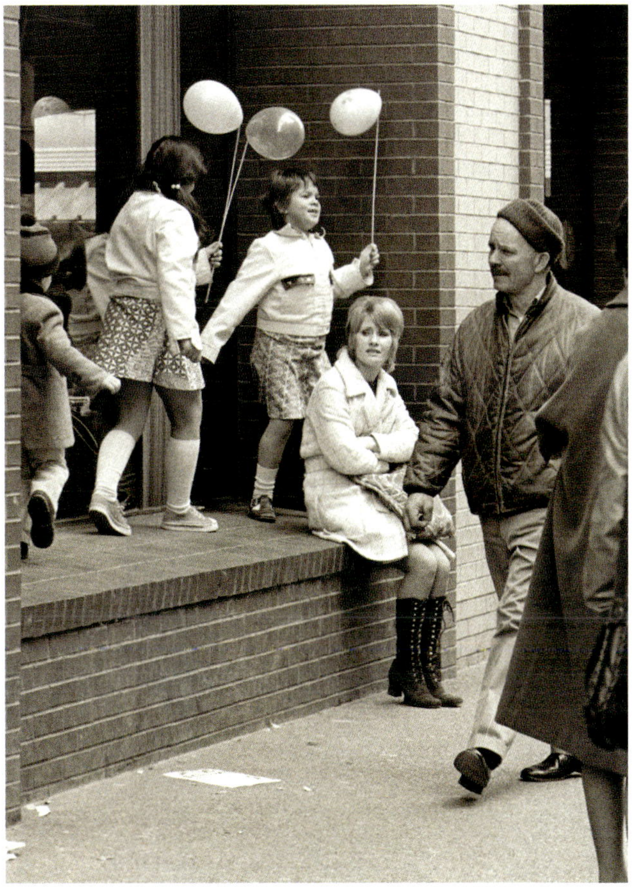

Above: Kids and mom waiting for a bus

Opposite: Young men walking by Alexander Calder's *The Spinner*—commissioned by Dayton's department store in 1967—on Nicollet Mall

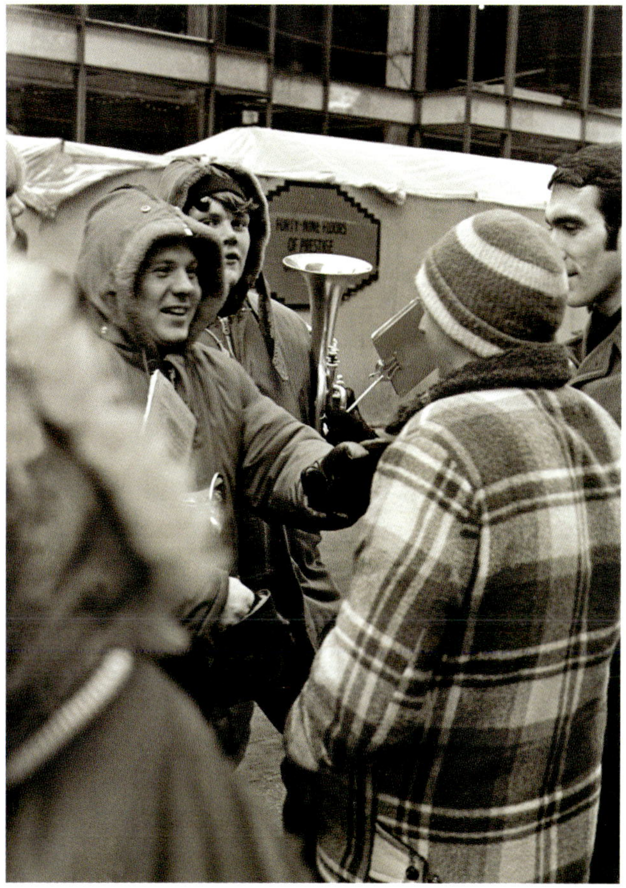

Street musicians performing on the mall

IDS

One ongoing story told in the images of Minneapolis in the early 1970s is the rise of the IDS Center. Over the course of two years, until its completion in 1972, Mike's photos mark, with increasing interest, the structure's rise to the top of the skyline. For more than forty years, the art deco Foshay Tower had been the tallest structure in town, and it was utterly dwarfed by this new, steel-and-glass building—a testament to postwar Minneapolis's prosperity and its growing role as a regional leader. Philip Johnson's design for the IDS Tower is sleek and sophisticated, an altogether modern statement that makes few concessions to the existing urban fabric. It was not, like the mills that had towered over the city in the previous century, a monument to manufacturing or labor. Nor was it, like the once-formidable city hall, a monument to governance. "IDS" was short for "Investors Diversified Services." This was a monument to the sort of high finance that would define the city's new identity.

In his photos, Mike pioneered a kind of Minneapolis-specific street photographic subgenre: the "IDS neck crane." The tower was so out of scale with anything else in the city that it invited enthusiastic gawking from Nicollet Mall below. For at least ten or perhaps twenty years, this was a sure way to separate the tourists from the townies while walking downtown: the tourists would inevitably be standing in the middle of the sidewalk, staring up. You see less of that today, but it's still out there.

A columnist from the local paper visited the top of the IDS right before it opened and reported sadly on the scene below: "Downtown looks like a giant parking lot with a few buildings tossed in for comic effect. . . . Freeways suture the landscape." The IDS changed the way the city looked not just from below but from above. "Our city's planners and zoners and developers should spend some contemplative hours looking at their problems from this elevation," the columnist suggested.

At the time of its debut, public opinion on the new skyscraper was somewhat mixed, though generally favorable. The building, many thought, made Minneapolis seem like a real city. A poll in the *Star* was split about fifty-five/forty-five between those impressed and those with reservations, the "impressed" side having the statistical edge. Affection for it grew over time, especially as the rest of the skyline caught up. The tower is now one of the most beloved features of the urban landscape. It has taken on an untouchable quality. When the new First Bank Place (now known as the Capella Tower) challenged its dominance for the title of highest skyscraper in the state in the early 1990s, there was something of an outcry. Let the IDS be the tallest, people said.

Another consequence of the tower rising so high is that it connected the Twin Cities visually unlike anything else had previously. From certain vantage points in St. Paul, one had barely been able to see the Foshay peeking above the tree line. But the IDS was clearly visible from deep in the heart of Minneapolis's easterly twin across the river. You could see it easily from Highland Park or Merriam Park, residential enclaves of St. Paul that historically had been as spiritually distant from Minneapolis as Lake Michigan or North Dakota.

"One year, I looked west and there stood a stark pillar of a building, rising higher than anything we'd ever known in this region of the country," wrote broadcaster and St. Paul native T. D. Mischke in a 2013 essay for *MinnPost*. "They called it 'IDS,' but that's not the term Uncle Kenny used as he stood with me staring across the fast flowing water. 'Tommy boy,' he said, 'that there is Minneapolis giving us the finger; something they've been wanting to do for some time now.'"

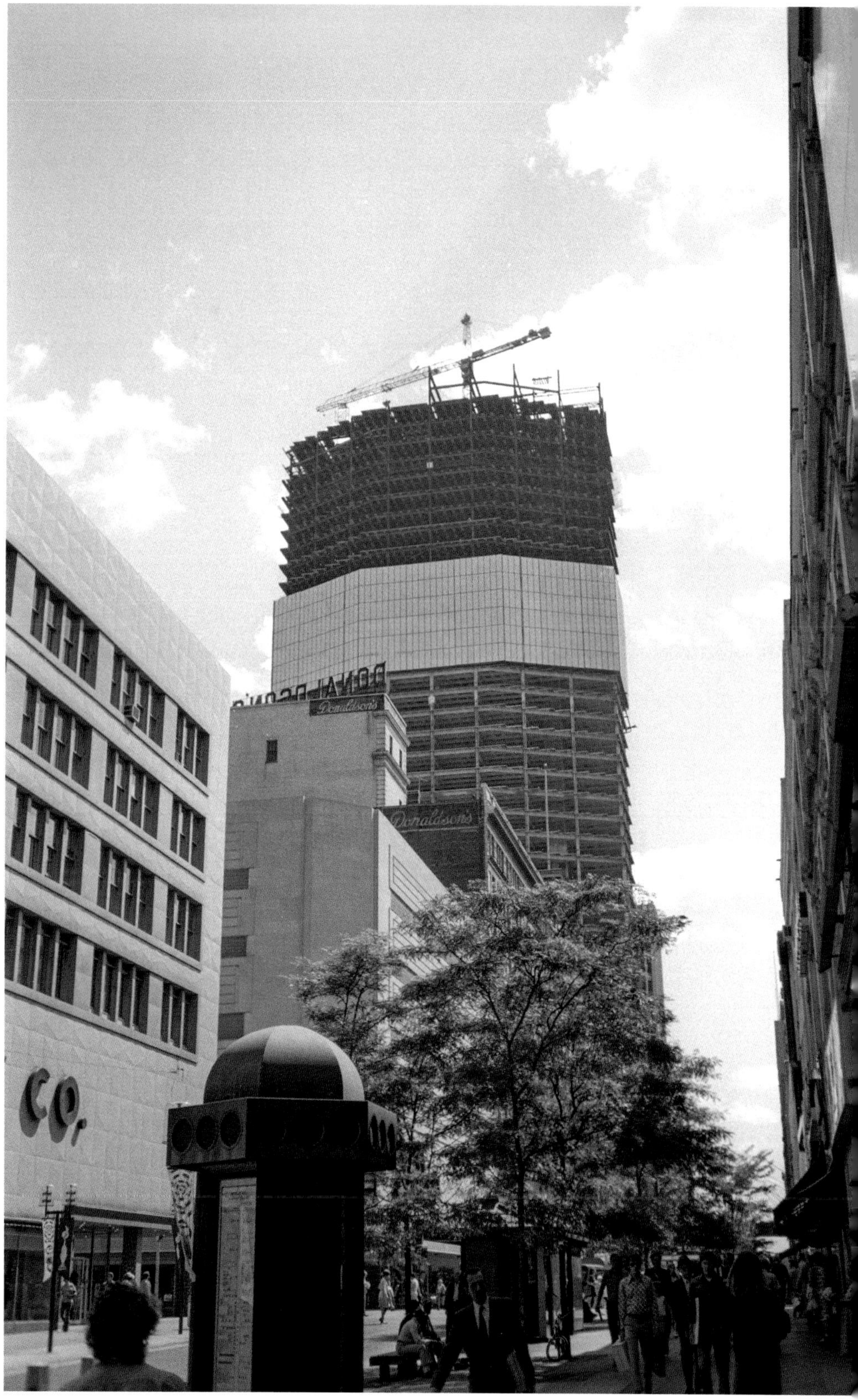

The IDS Center under construction on Nicollet Mall

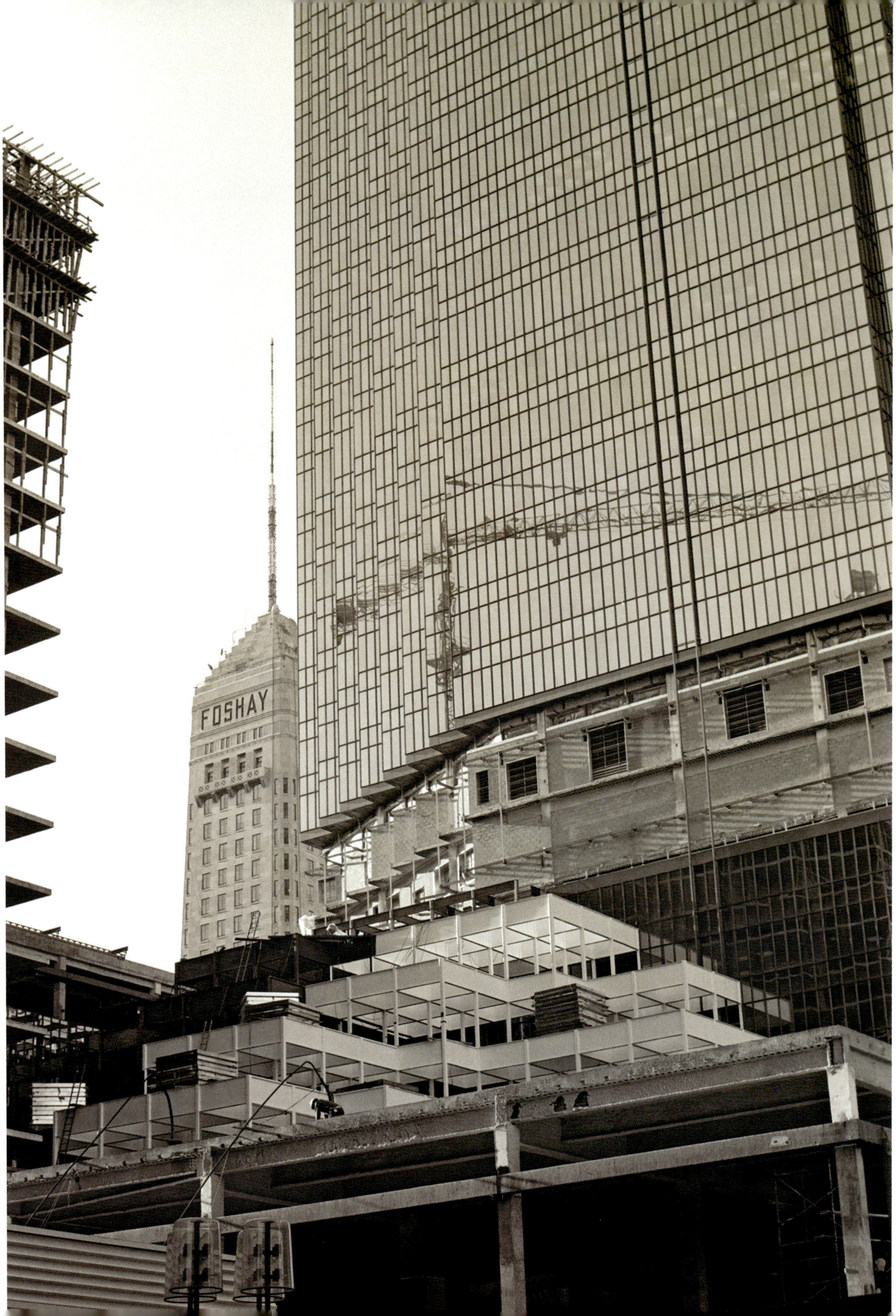
FOSHAY

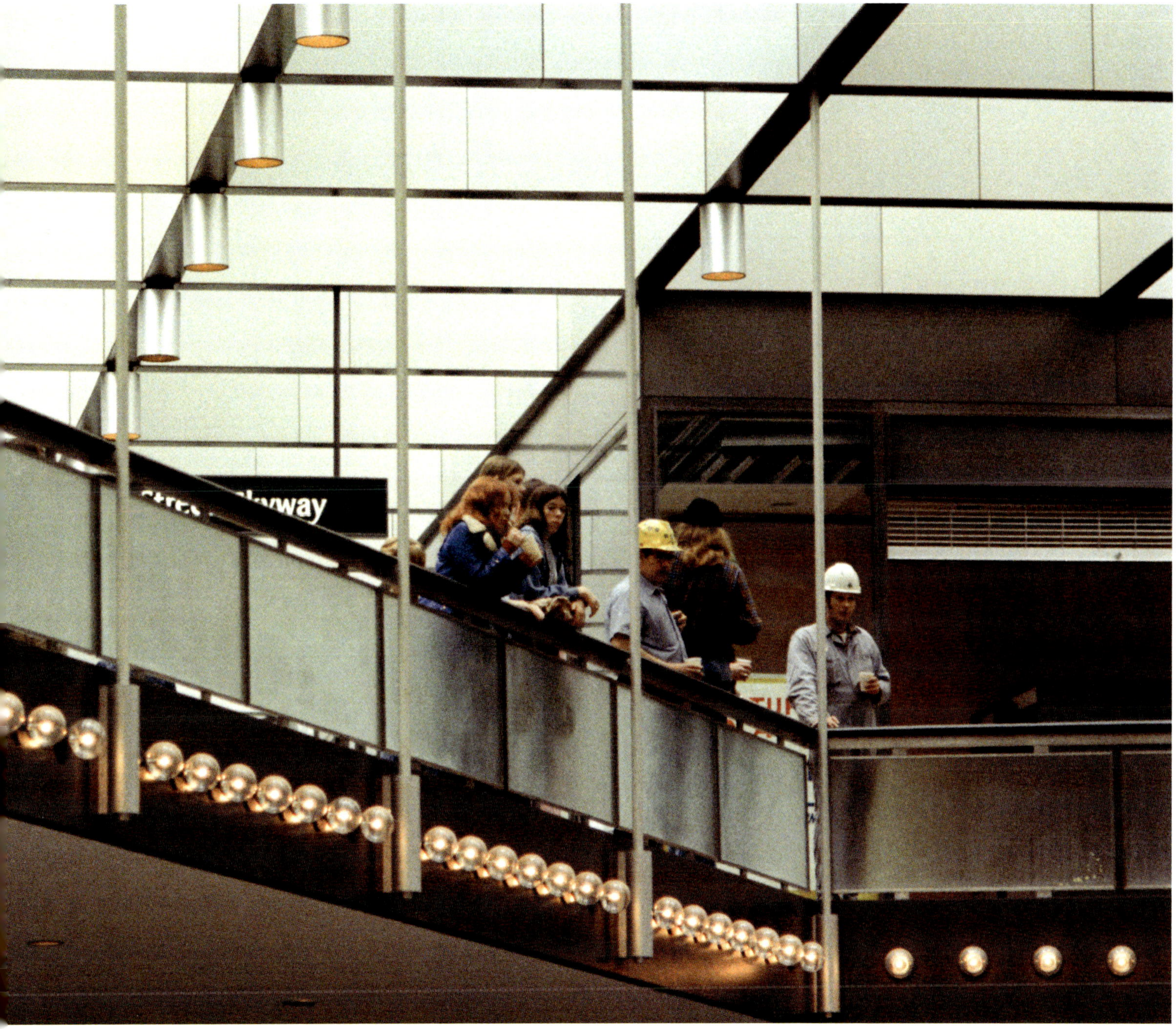

Above: Visitors and workers checking out the Crystal Court in the IDS Center

Opposite: The Crystal Court and the IDS under construction, with the Foshay Tower in the background

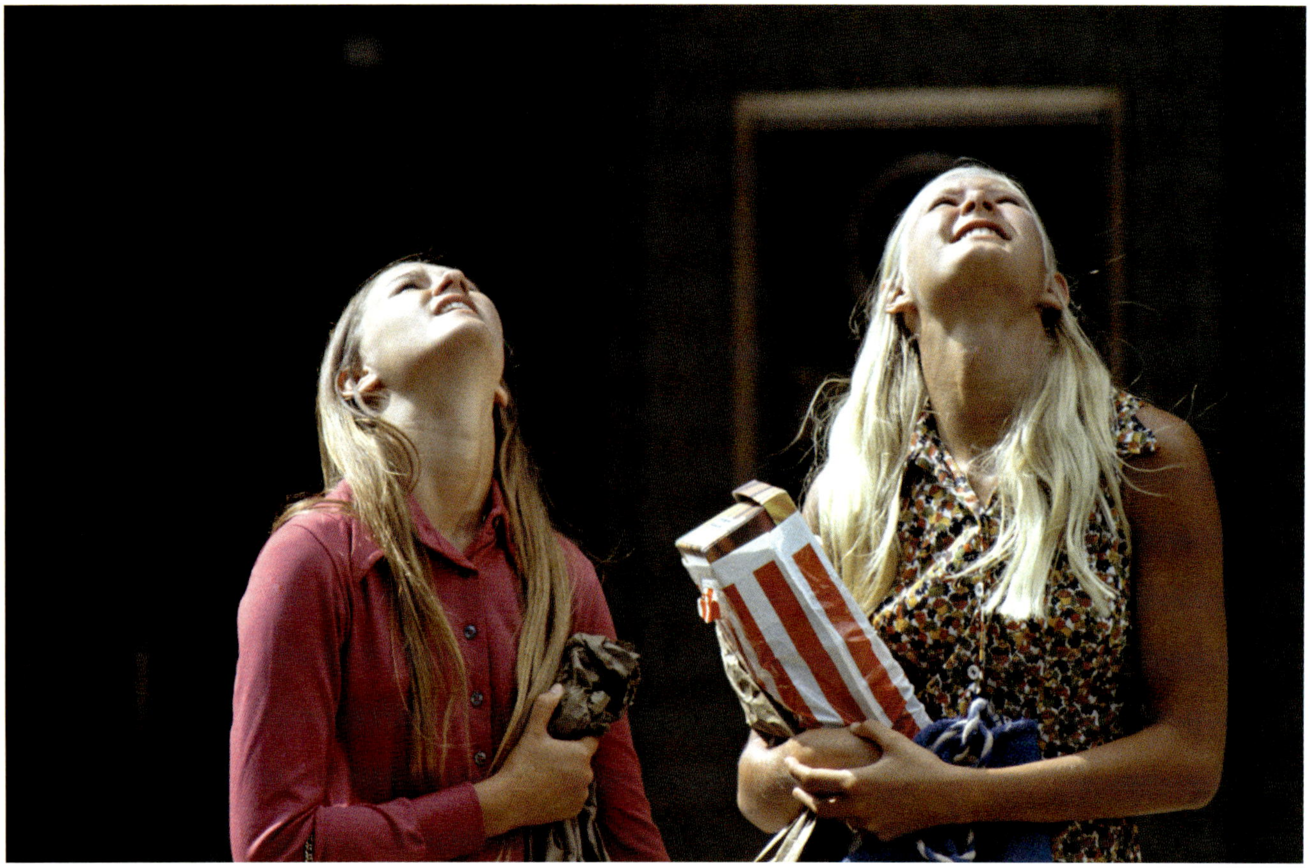

Above: The IDS neck crane

Opposite: The nearly completed IDS Tower from below

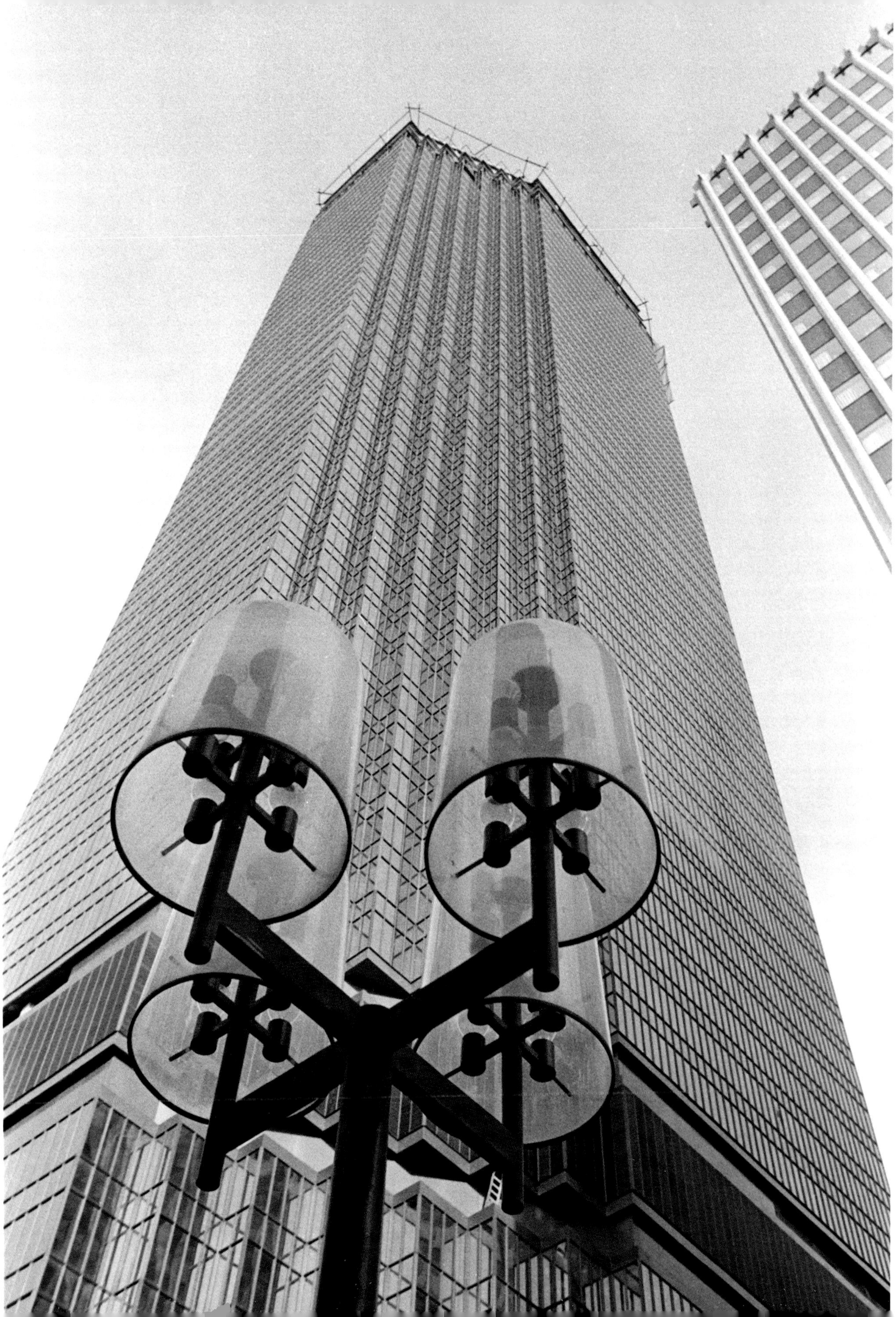

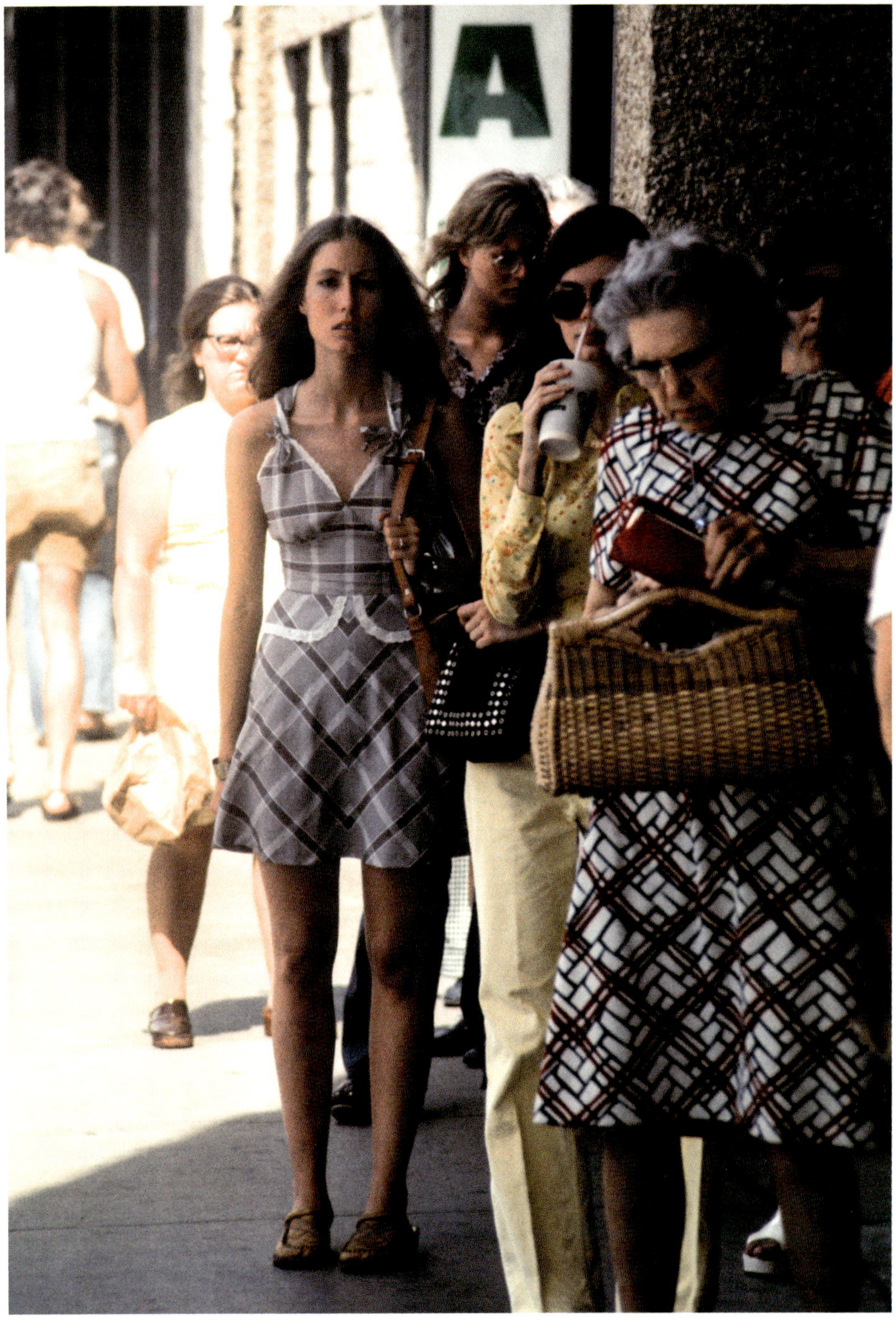

Women young and old waiting on Nicollet Mall

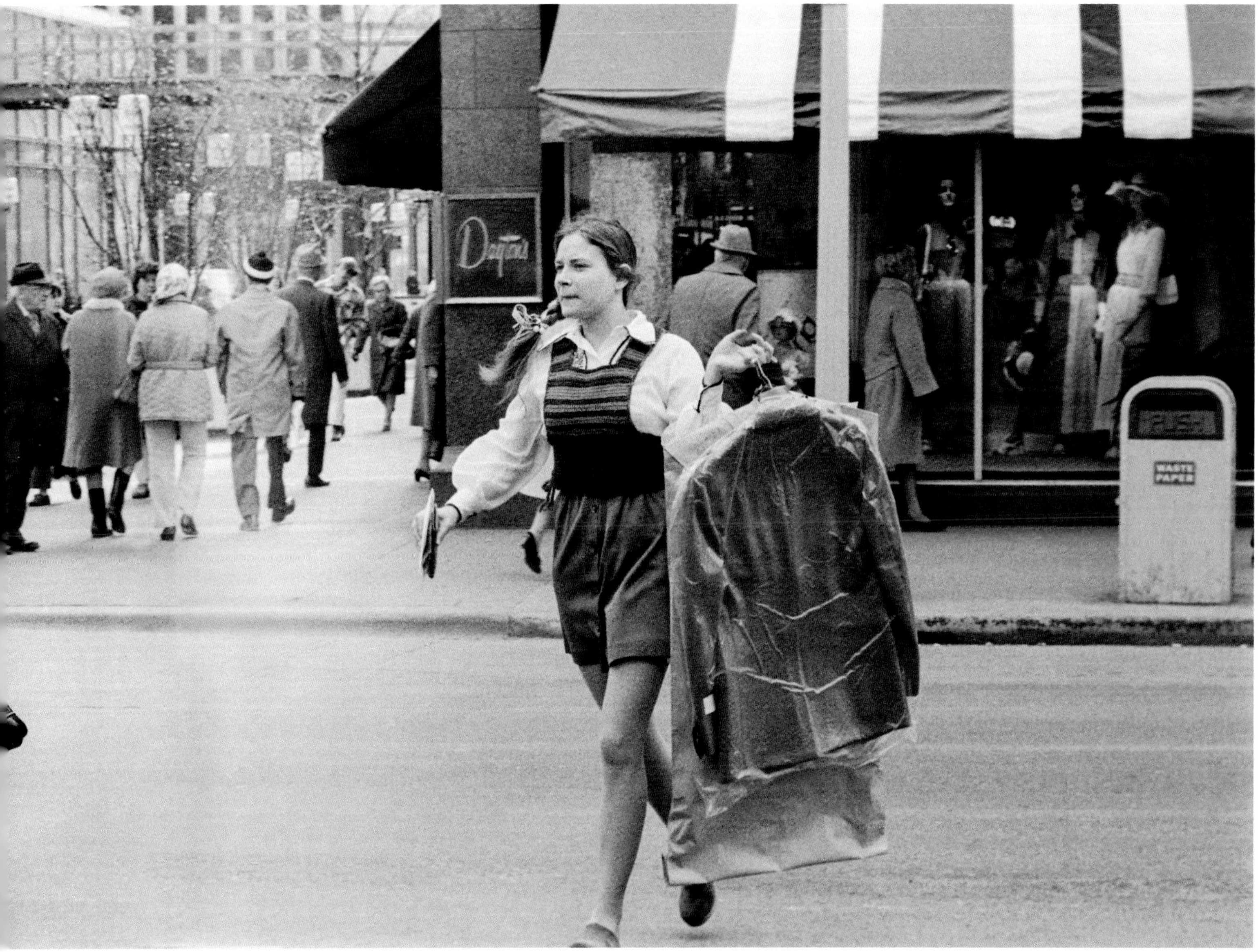

A successful shopping trip to Dayton's

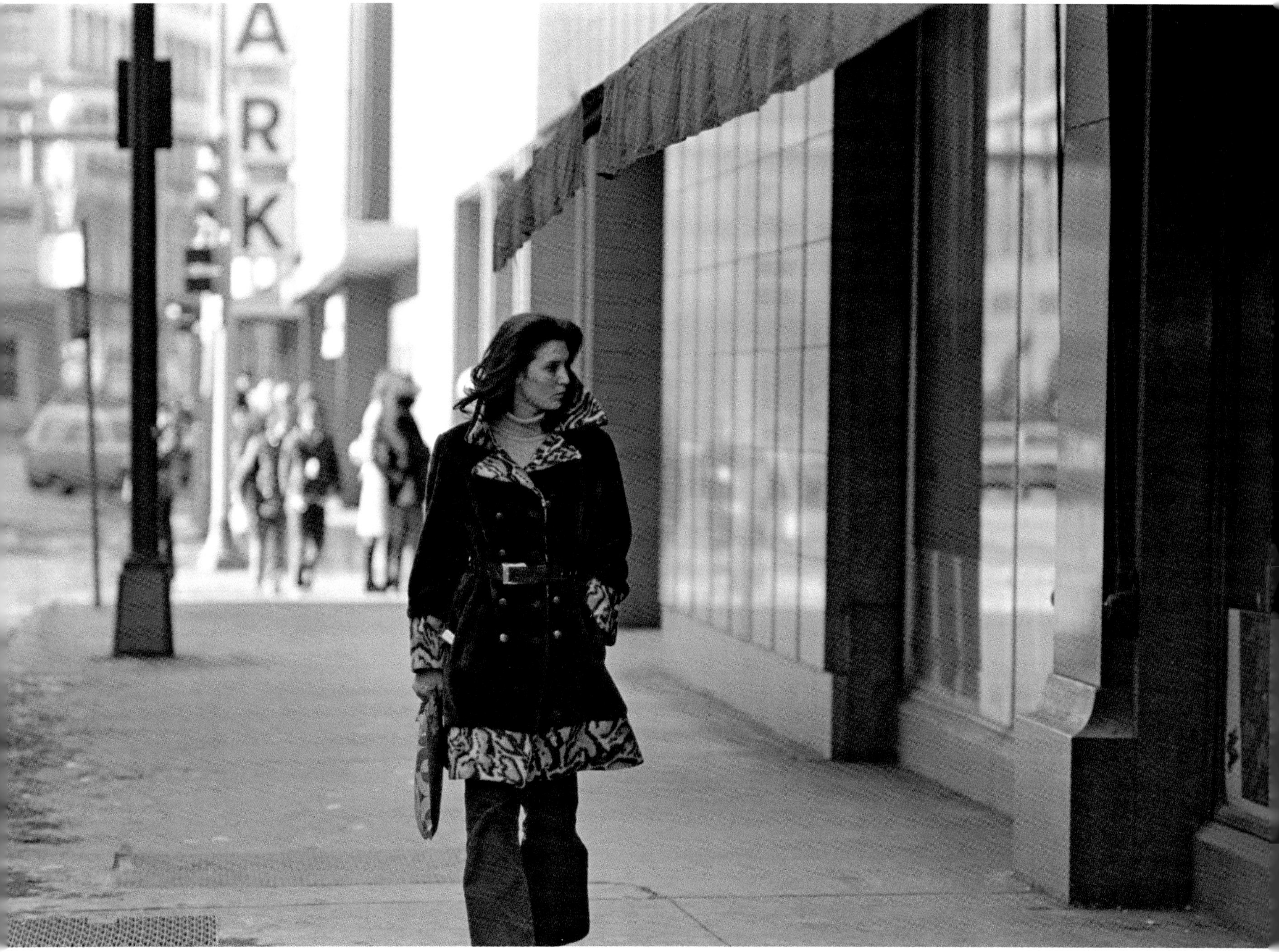

A Dayton's bag—the ultimate fashion accessory

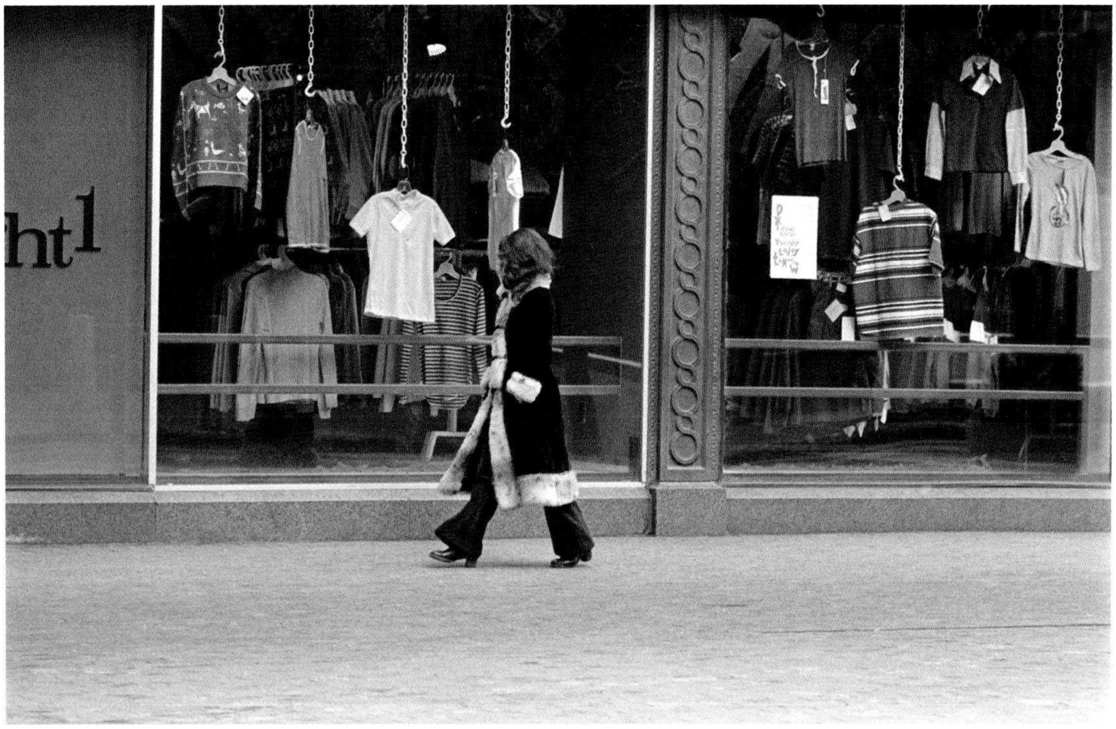

Window shopping at Dayton's

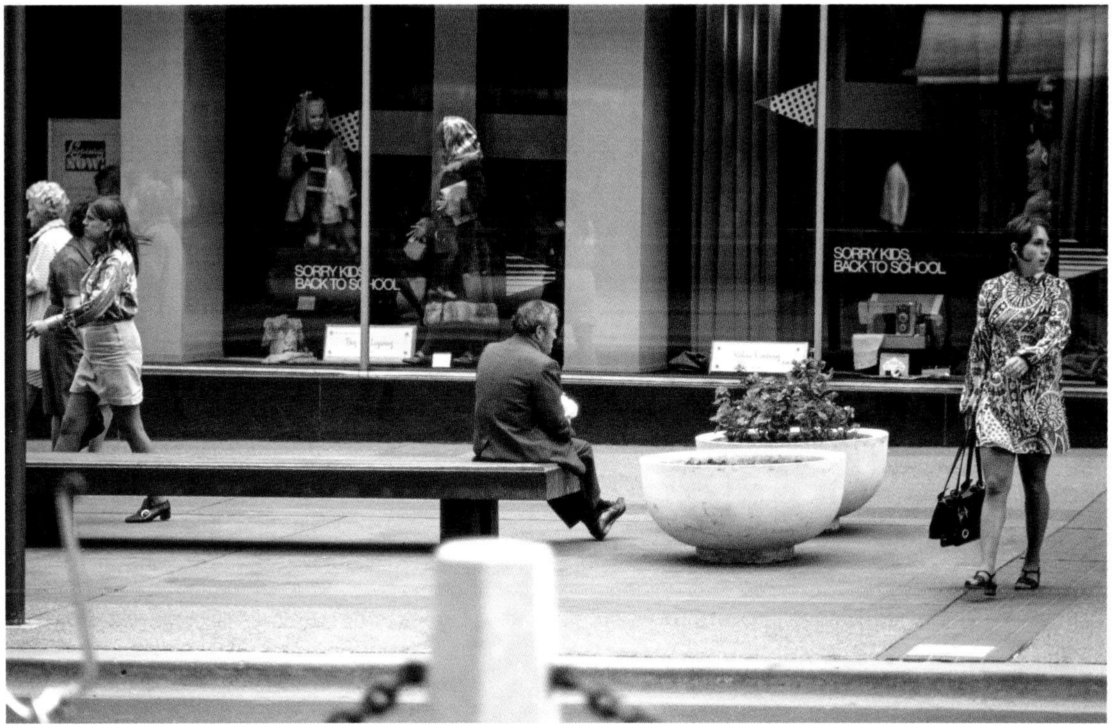

"Sorry Kids, Back to School" window display at Donaldson's

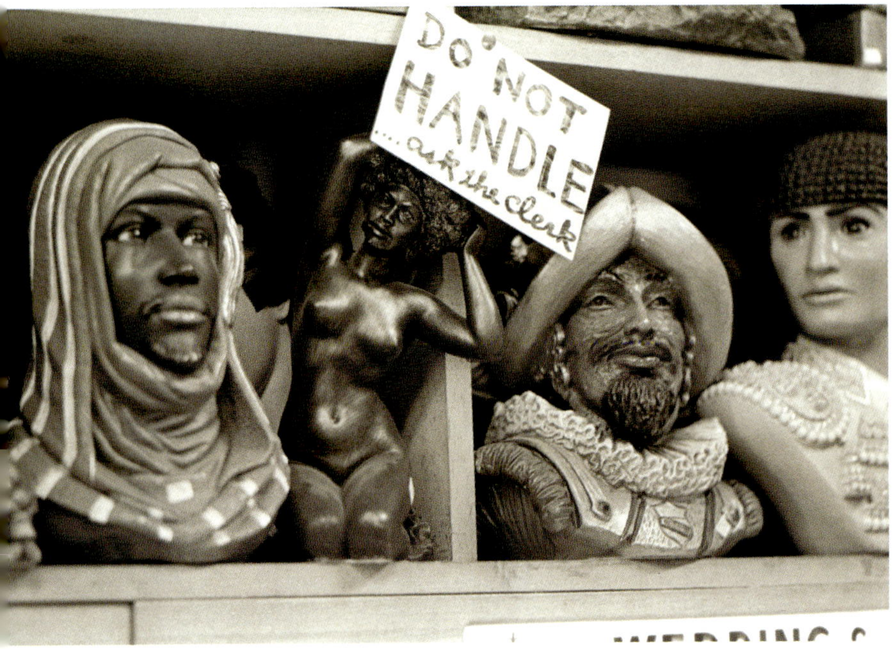

Sculptures and figurines in a window display

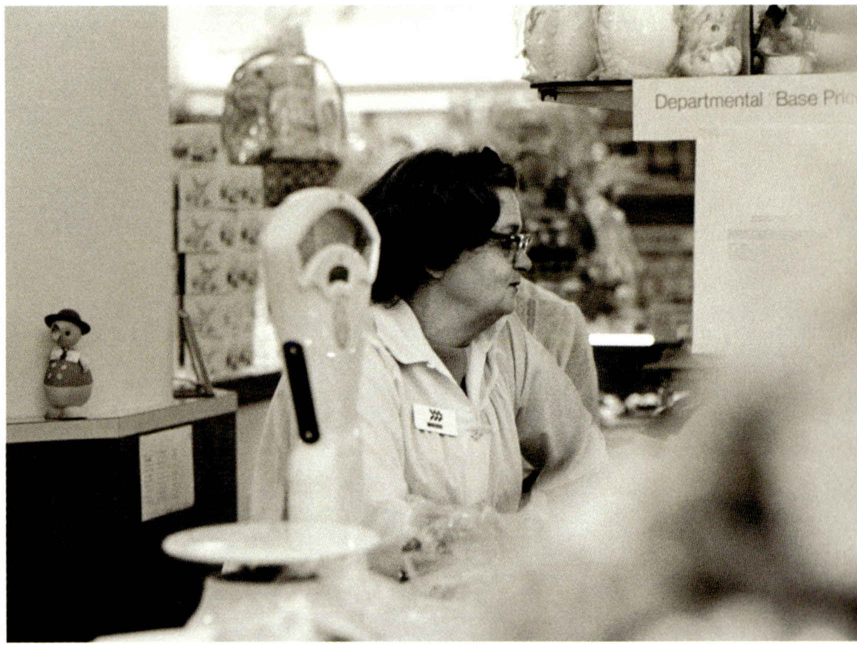

An employee at the Dayton's candy counter

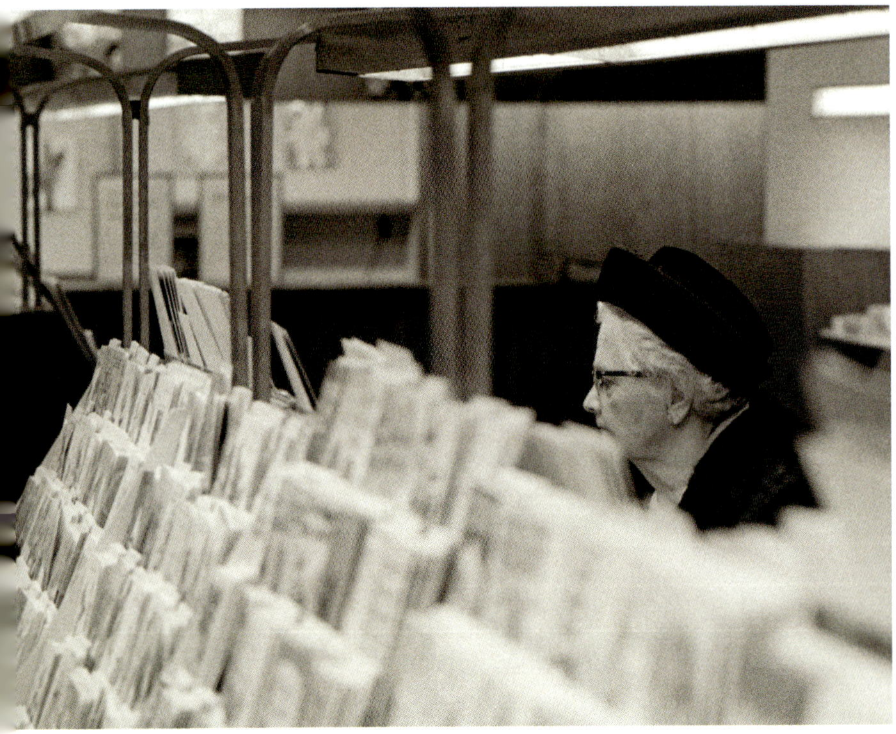

Shopping for the perfect greeting card

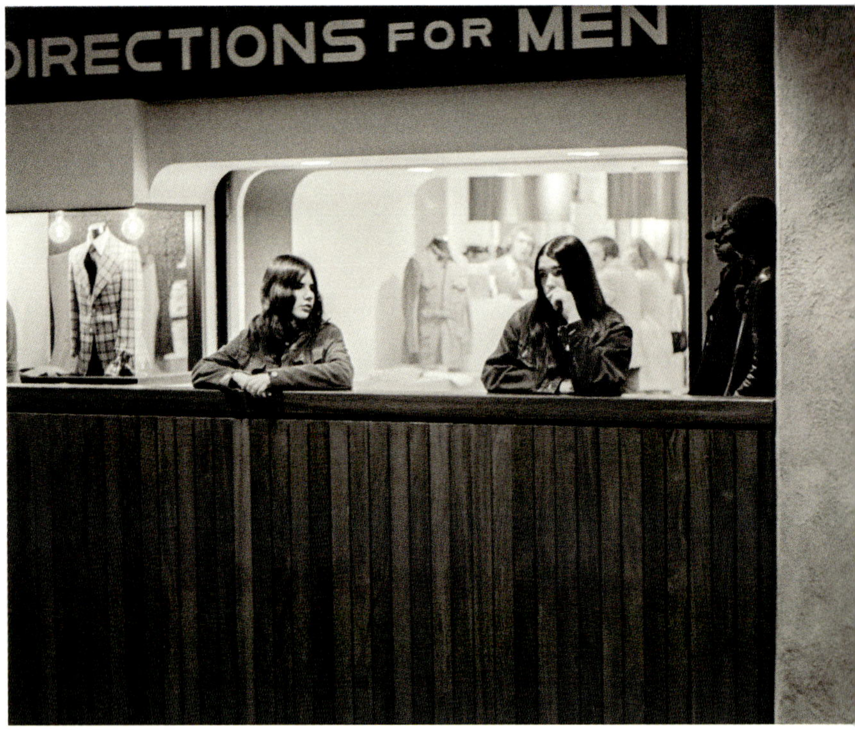

Outside the Directions for Men store in LaSalle Court

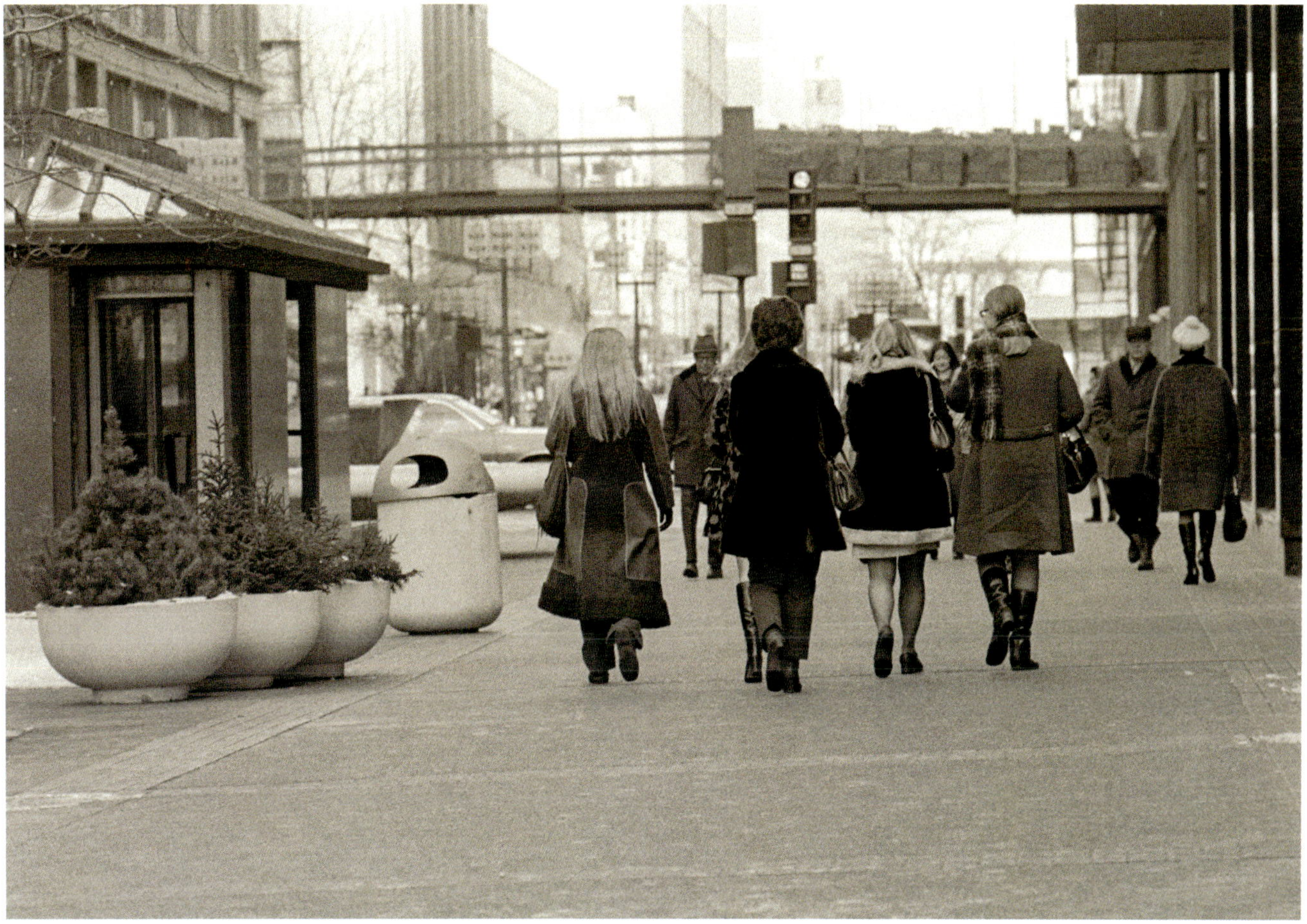

Strolling on the mall, in front of the Midwest Federal building near Eighth Street—the skyway seen here under construction runs between Dayton's (now Macy's) and the IDS Center

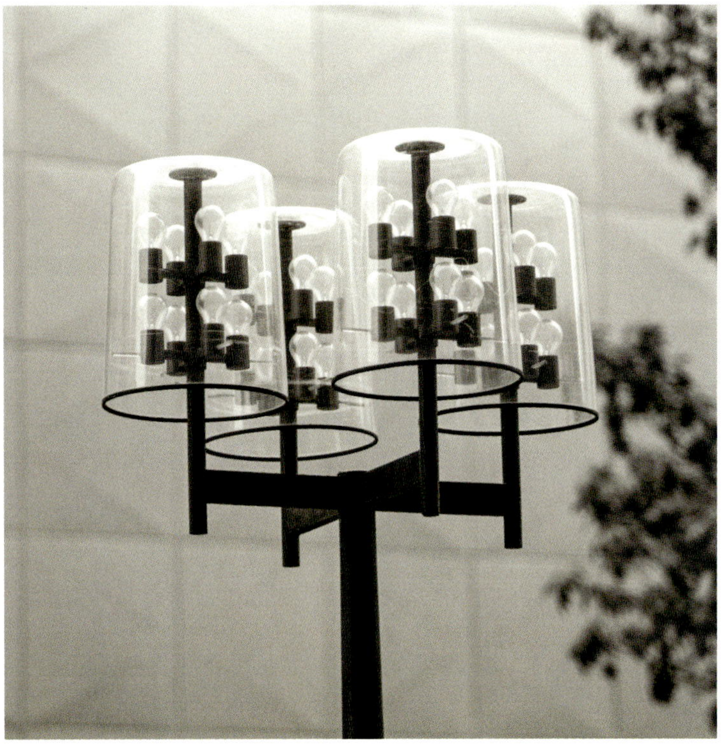

Above: A classic Nicollet Mall streetlight

Opposite: Kids contemplating the fountain at Nicollet and Eighth Street

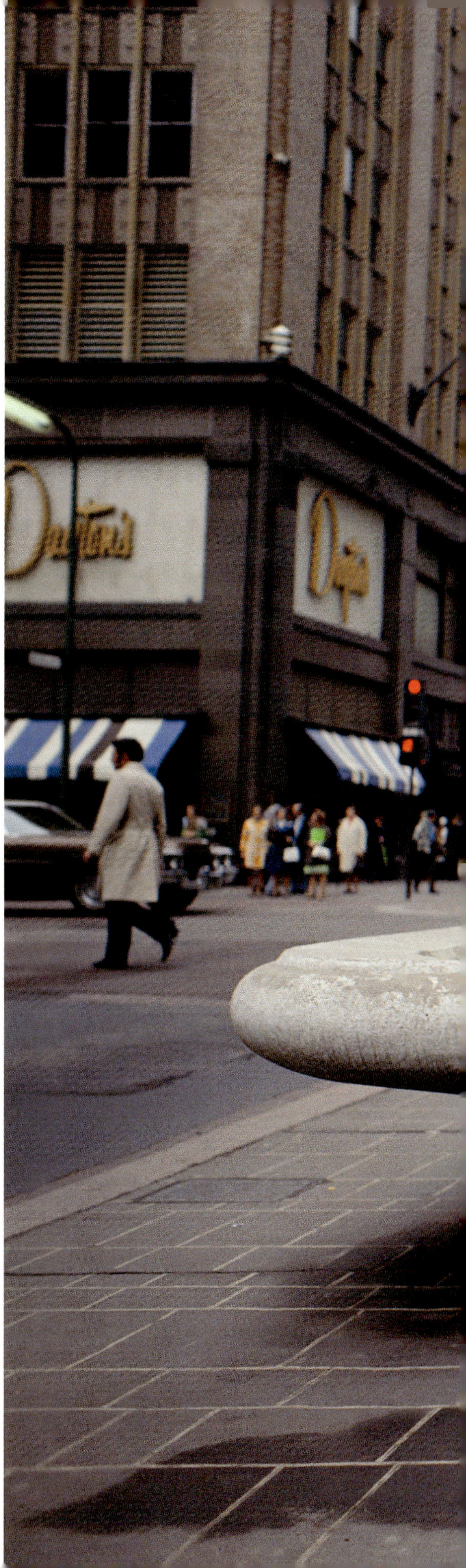

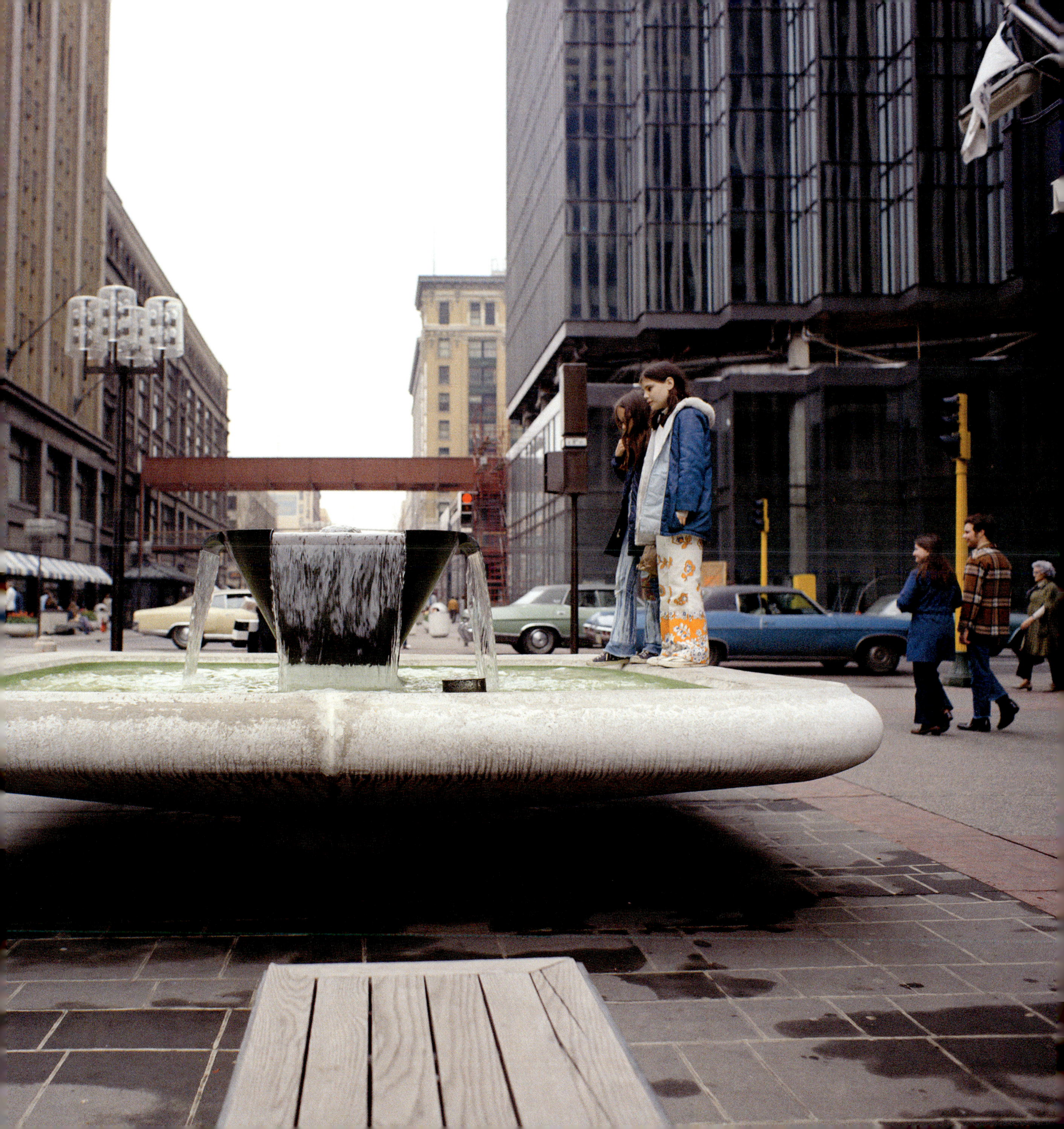

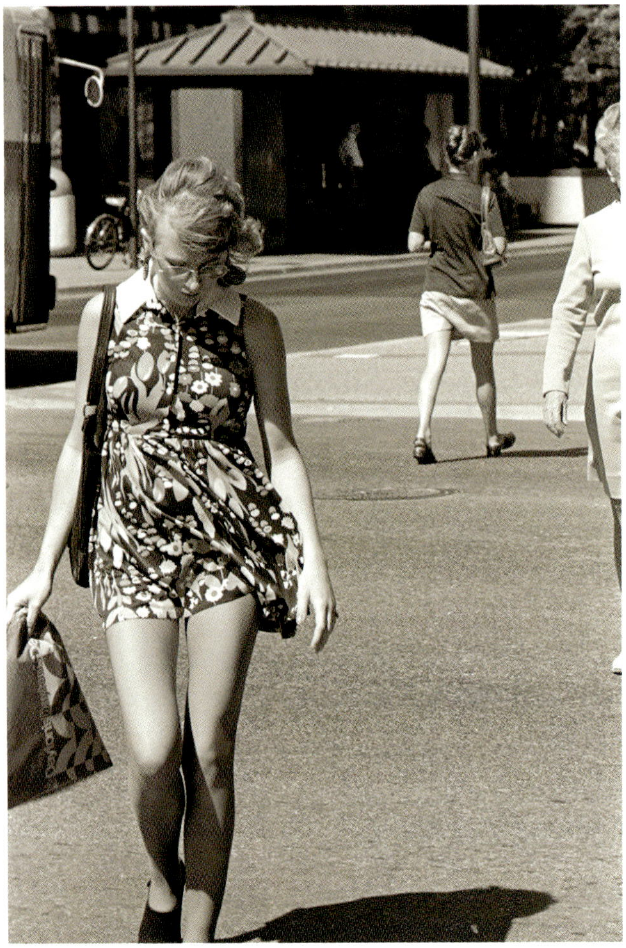

Another satisfied Dayton's shopper

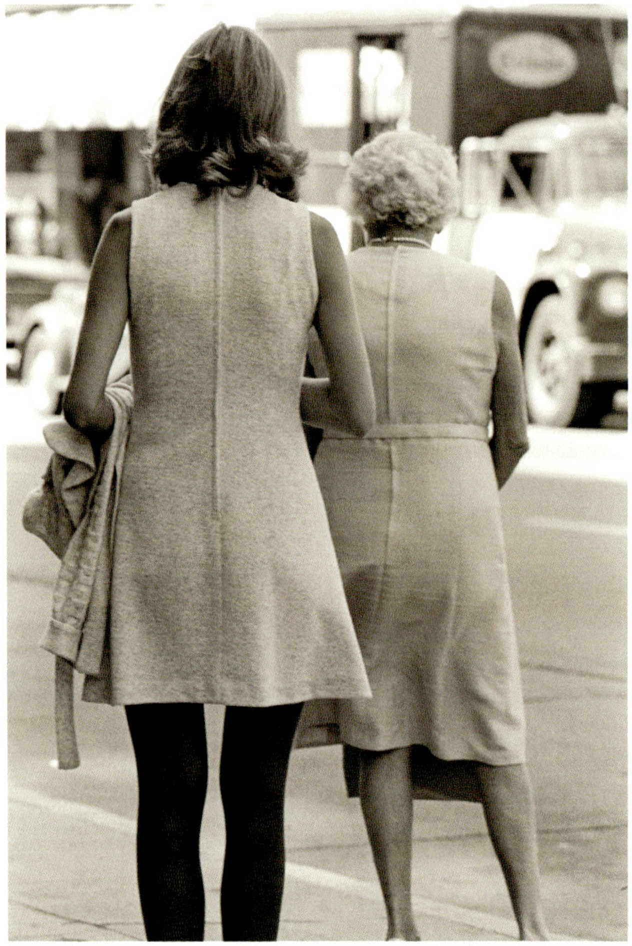

Waiting to cross the street

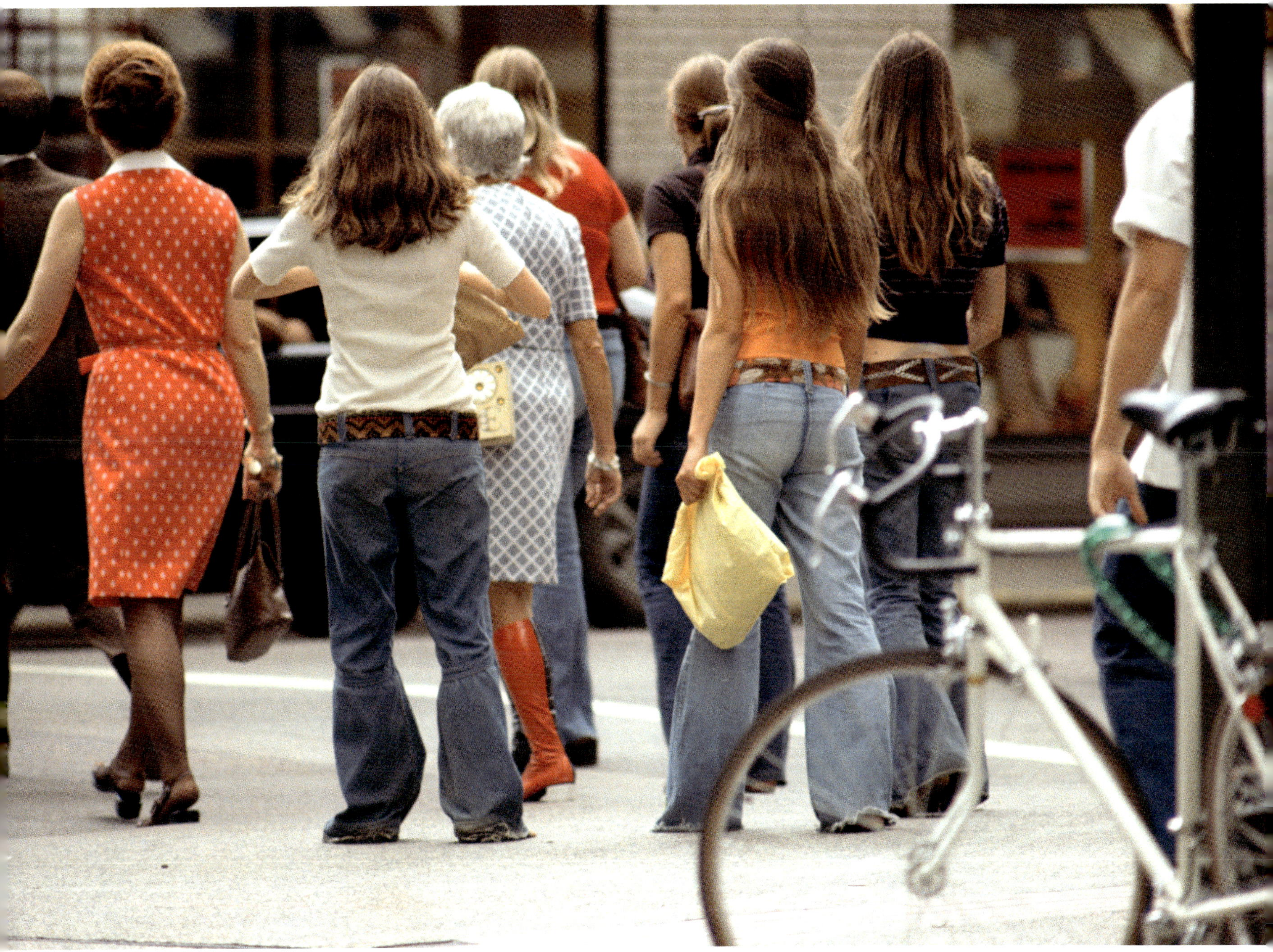

Ultimate 1970s fashion: bell bottoms and hip huggers

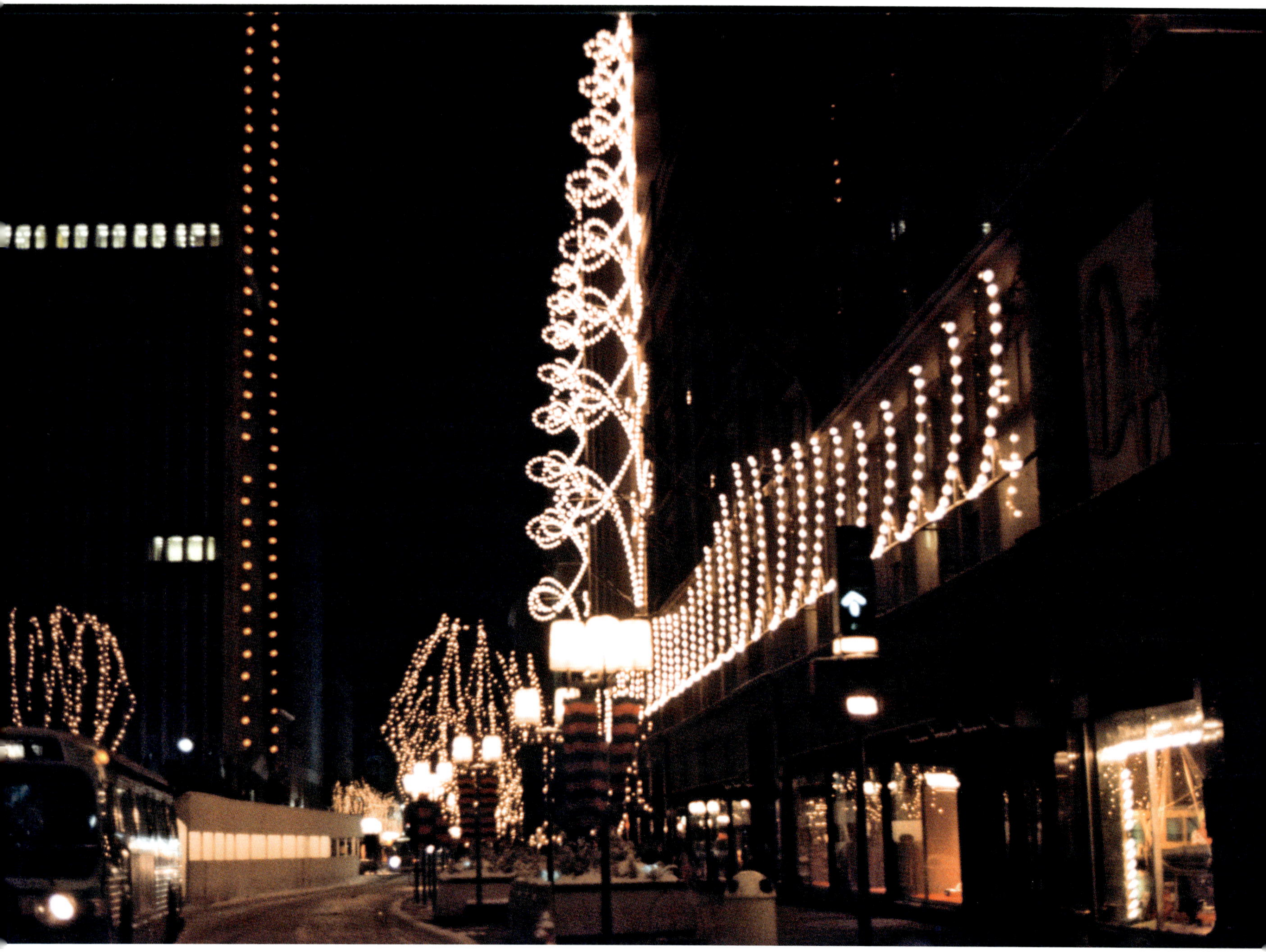

Dayton's and Nicollet Mall lit up for Christmas

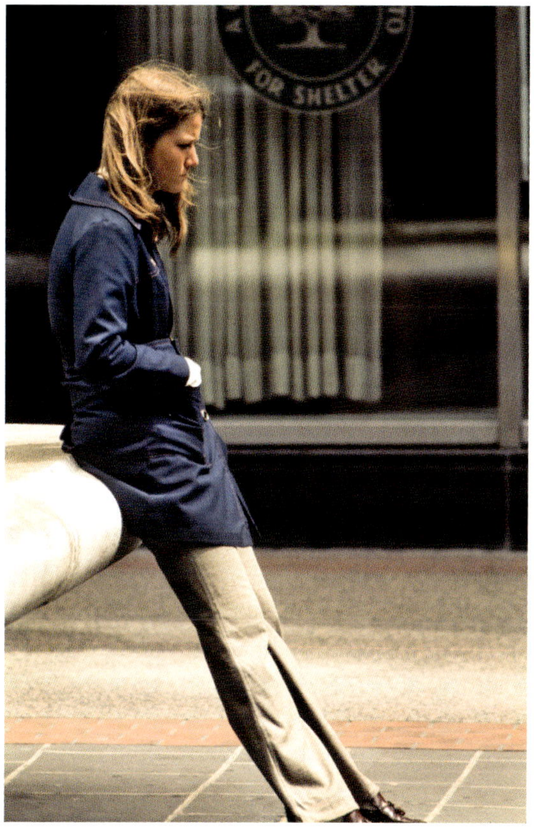

Taking a break on the mall

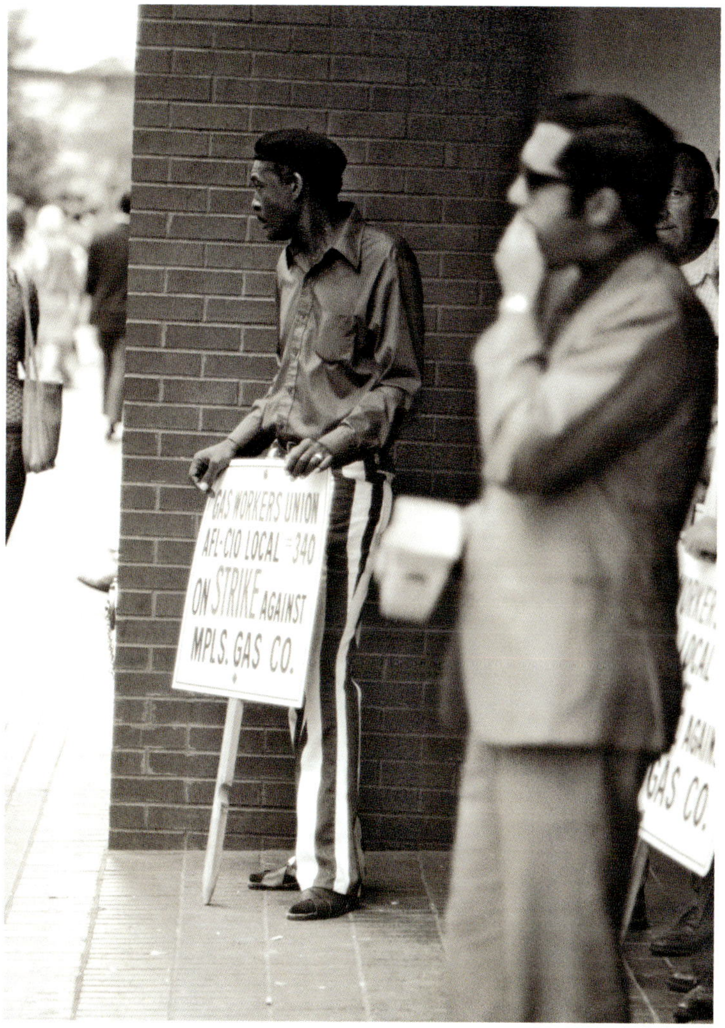

Union workers striking outside of Minnegasco

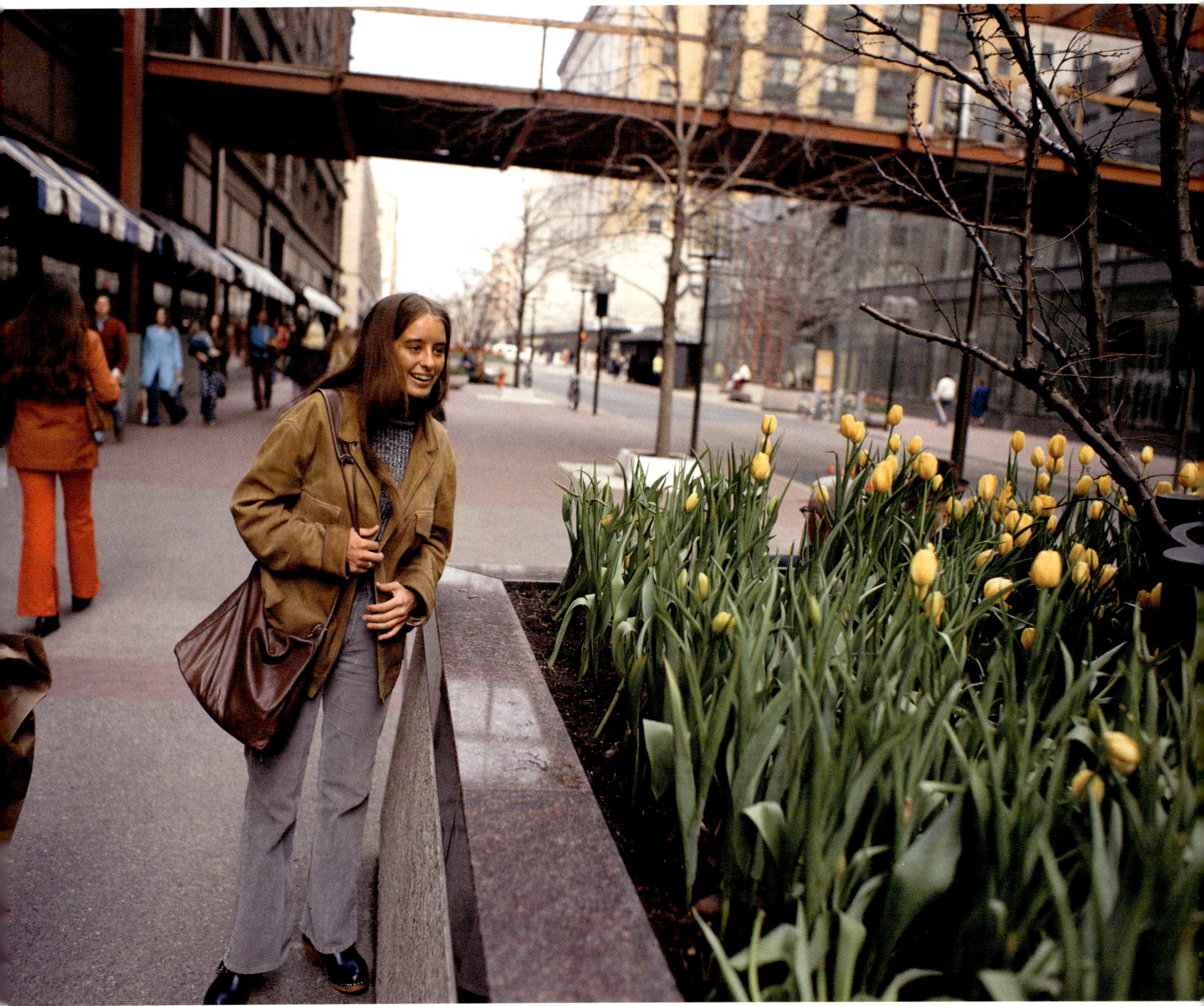

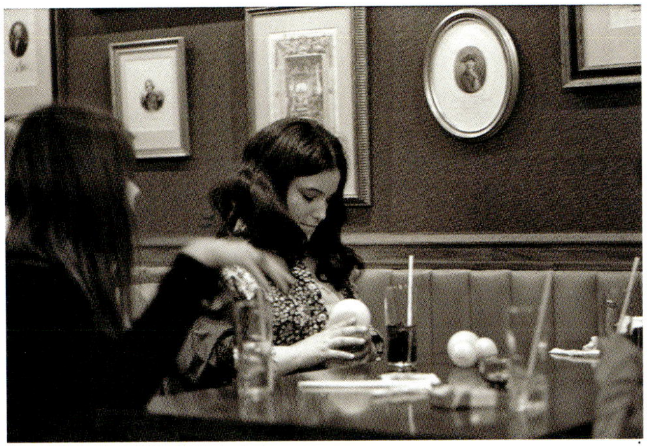

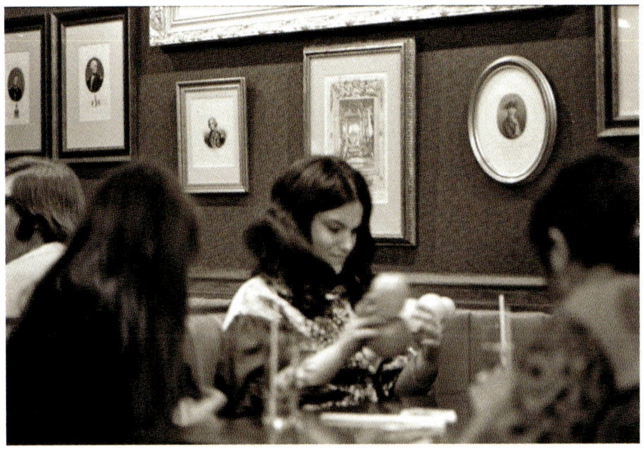

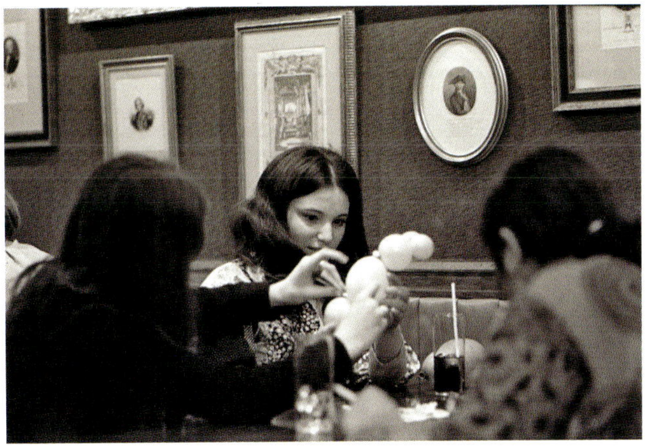

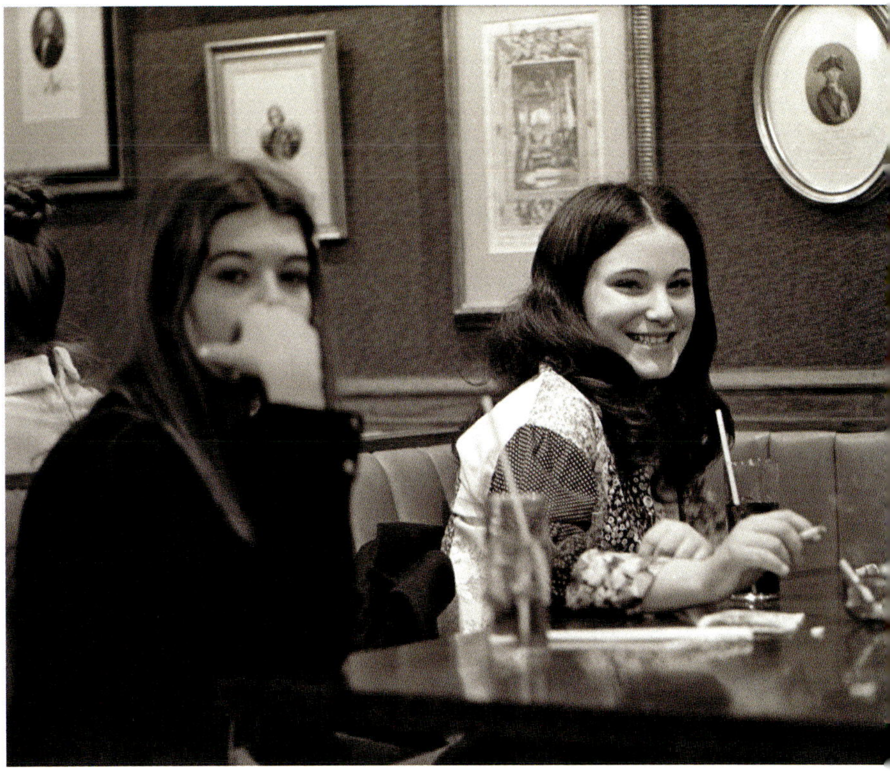

This page: Friends hanging out at the Harvest House cafeteria, upstairs from Woolworth's in the IDS Center

Opposite: Stopping to admire the tulips on the mall

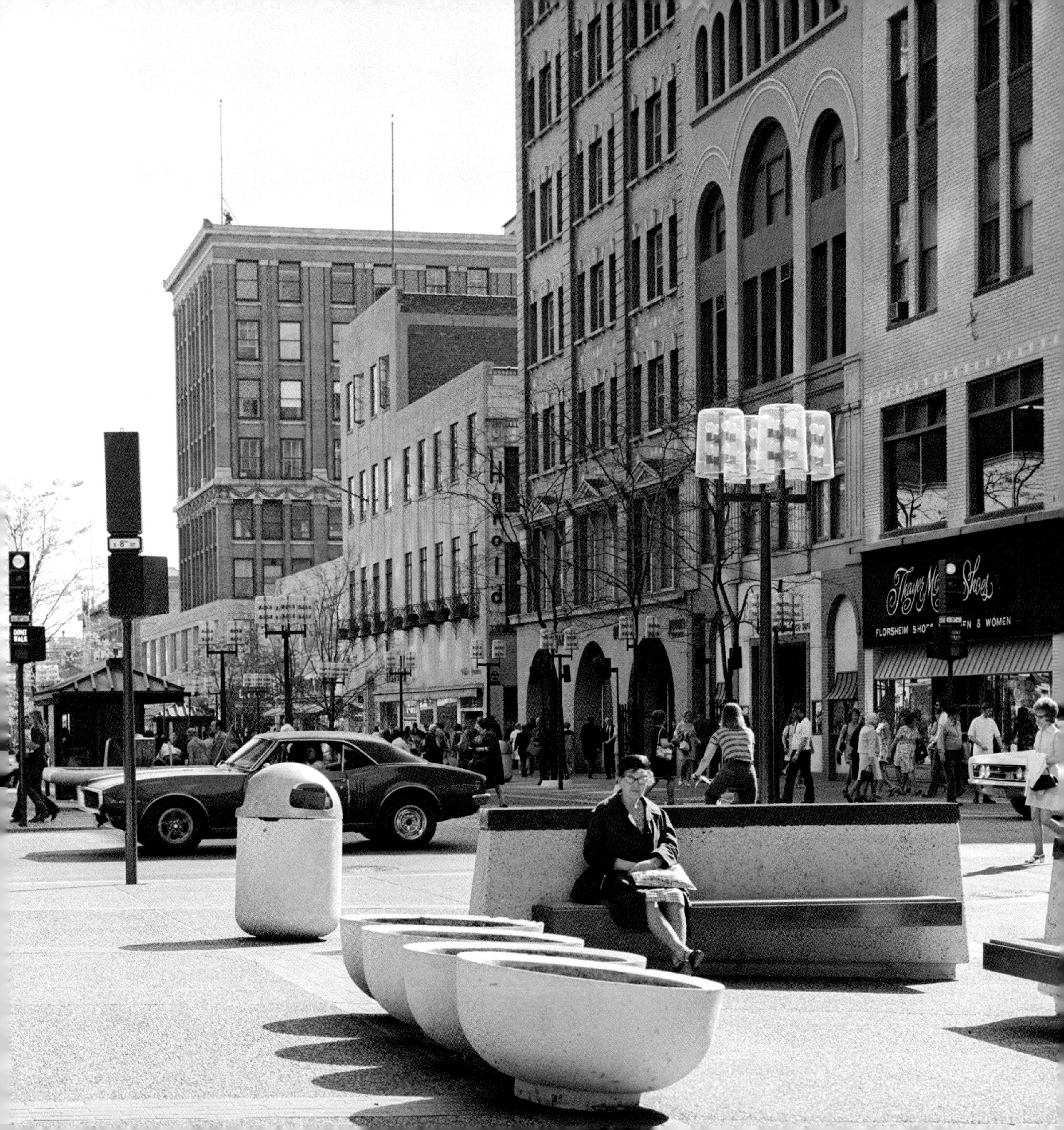
DONT WALK
Harold

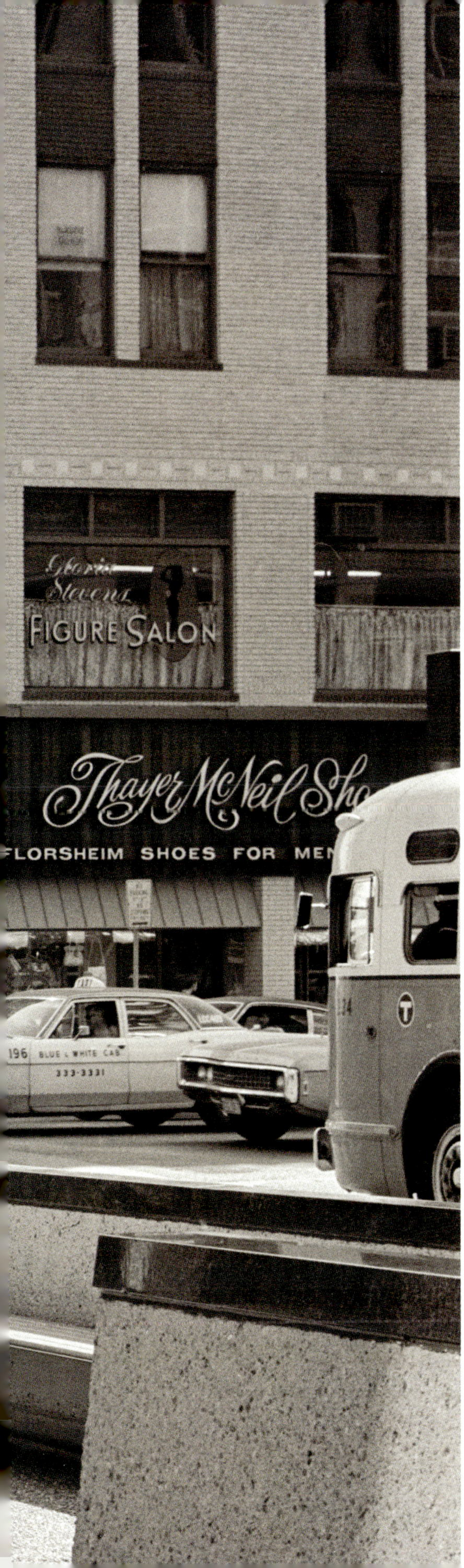

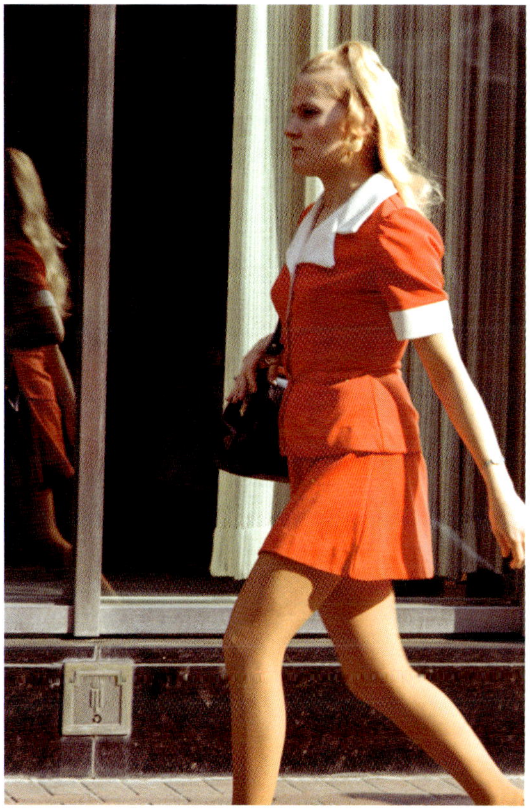

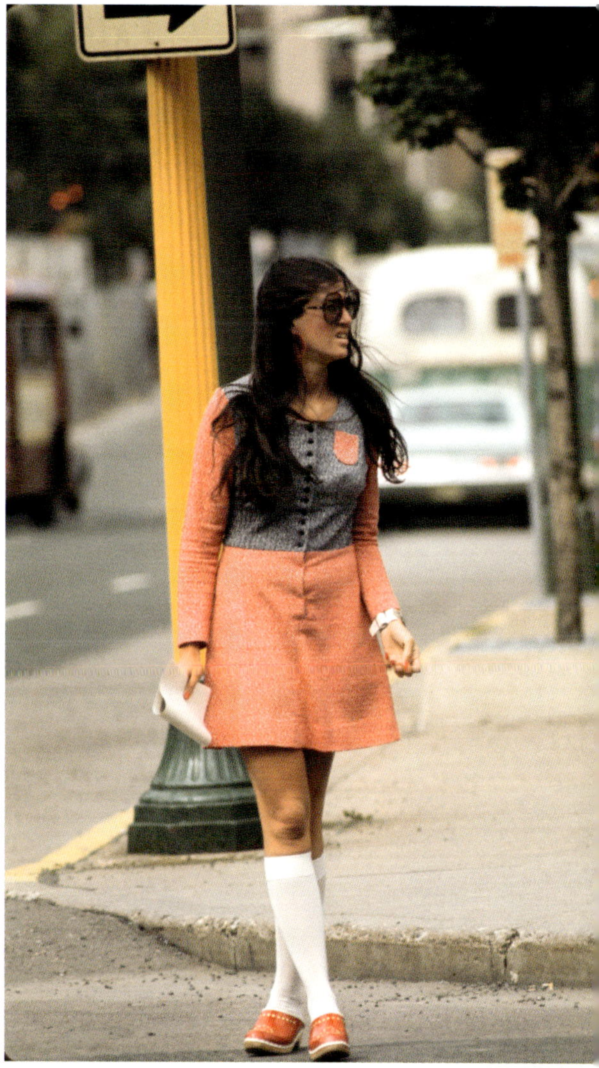

This page: More stylish young women of Minneapolis

Opposite: Action at the corner of Eighth and Nicollet

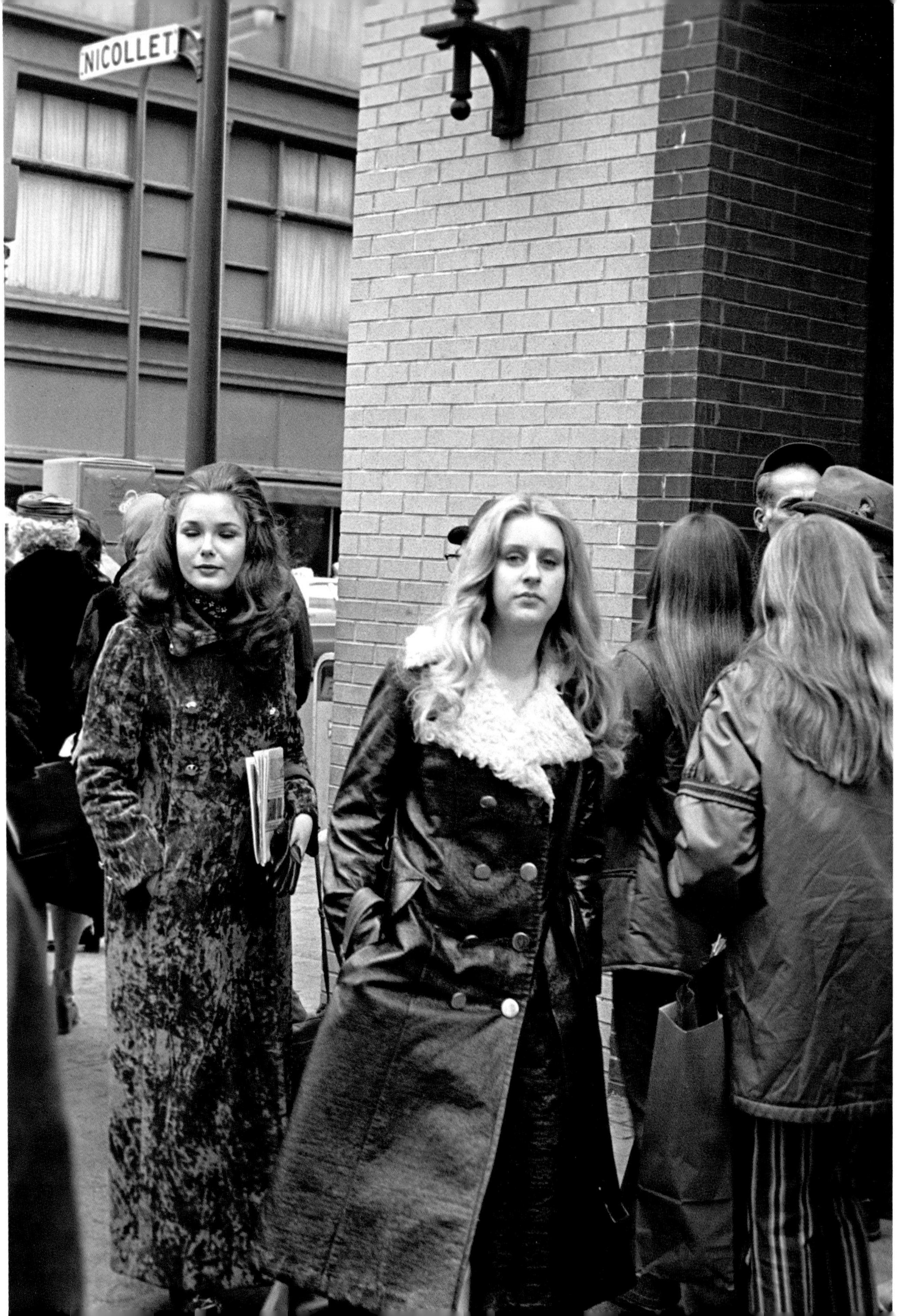
NICOLLET

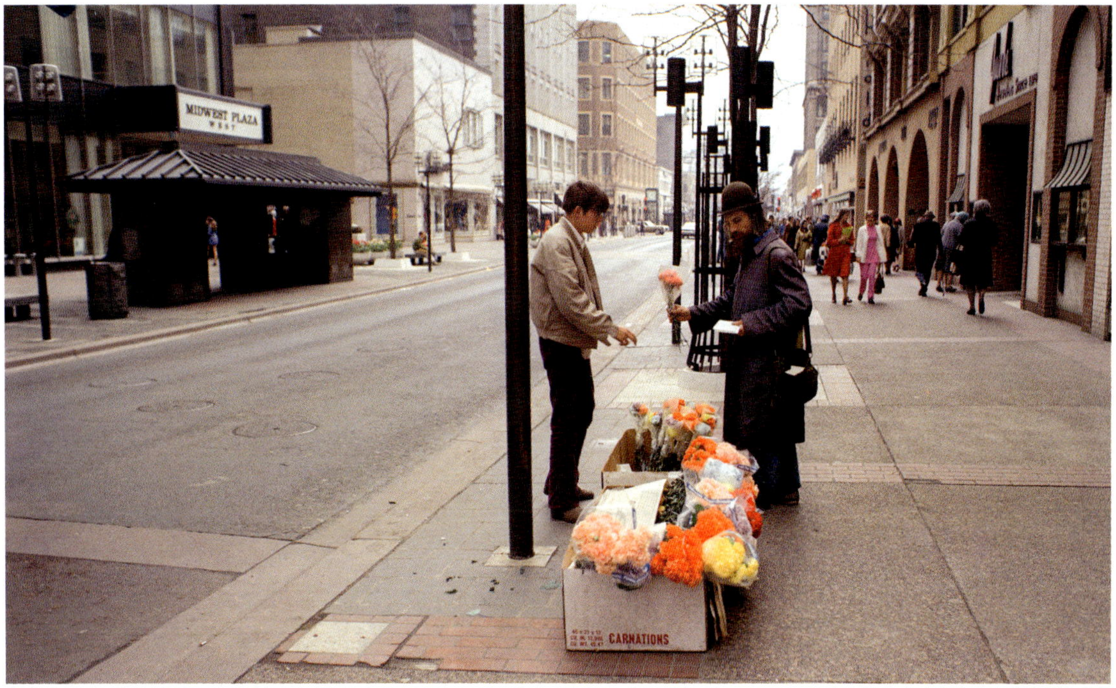

Above: Selling carnations across from Midwest Federal plaza

Opposite: Fashionable coats on Nicollet

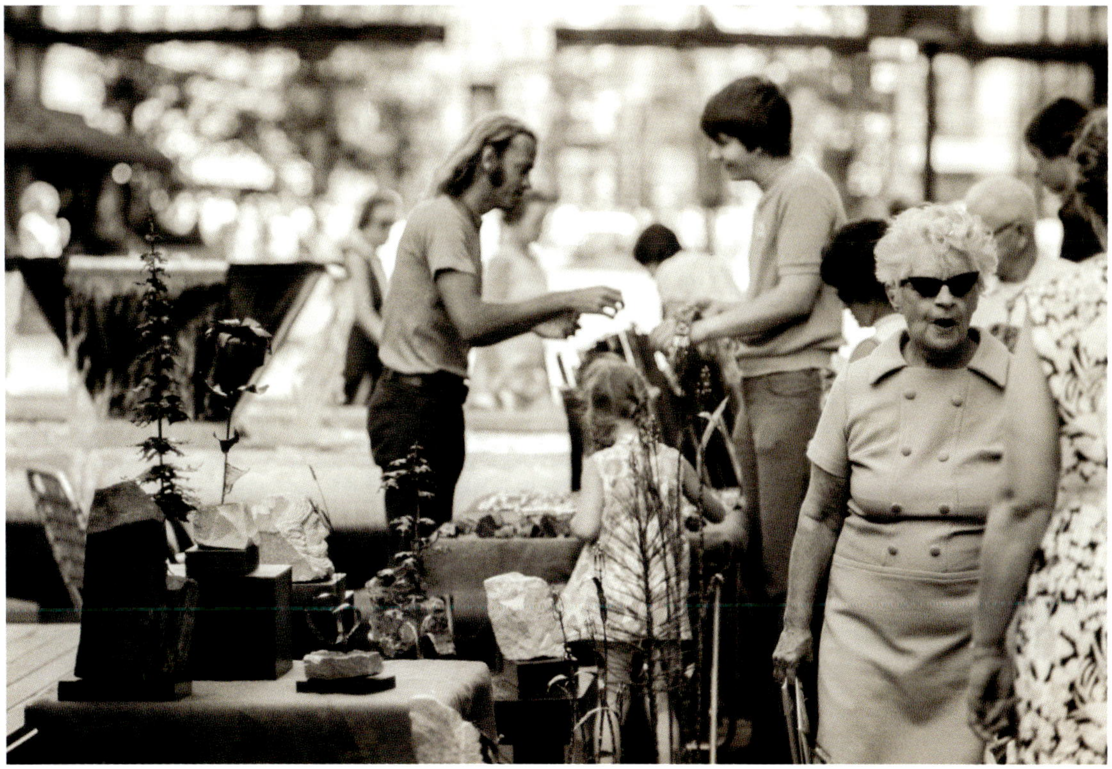

Art sale on the mall—the sort of public use that Nicollet Mall was designed to accommodate

BROWN PHOTO

The downtown location for Brown Photo, at Ninth and Nicollet, was the flagship store for ten locations around the metro. By the early 1970s, Brown was a dominant enough force on the local photo scene to have its own large satellite location at the state fair. "It was more of a down-home place," photographer Stuart Klipper says of the chain. The downtown store, however, had more in common with Jay's Cameras than it might have had with one of its suburban locations. Though still regarded as somewhat middle of the road, the Brown on Nicollet serviced a higher-end, more professional class of hobbyist. "I'm sure they sold a lot of cameras to doctors," recalls Klipper.

Brown Photo had started in the 1930s as a mail-order photo finishing business based in North Minneapolis, advertising in the backs of specialty magazines and developing film for amateur photographers all over the Upper Midwest. A large number of these clients were rural photographers in outstate Minnesota and the Dakotas who couldn't get their work printed professionally in their nearby small towns. Beginning after World War II, Brown expanded from its northside base to open stores elsewhere in the metro, with a particular focus on the new malls and shopping centers sprouting up in and around the suburban "Dales"—Robbinsdale Shopping Center and Southdale Mall in tony Edina were two of their earliest locations. In addition to cameras, Brown sold a lot of affordably priced equipment for the hundreds of amateur darkrooms that were popping up in basements and garages around the Twin Cities metro. It was the sort of place you'd go for an in-store demonstration on a Sunday afternoon and come away with a new enlarger, some printing paper, and a couple gallons of Dektol.

Though it had a somewhat middle-of-the-road reputation, Brown was staffed by enthusiastic, young employees who were well connected in the photo community. One of them was a young man named Dave Harris, the Brown Photo employee pictured on page 102. The photo is more like a picture of a friend than of a professional acquaintance. The friendship that he and Mike struck up is a good example of the sort that can be fostered by an independent business. Initially, they'd met when Mike was looking at a used Nikon F with a special lens ("I'm sure I made a pest of myself by stopping in several times to look at it"). At $400, it was too expensive to buy outright, but Dave worked out a financing plan with Mike, and he was able to take it home.

Eventually, Dave would offer Mike the chance to borrow all sorts of new equipment. "He was always very accommodating whenever some new gear caught my eye," Mike recalls. "In hindsight, it's rather amazing that he would let me borrow all this very expensive equipment with only my signature on a 'loaner' invoice. But it was a great opportunity to try things I couldn't afford to own."

When Mike got married a few years later, in 1975, Dave was the wedding photographer.

Opposite: Brown Photo, on the corner of Ninth and Nicollet, in the Medical Arts Building

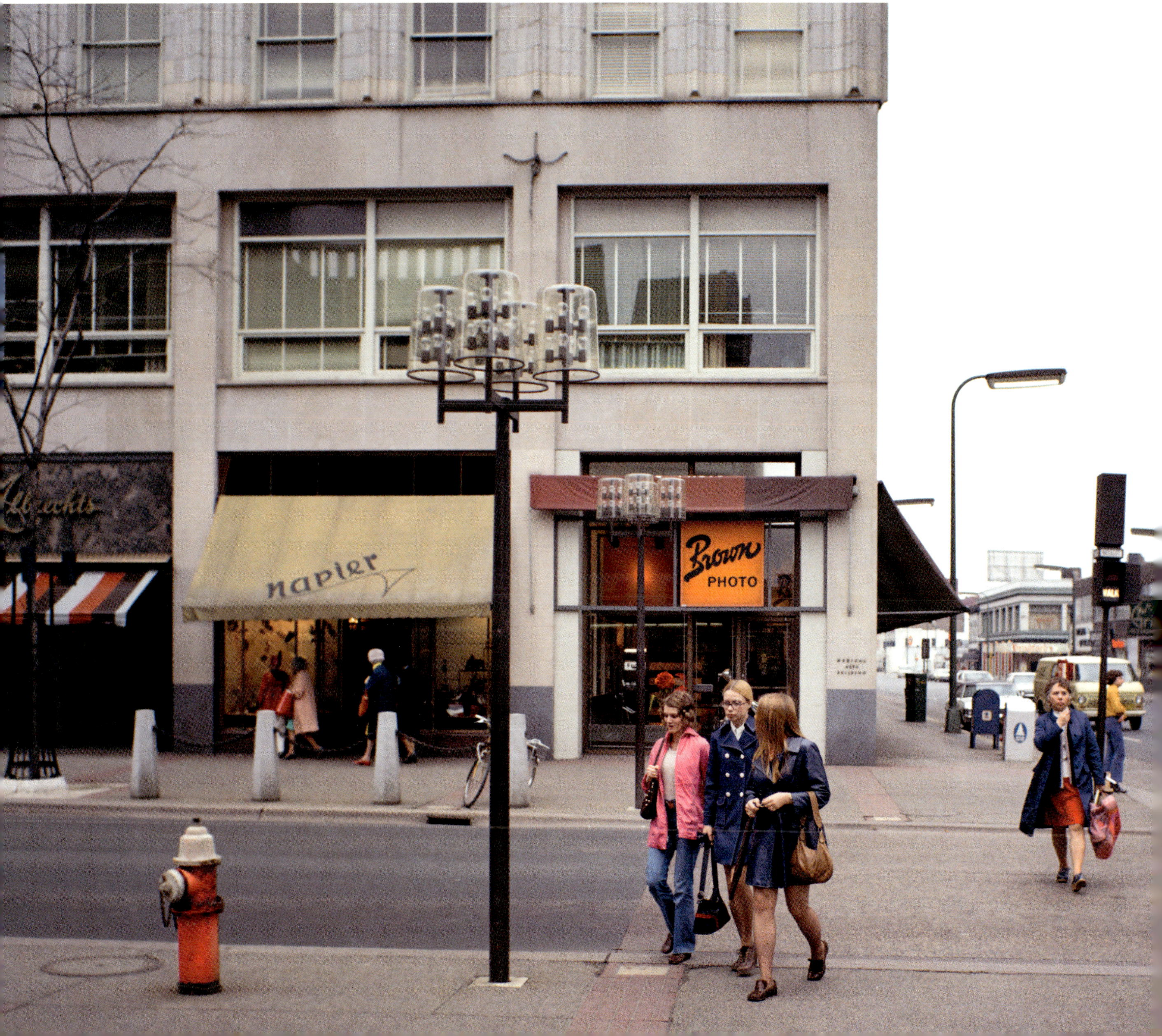
napier
Brown
PHOTO

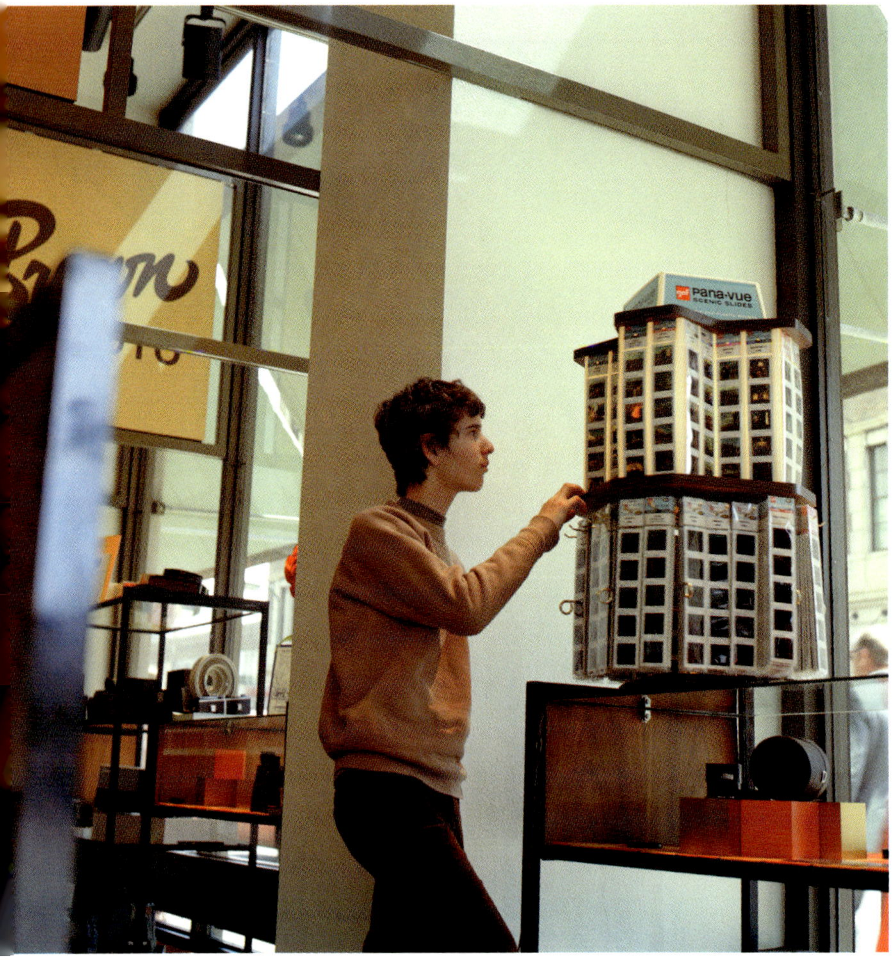

Browsing the "Pana-vue Scenic Slides" at Brown Photo—buy a slide of the IDS Tower or Minnehaha Falls while on vacation in Minneapolis, and take it home to show your family and friends in the obligatory vacation slide show

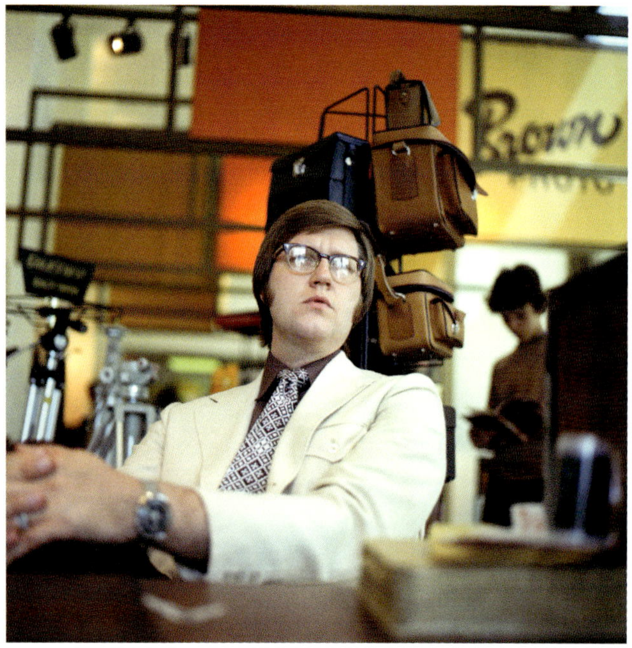

Dave Harris, ace camera salesman, at Brown Photo

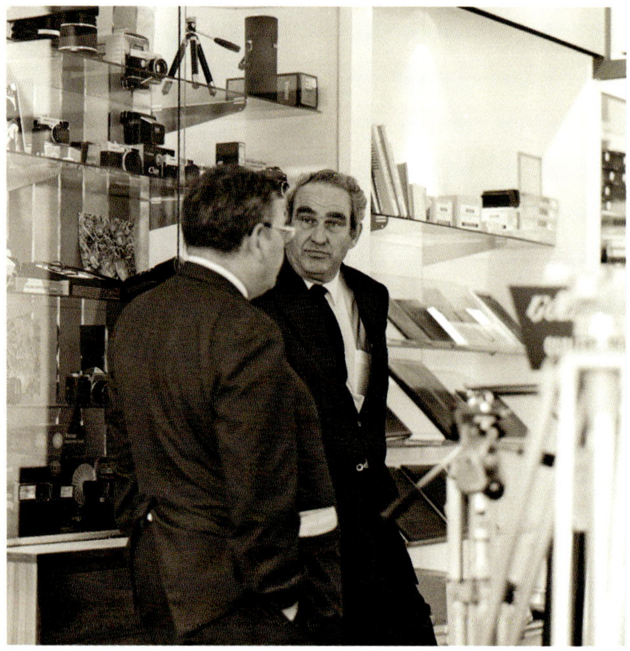

Above: Two salesmen at Brown Photo

Opposite: A woman wearing a fur coat crossing Nicollet

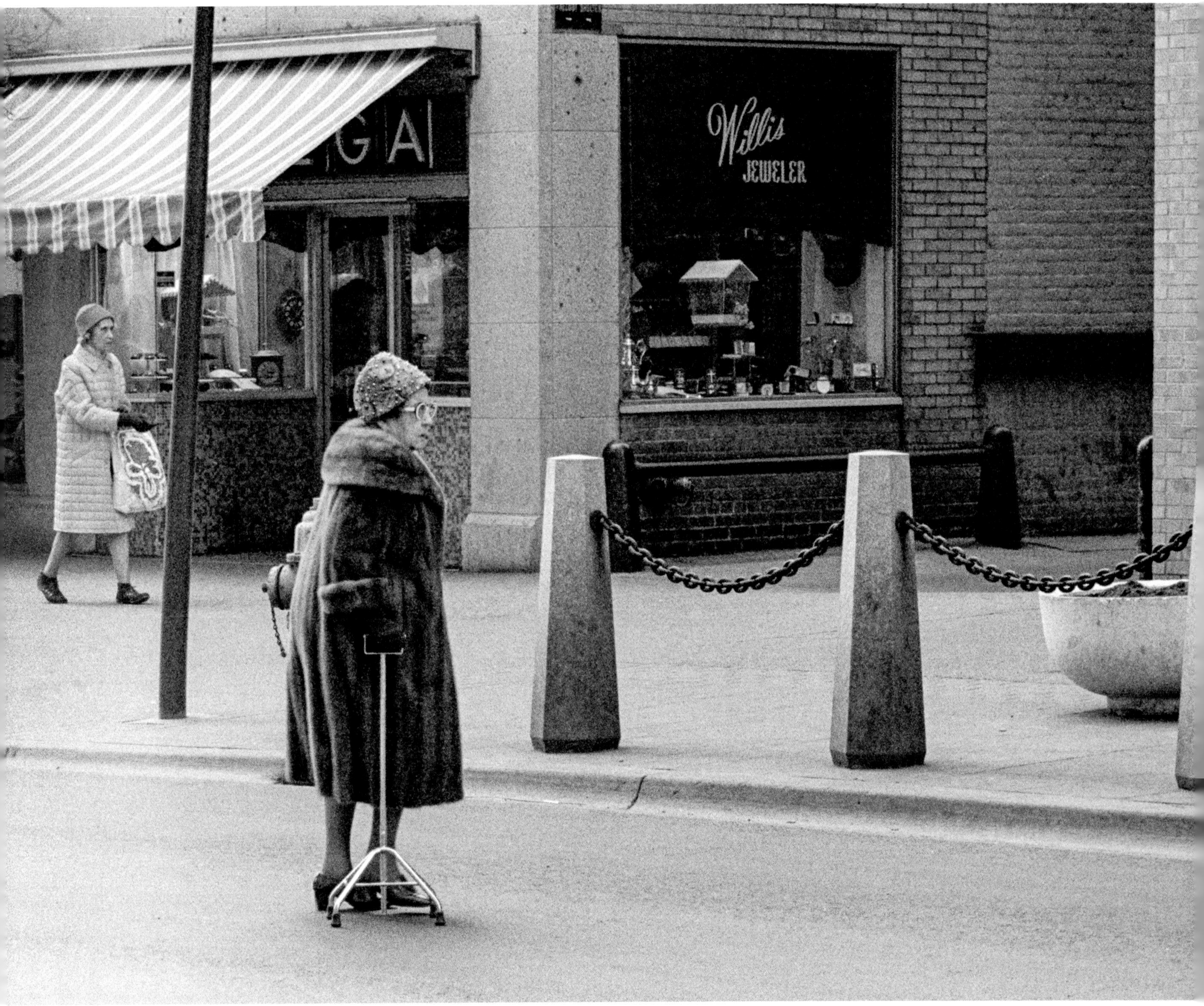
EGA
Willis
JEWELER

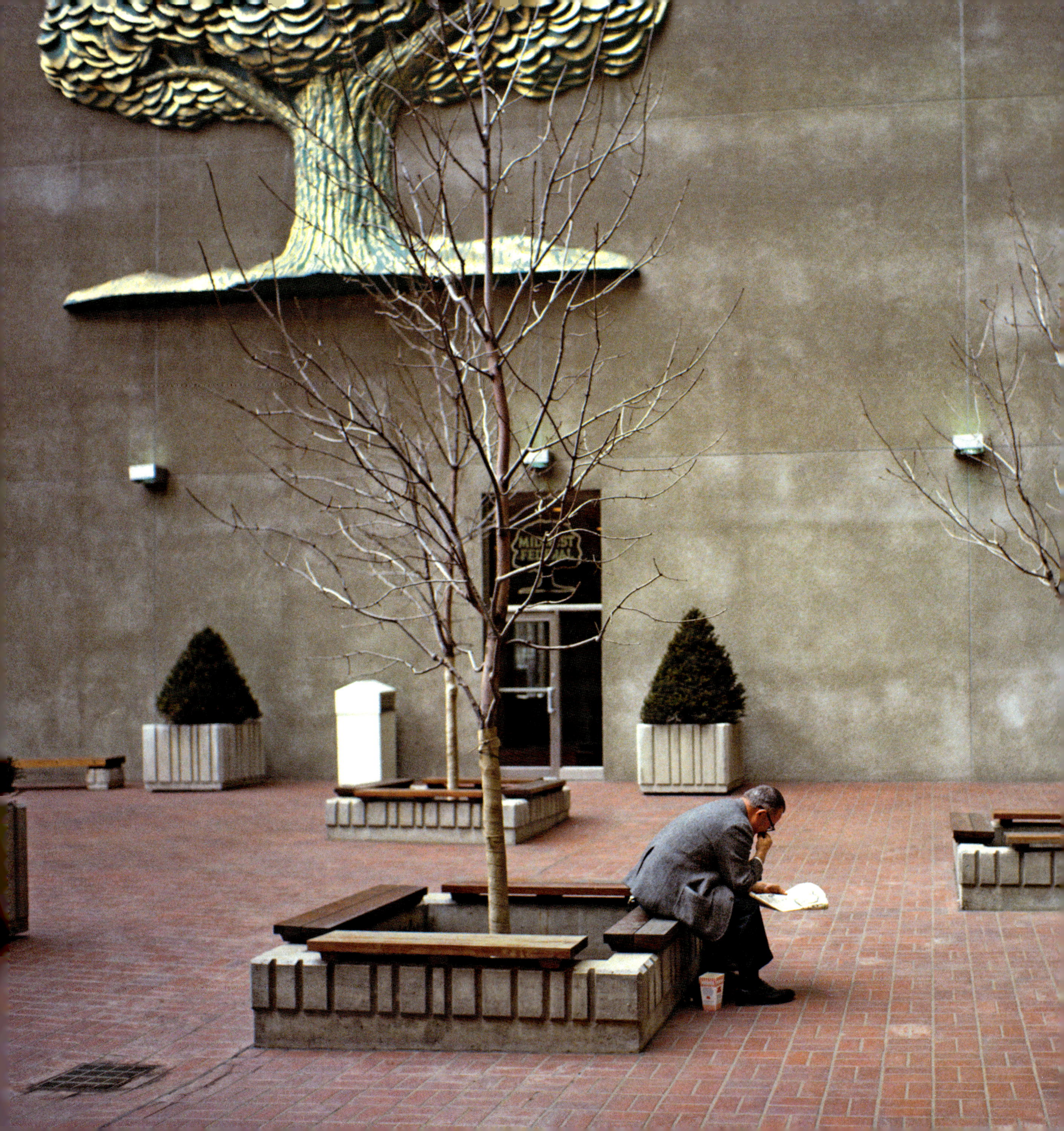

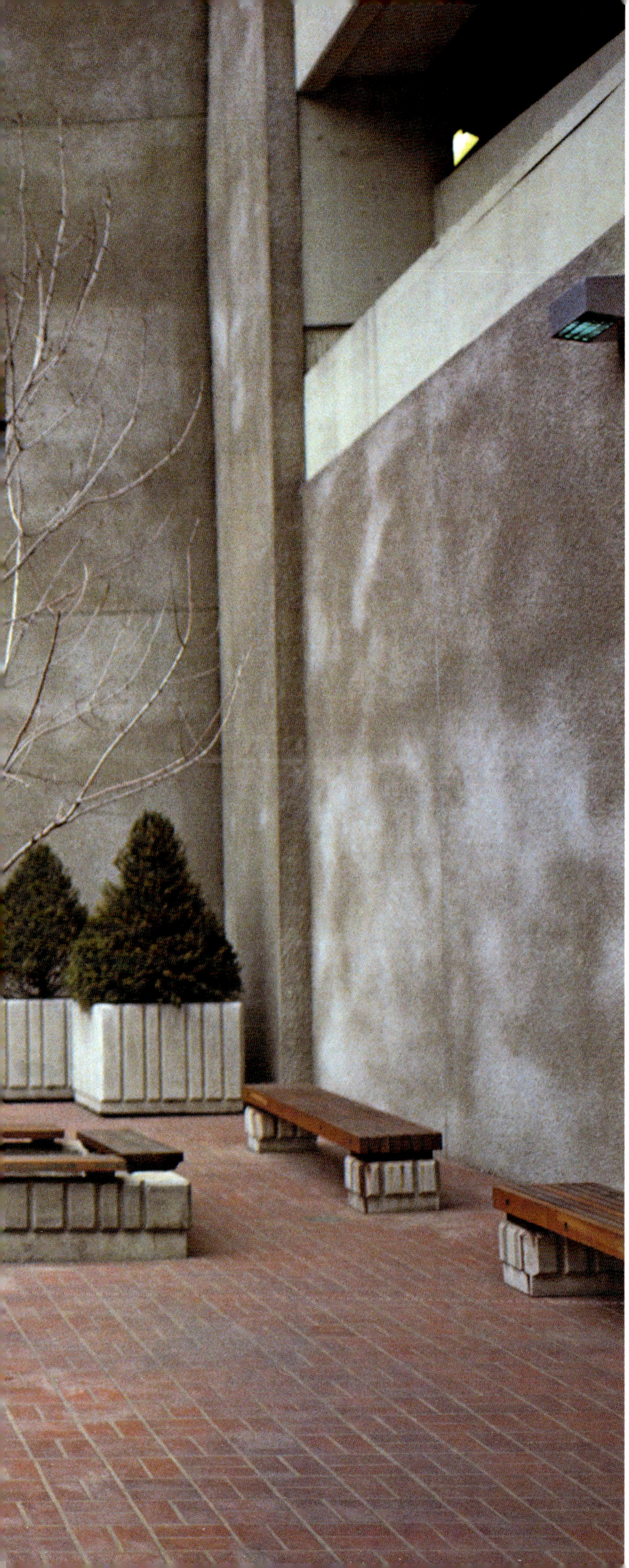

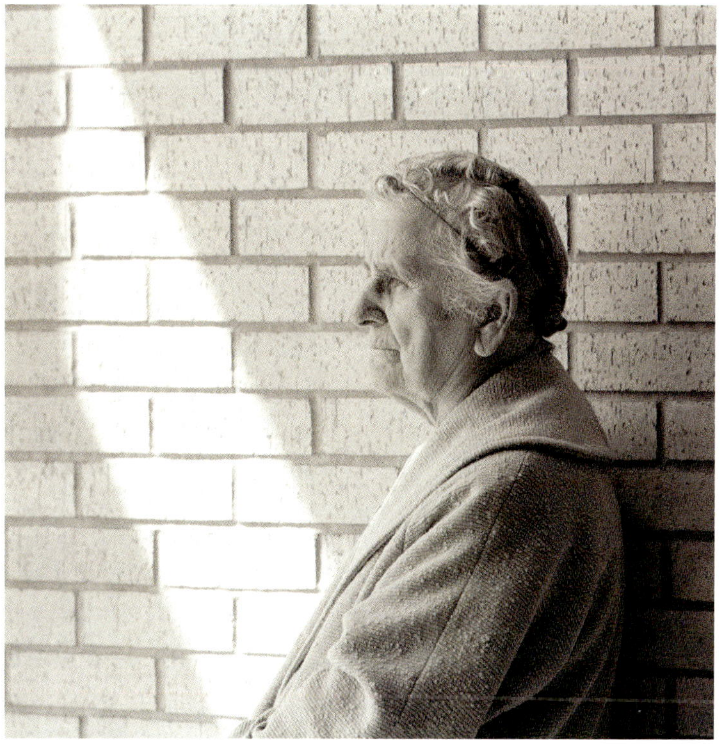

Above: Deep in thought

Opposite: Reading the paper in Midwest Federal plaza

RED BUSES

Red buses were, in their time, as iconic a symbol of the Twin Cities as the skyways were. Introduced by the Metropolitan Transit Commission in 1970 in the wake of rapidly declining transit use and rapidly increasing suburbanization, the red buses were meant to reintroduce Twin Citians to mass transit, adding a touch of the whimsical and exotic to a form of transportation that had historically been regarded as second rate. "The red was chosen for its 'cheerfulness,'" noted a *Star* article from that year, though there was some dissent on the commission; apparently some members said the color choice "smacked of 'danger,' 'communism,' and fire engines." One commissioner sardonically commented that red would be appropriate, since they'd probably operate at a deficit. (On the topic of revenue, the commission also decreed the buses would be ad free. This policy didn't last. One can spot any number of ads on the buses in Mike's photos.)

The buses proved popular. As is evident from color photos, the color scheme ably cut through the rest of the city's visual noise. Convincing Twin Citians, increasingly attached to their cars, to give the buses a try was consistently an uphill battle, however. The morning papers regularly featured stories of little tweaks and adjustments to the system made here and there. Even something as granular as the seat materials didn't escape notice. "Riders complained of the slippery, hard seats on last year's model," reported the *Tribune* in 1973. They were replaced with foam-padded seats in the newer buses.

One of the most innovative developments in public transit between the end of the streetcar era and the launch of the light-rail system in the mid-2000s were the agile, fire-red Quick Transit (QT) minibuses that shuttled workers, shoppers, and anyone else up and down Nicollet Mall and through the rest of downtown every six minutes—"Loop the Loop on the QT," the ads said. One *Star* columnist noted with some surprise that he came across his boss, *Star* and *Tribune* publisher John Cowles, enjoying the ride in one of these "tomato red rascals" on a weekday afternoon. The buses were so convenient that even one of the wealthiest men in town wanted to jump on board.

Downtown traffic, then as now, was trouble. Columnist Barbara Flanagan, ever the advocate for the pedestrian, half-seriously suggested mass action: "Should we ride on city hall and demand equal space on our streets and roadways for buses and bikes?" she wrote in 1972. "Maybe, though, we'll have to leave the bikes and buses behind and march pedestrian-style. The way auto and truck traffic is tangled downtown nowadays, the only fast way to go is on foot."

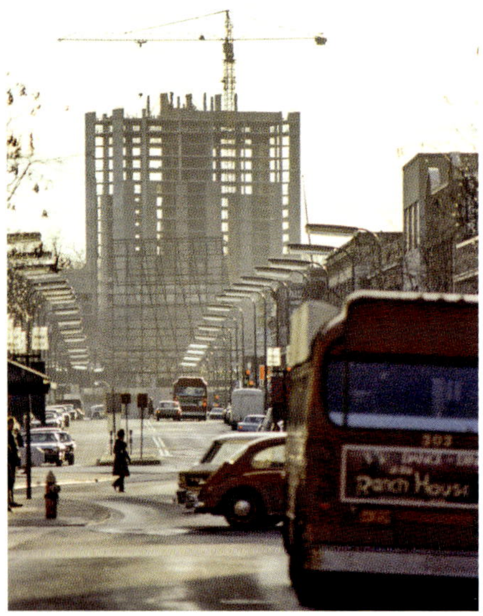

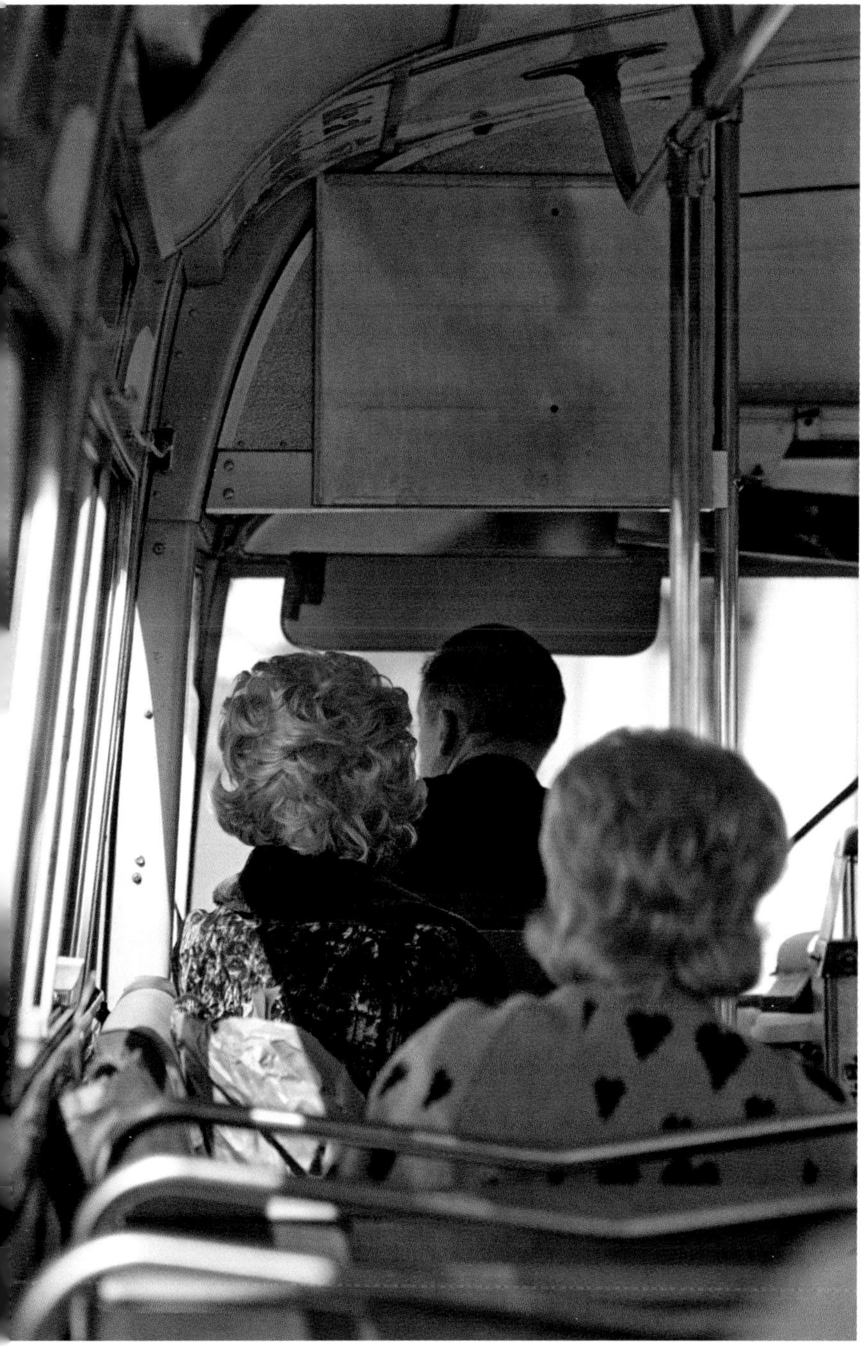

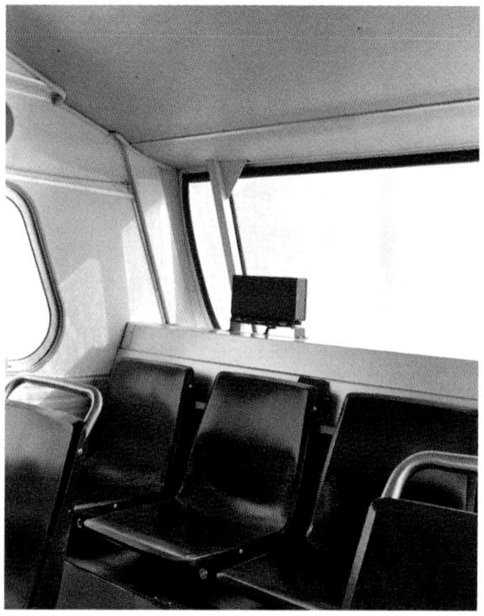

The hard plastic seats of the "big red bus," before the transit commission got rid of them at the public's behest

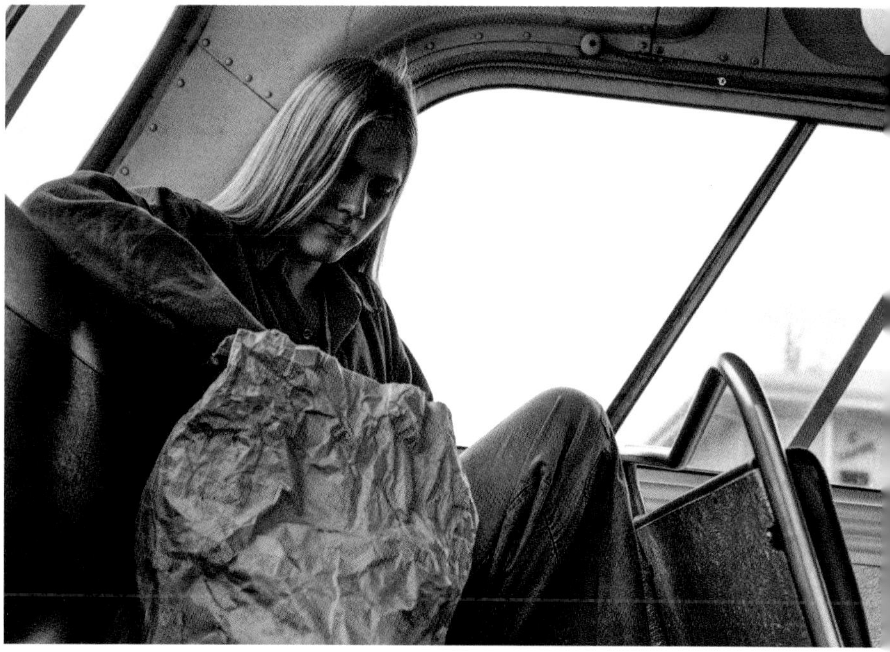

Above: Heading downtown on the 4A bus

Opposite: Looking south on Nicollet from Ninth Street, with the city's new red buses

Riding in the back row

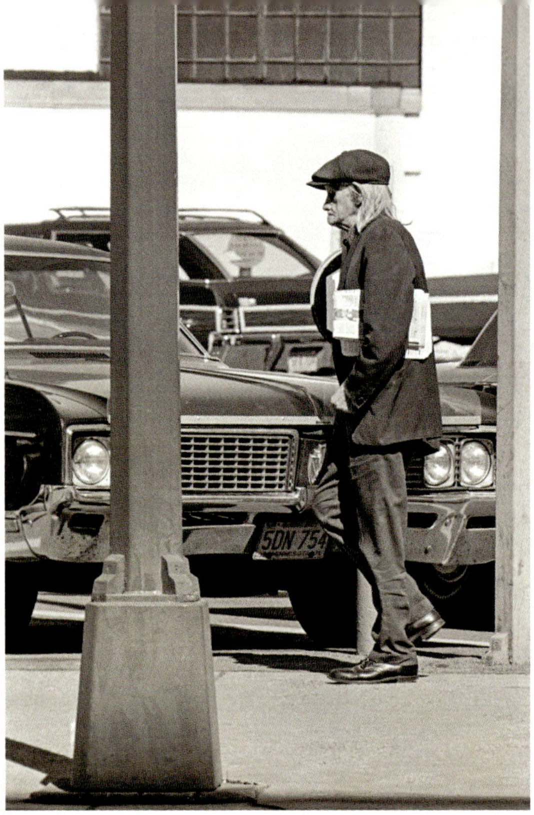

An elderly man on the move

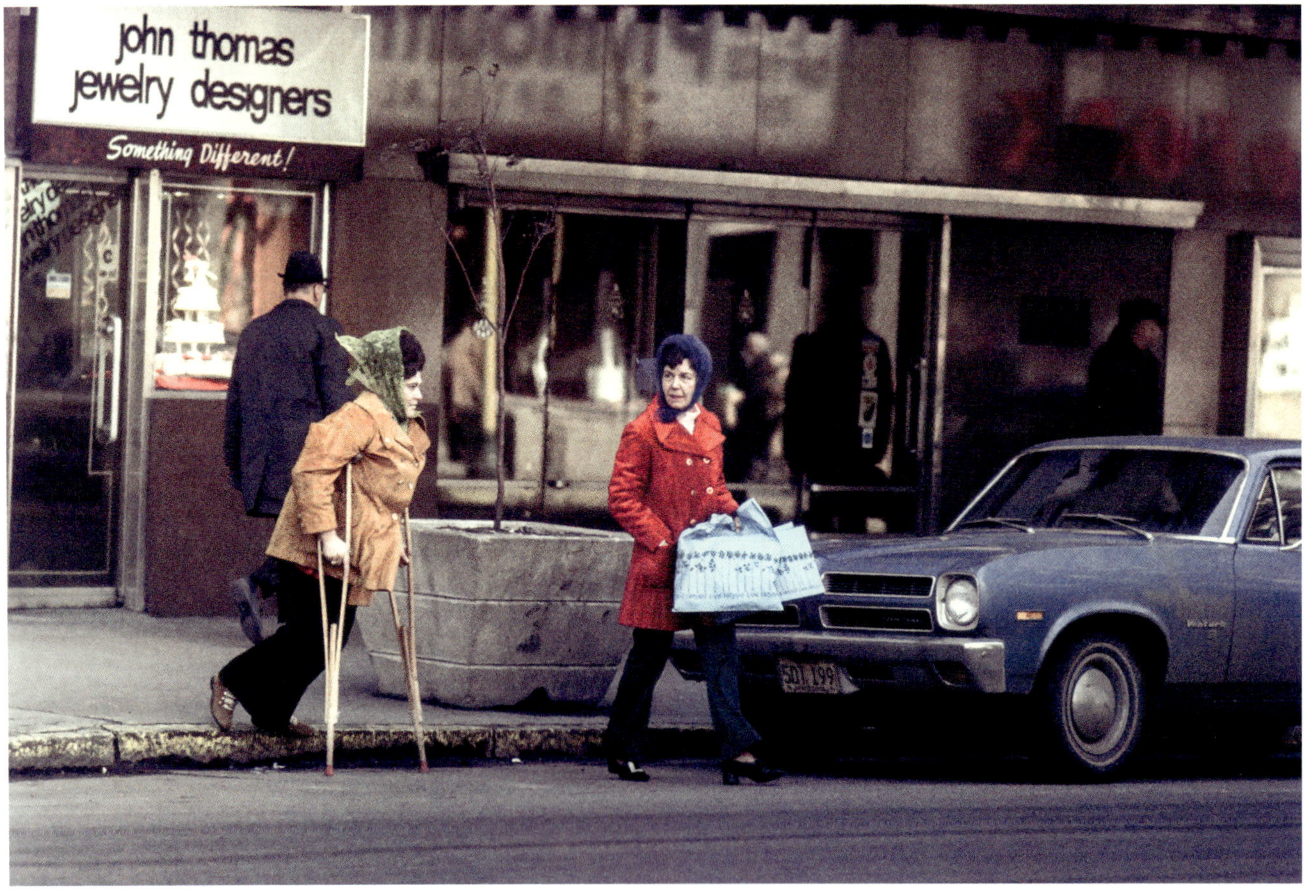

Jaywalking shoppers

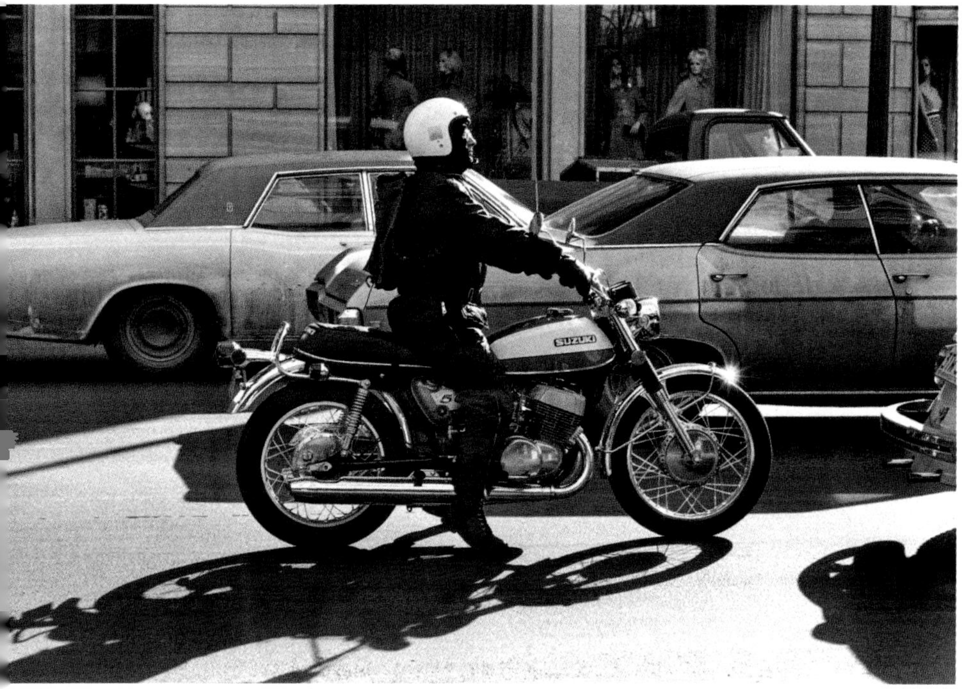

A Suzuki rider waiting in front of the Young Quinlan Building

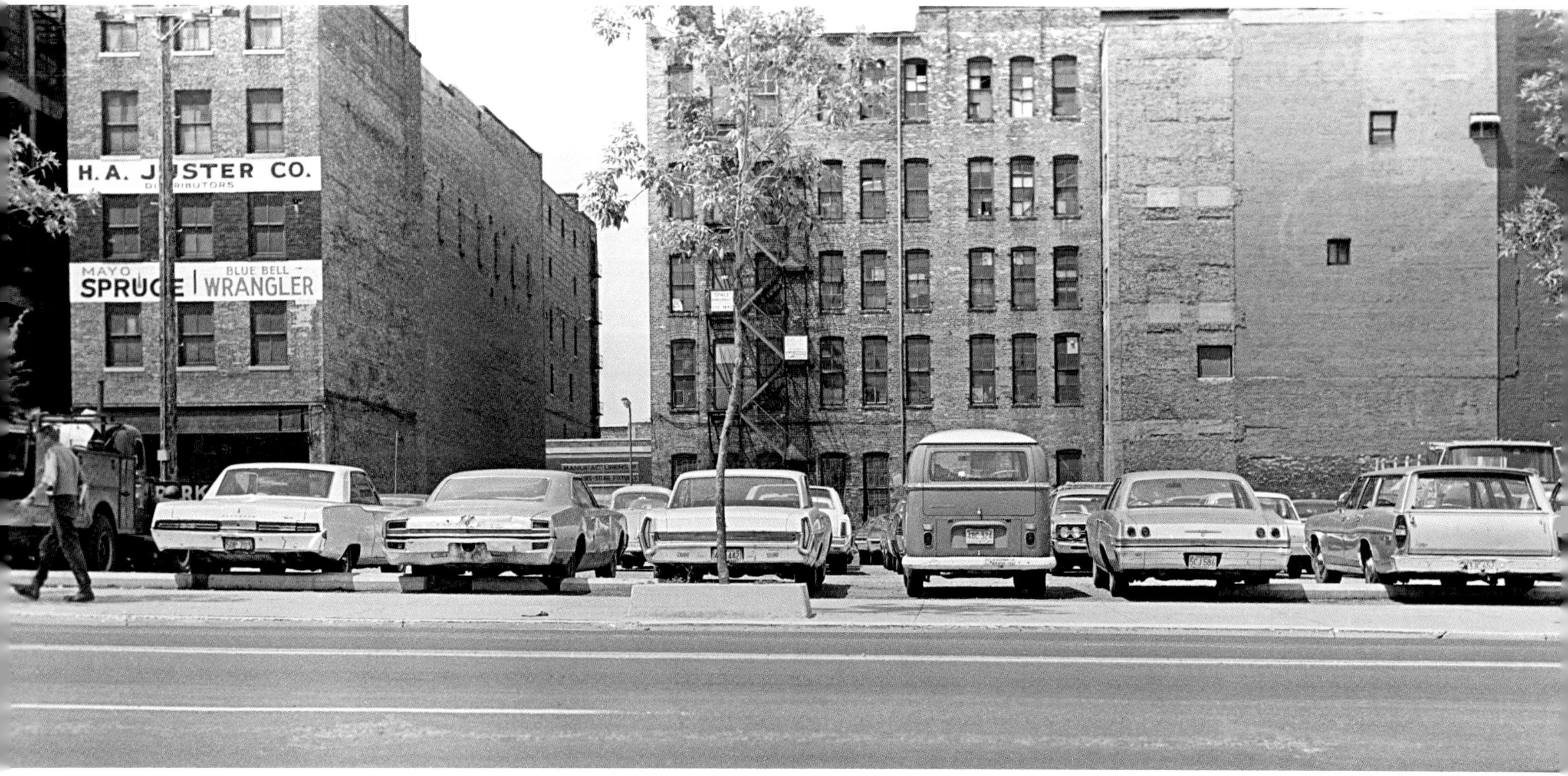

A parking lot on Hennepin Avenue. “Lakes are Minneapolis’s most noticeable landmark from the air,” wrote columnist Barbara Flanagan in 1973. “The other, unfortunately, is blocks of unsightly parking lots.”

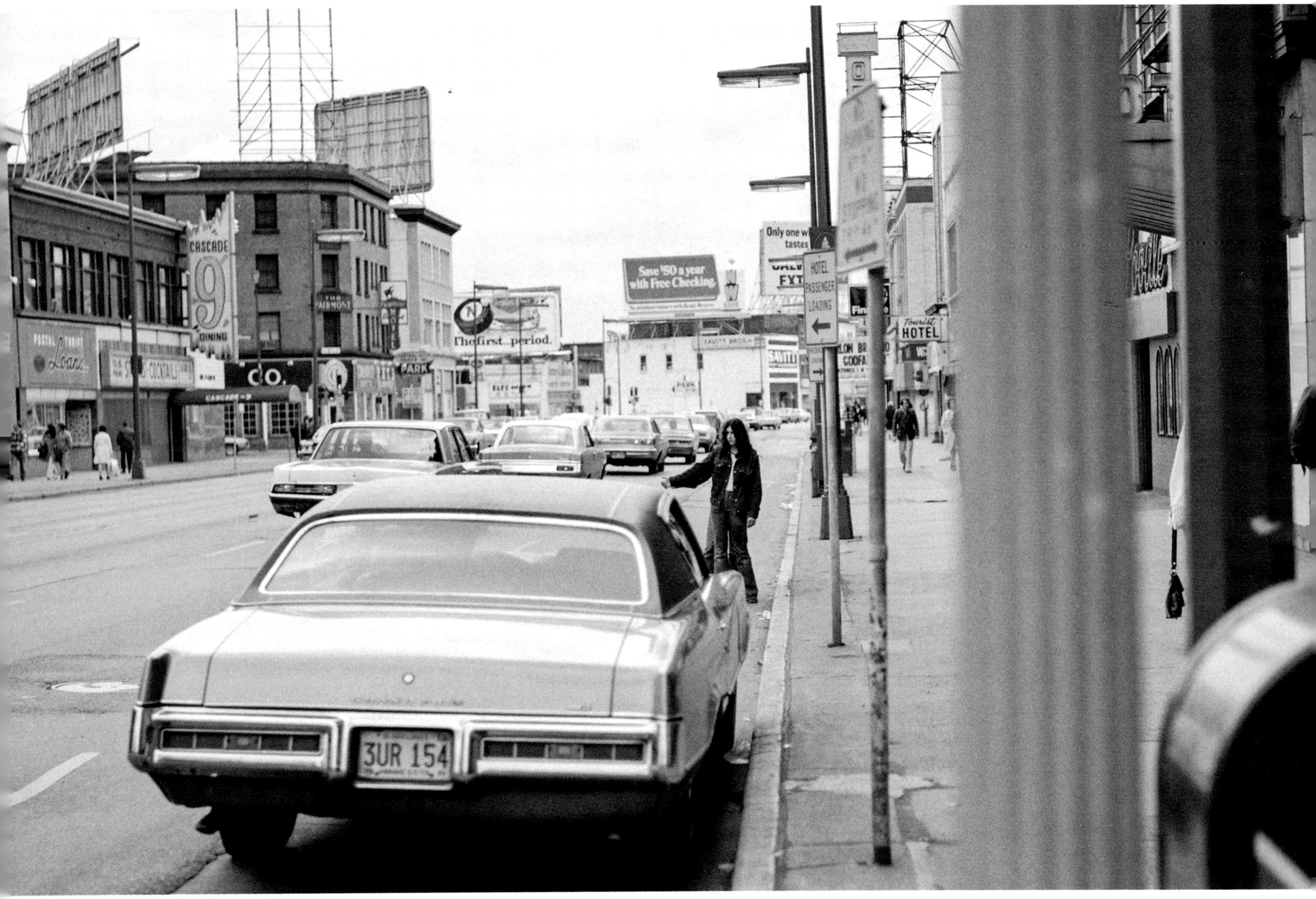

Hitchhikers on Hennepin between Eighth and Ninth Streets, with the Cascade 9 restaurant—notable for its shish kebabs and Dixieland jazz—in the background

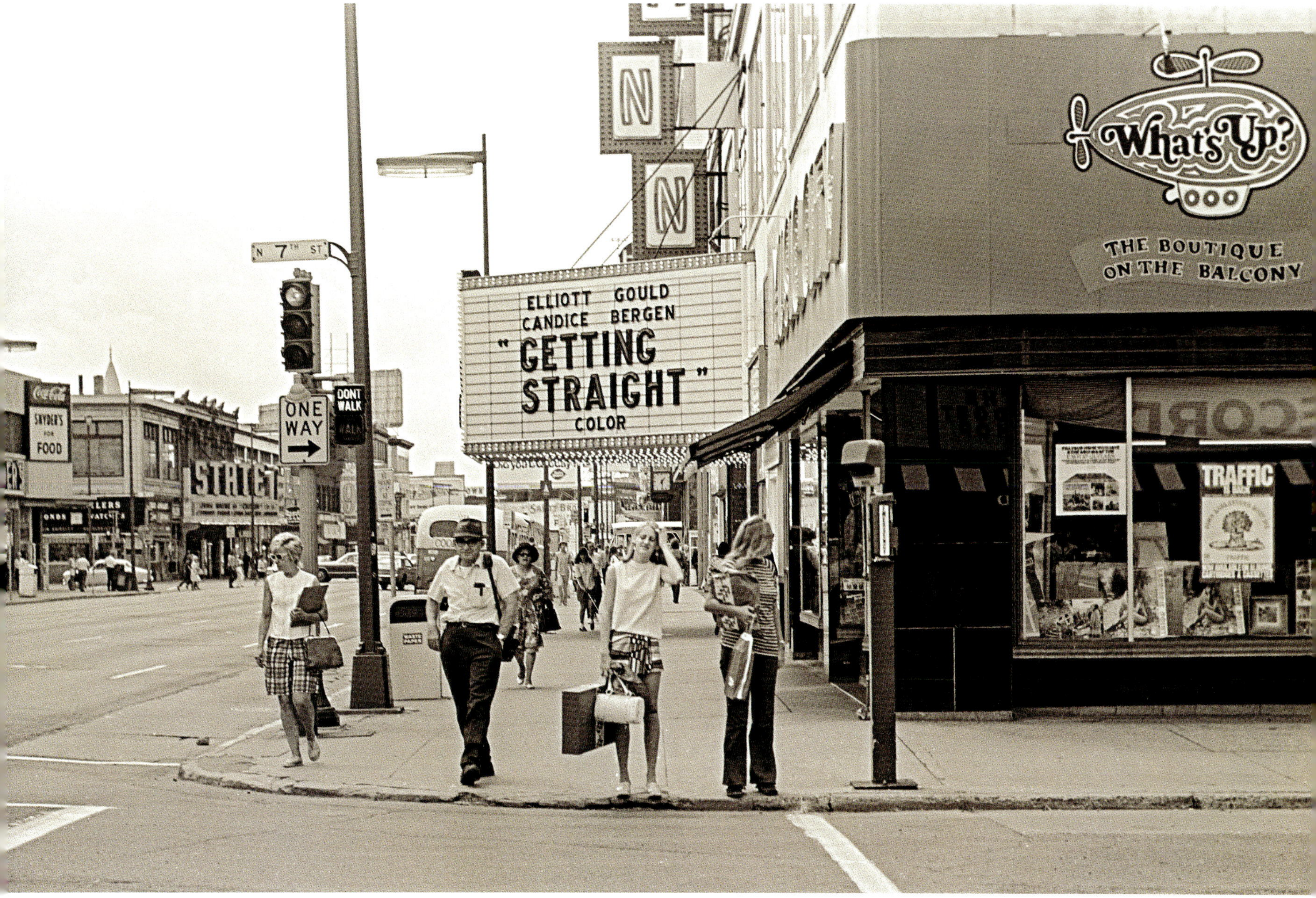

Getting Straight, starring Elliott Gould and Candice Bergen, at the Mann Theater at Seventh and Hennepin, June 1970

MOVIE THEATERS

In addition to being a document of a feature of downtown life that has vanished completely from the early-twenty-first-century city, the presence of so many theaters in Mike's streetscape photos gives us a unique way to date these images down to the week. In addition, it also gives us a way to imagine the types of conversations some of the pedestrians and bus riders in these photos may have been having. This was an era when options for entertainment were quite limited—only four TV channels and all that—and the local newspapers held some serious sway in setting the tone of the cultural conversation. It's been suggested that *Star* critic Don Morrison's rave review and subsequent championing of Hal Ashby's beloved cult comedy *Harold and Maude* was one of the factors leading to its unprecedented two-year run at the Westgate Cinema in Edina, after it closed at the Downtown World.

The 1970s is justifiably known as a golden age for American cinema, and that claim is supported by the many now-legendary movies on some of these marquees: the aforementioned *A Clockwork Orange*, for starters, and if you peer closely enough at the marquees in the distant background of some of these images, you'll also find *The Godfather* and *The French Connection*. However, a lot of these shots are a good reminder that it wasn't all gold. (Examining closely, you'll also find Carl Reiner's justifiably forgotten *Where's Poppa?*, starring George Segal and Ruth Gordon.) Some of the films featured on the marquees in these images have slipped into utter obscurity, even among the most dedicated film fans. That includes movies starring some of the great film stars of the day, such as Elliott Gould, who made some of the best films of the era between 1969 and 1975. They couldn't all be winners, of course. At the Mann Theater, we find him in Ingmar Bergman's first English-language film, *The Touch* (see page 114). (Of the stilted dialogue, *Tribune* critic Will Jones asked: "Has it somehow sounded better in Swedish, and have the writers of English subtitles been rescuing those Swedish actors with their translations?") Even more obscure than that is one that came a year later, Gould and Candice Bergen in 1971's *Getting Straight* (see page 111), another relative flop from the middling period in Gould's career following *Bob & Carol & Ted & Alice* and *M*A*S*H*. (Ben Kern at the *Tribune:* "The only real individualizing and, hence, engaging thing about the film is the character of Harry, excellently done by Elliott Gould.")

One distinctly period-specific sight is *Beyond the Valley of the Dolls*, which opened at the Orpheum in July 1970. Skin-flick kingpin Russ Meyer's rock and roll–flavored schlock epic, penned by none other than Roger Ebert, is now deemed one of the great cult films of all time. Predictably, this classic of the "sexploitation" genre opened locally to some of the worst reviews in memory ("Roger Ebert has so completely given up hope of future respect as to give his name of co-author," writes Don Morrison of his midwestern colleague). Jacqueline Susann, whose *Valley of the Dolls* this film was supposedly a loose sequel to, happened to be in town on a book tour when the movie opened. Will Jones from the *Tribune* caught up with her to get her take. "They brought in this Russ Meyer, who's made all those skin films," she complained. "He chose my title, but it's not my script. It's just another one of those Russ Meyer films, with nobody in it that you've ever heard of."

Despite being such a vibrant period of cinematic creativity, the early 1970s was also the last hurrah for the old downtown movie houses. As Dave Kenney explains in his terrific 2007 account of local cinematic history, *Twin Cities Picture Show*, "The top movies always opened at the downtown theaters. When they finished their first runs, they moved on to subsequent-run theaters—usually in the neighborhoods beyond downtown or in the suburbs. The downtown theaters' stranglehold on first-run motion pictures made them the destination of choice." By the early 1970s, the neighborhood and suburban theaters were starting to bid successfully for first-run movies, giving filmgoers in a metro area increasingly oriented around the suburbs an option to skip downtown altogether.

The nail in the coffin was *Jaws* in 1975, which opened at one downtown theater but also at the Cine Capri in far-flung White Bear Lake. The box office in the suburbs matched that of the downtown theater. The decline from there was precipitous. By the early 1980s, all but one of downtown Minneapolis's theaters—including all of those pictured in these images—had either shuttered or switched to the one format that still managed to draw a moderate crowd: pornos.

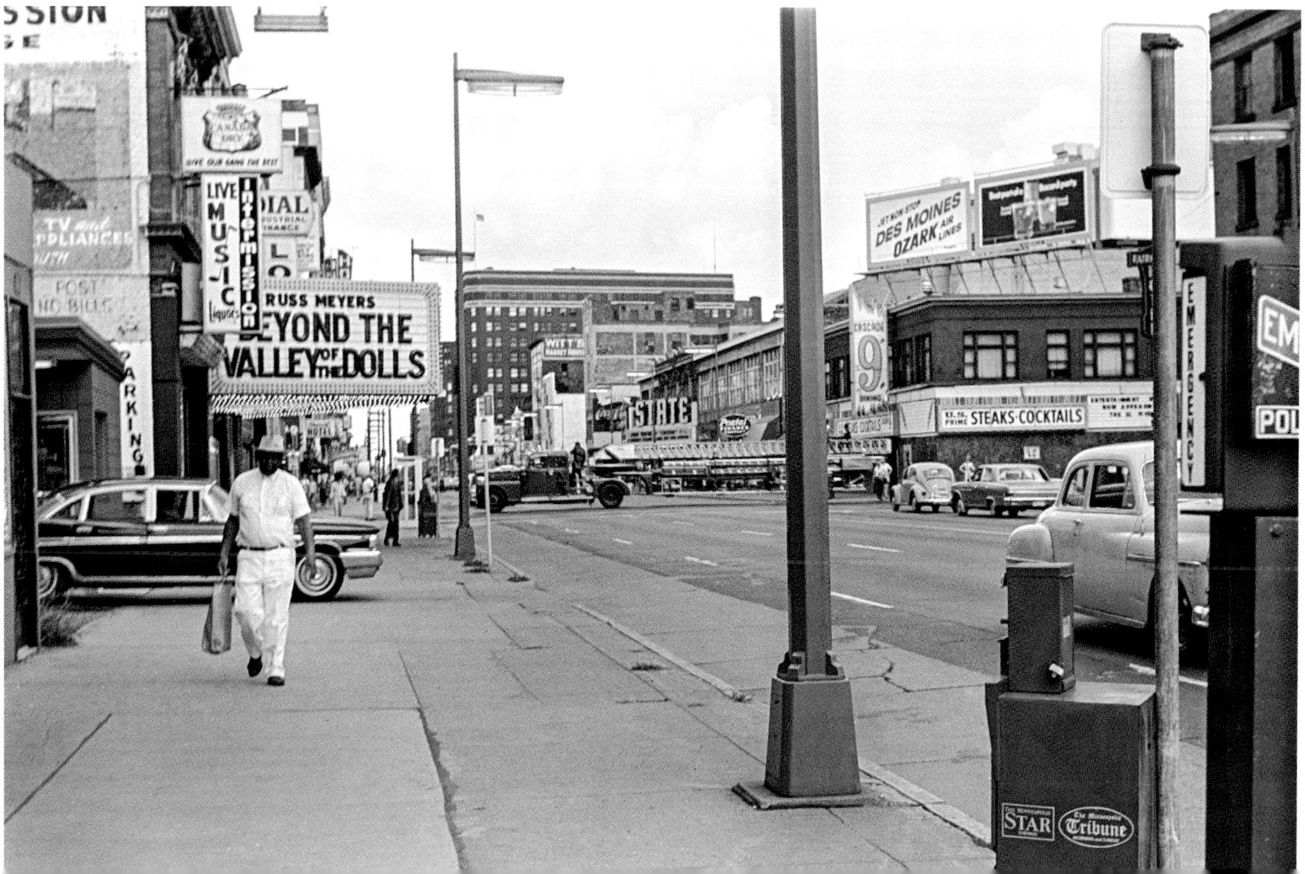

Hennepin Avenue near Ninth Street, with *Beyond the Valley of the Dolls* on the Orpheum's marquee

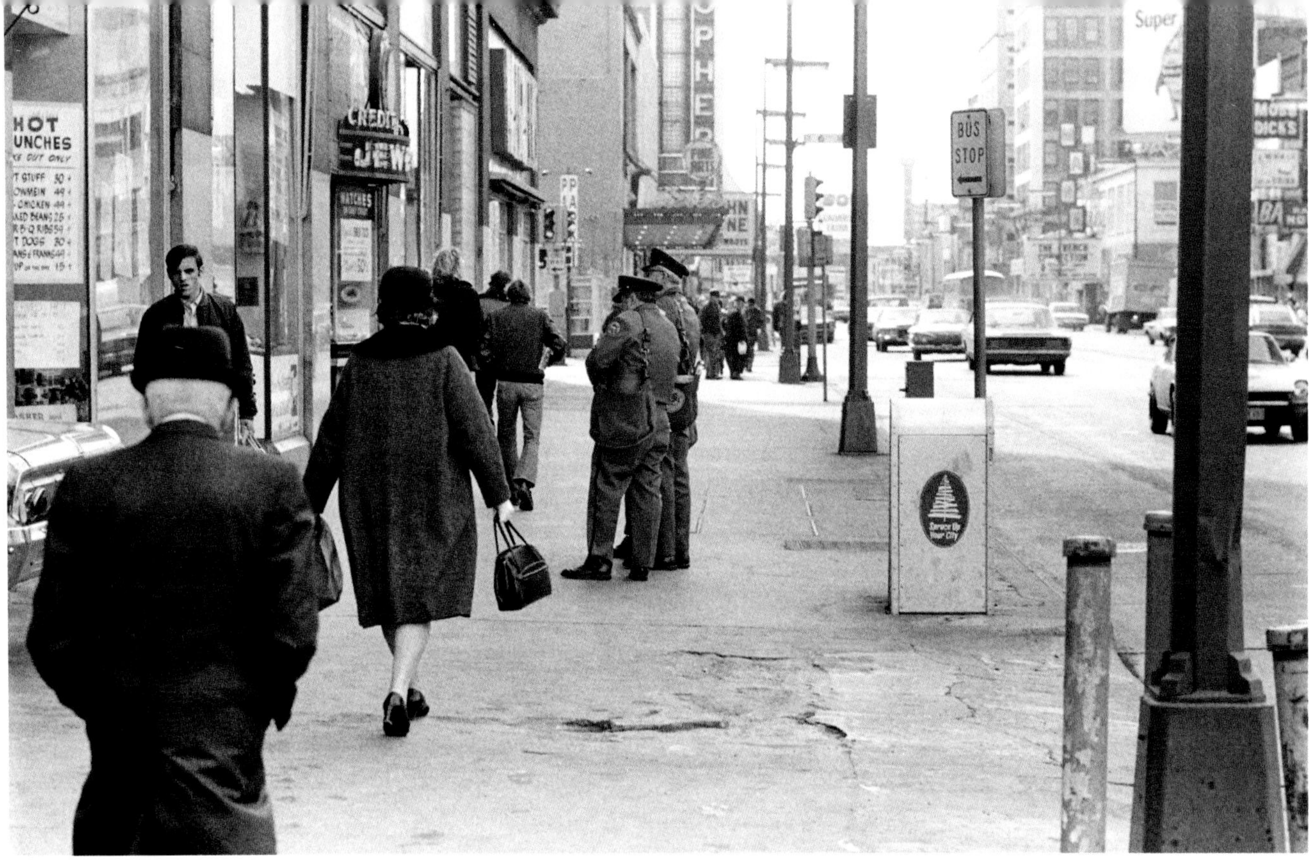

Hennepin Avenue activity near Sixth Street, across from the infamous Moby Dick's bar

Action at Hennepin and Seventh, with the Mann Theater and Music City

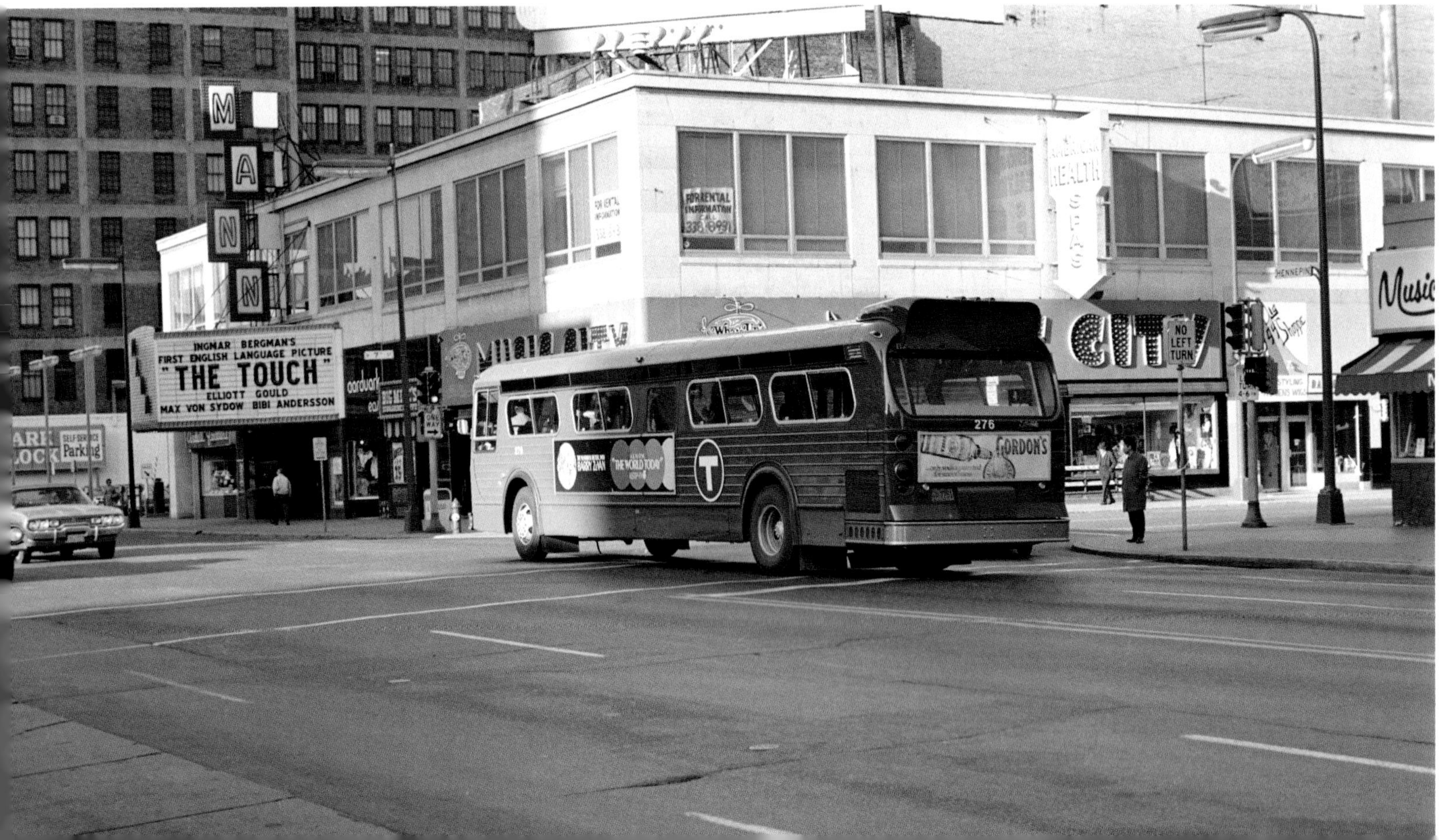

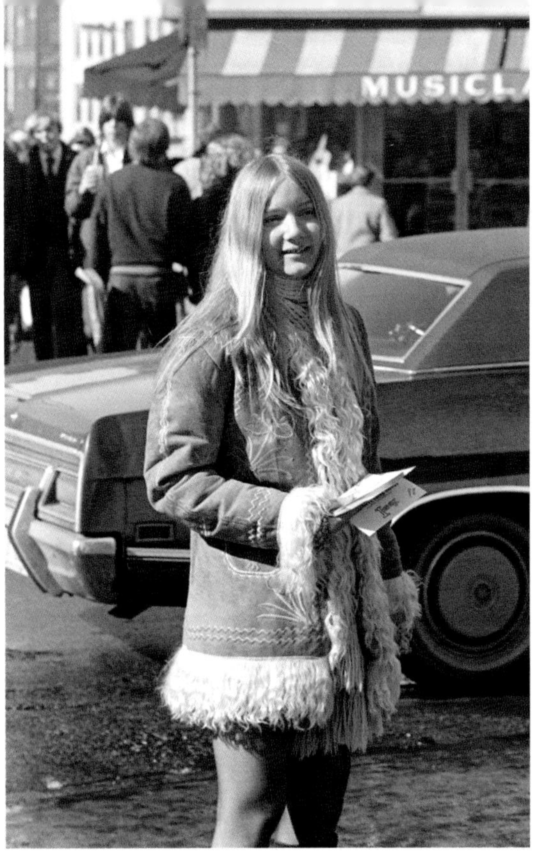

Handing out flyers on Hennepin

Browsing the folk music section at Musicland

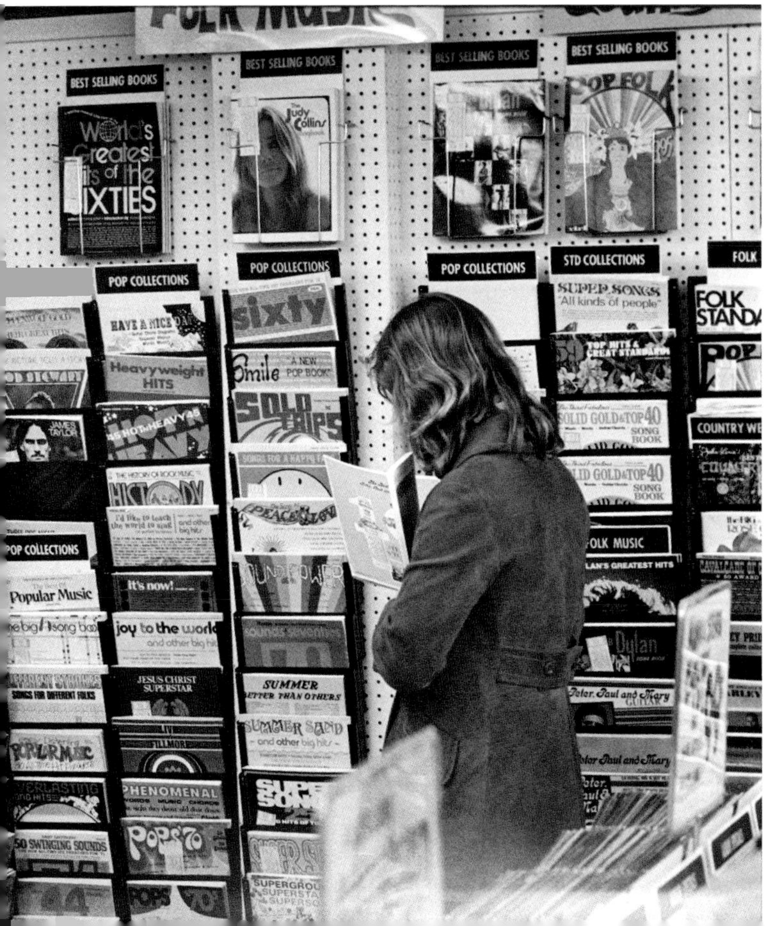

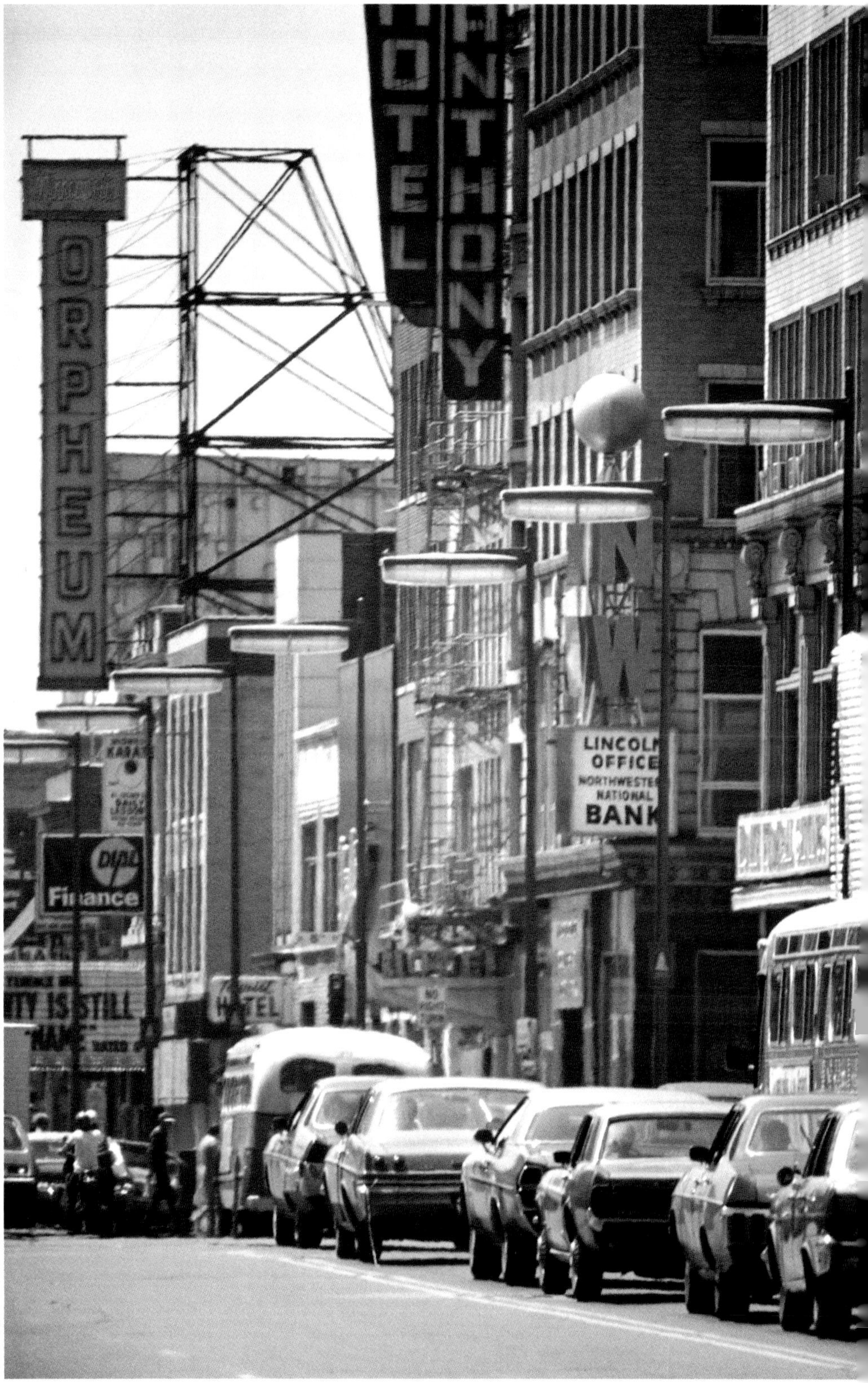

Looking south toward the Orpheum Theatre on Hennepin Avenue—the Hotel Anthony, between Eighth and Ninth Streets, was destroyed by a fire in December 1973

CENTURY CAMERA

The third of the core downtown photo shops frequented by aspiring photographer Mike Evangelist in the early 1970s was Century Camera, just a few blocks from Jay's and Brown on Ninth Street, a block off Hennepin. Century, which billed itself as the "Northwest's Largest Photographic Showroom," was a business that dated back to the early twentieth century and had roots on Minneapolis's north side. The founder, Harvey Goldstein, was staff photographer for the North High School newspaper and went on to shoot Gopher athletics for the University of Minnesota *Daily*. He opened Century Camera's first location in the heart of Dinkytown at 1327 Fourth Street Southeast in the late 1930s. Here it maintained a store and warehouse for many years. Over the course of the next three decades, in addition to its Dinkytown location, Century would have shops up and down Nicollet Mall, until about 1971, when the last downtown location, at 119 North Ninth Street, disappears from the city directory.

For some time, this store was reputed to be the largest photo shop in the Midwest outside Chicago. "Photography . . . has become more than a hobby, but big business," Goldstein told the *Minneapolis Star*. Century not only sold cameras and equipment to industrial and commercial photographers but also did big business in equipment rental and had half a dozen traveling salesmen on the road by the early 1960s. (The *Star* article also notes that by then, Goldstein had retired from professional photography: "he would be competing with too many customers.") "The rug merchants of the Minneapolis photo business," Mike says of Century. "The kind of place that would give you about fifteen seconds of browsing before asking if you were going to buy anything."

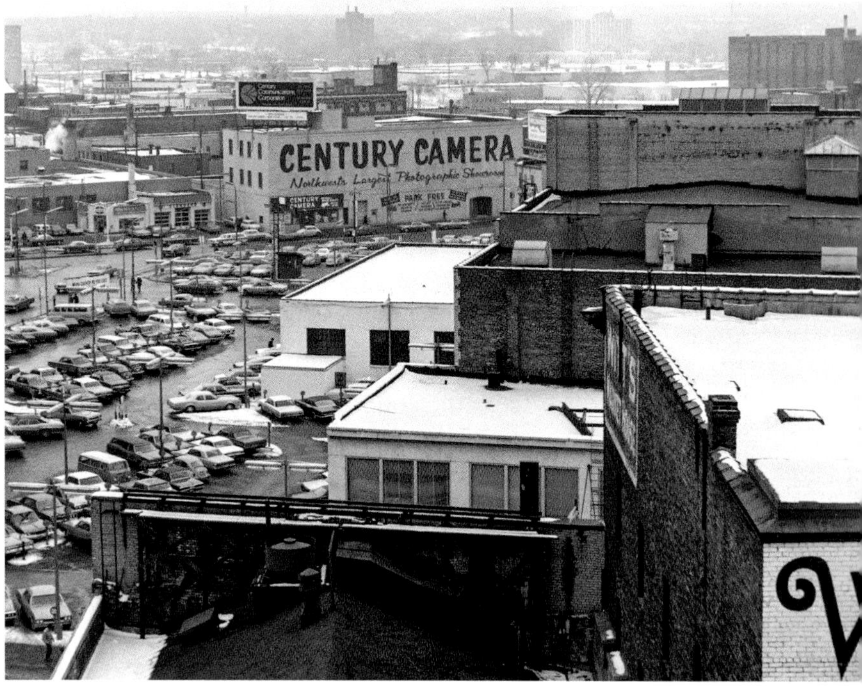

Century Camera, viewed from the top floor of the Dayton's parking ramp

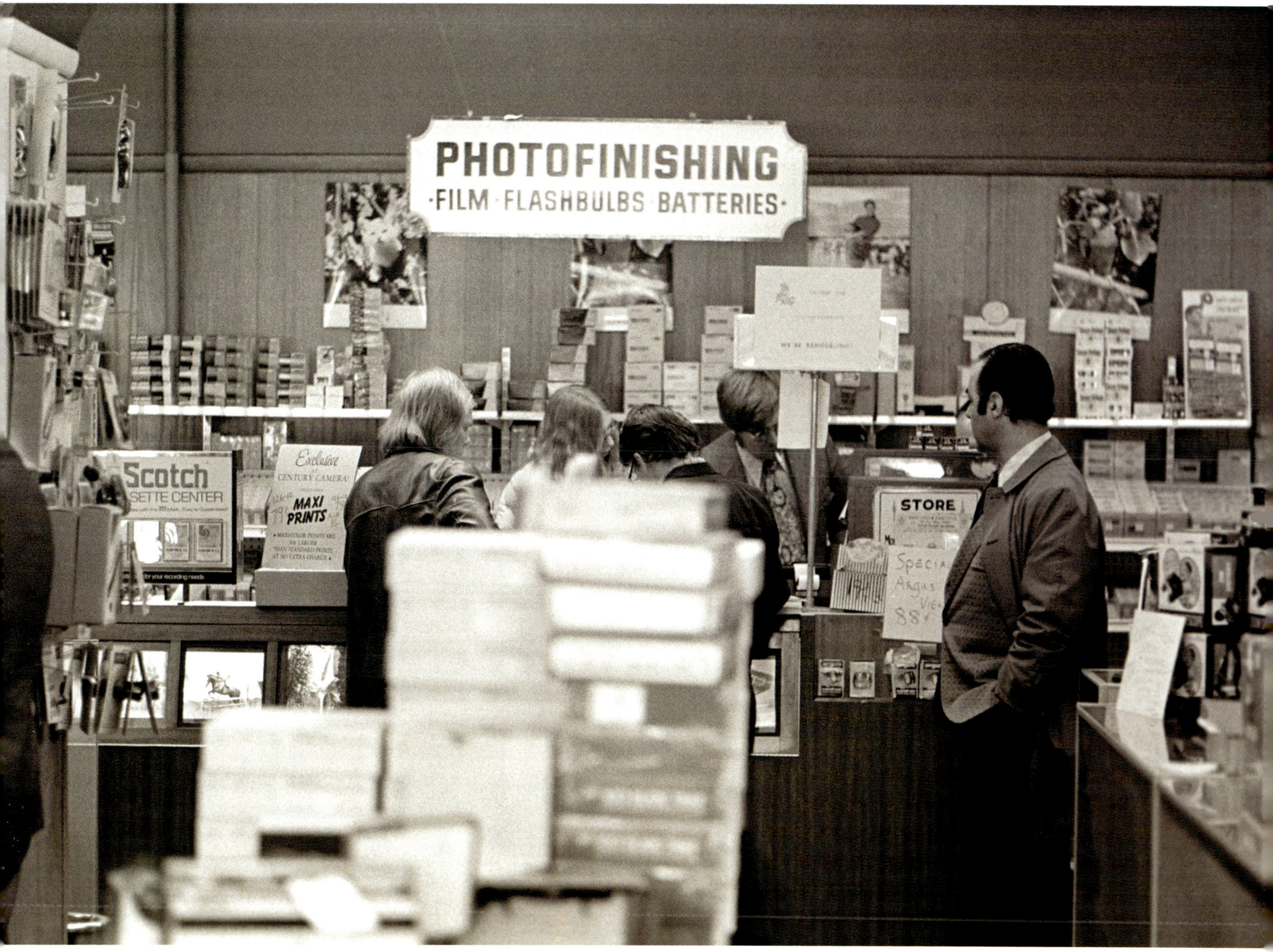

Shoppers and staff inside Century Camera

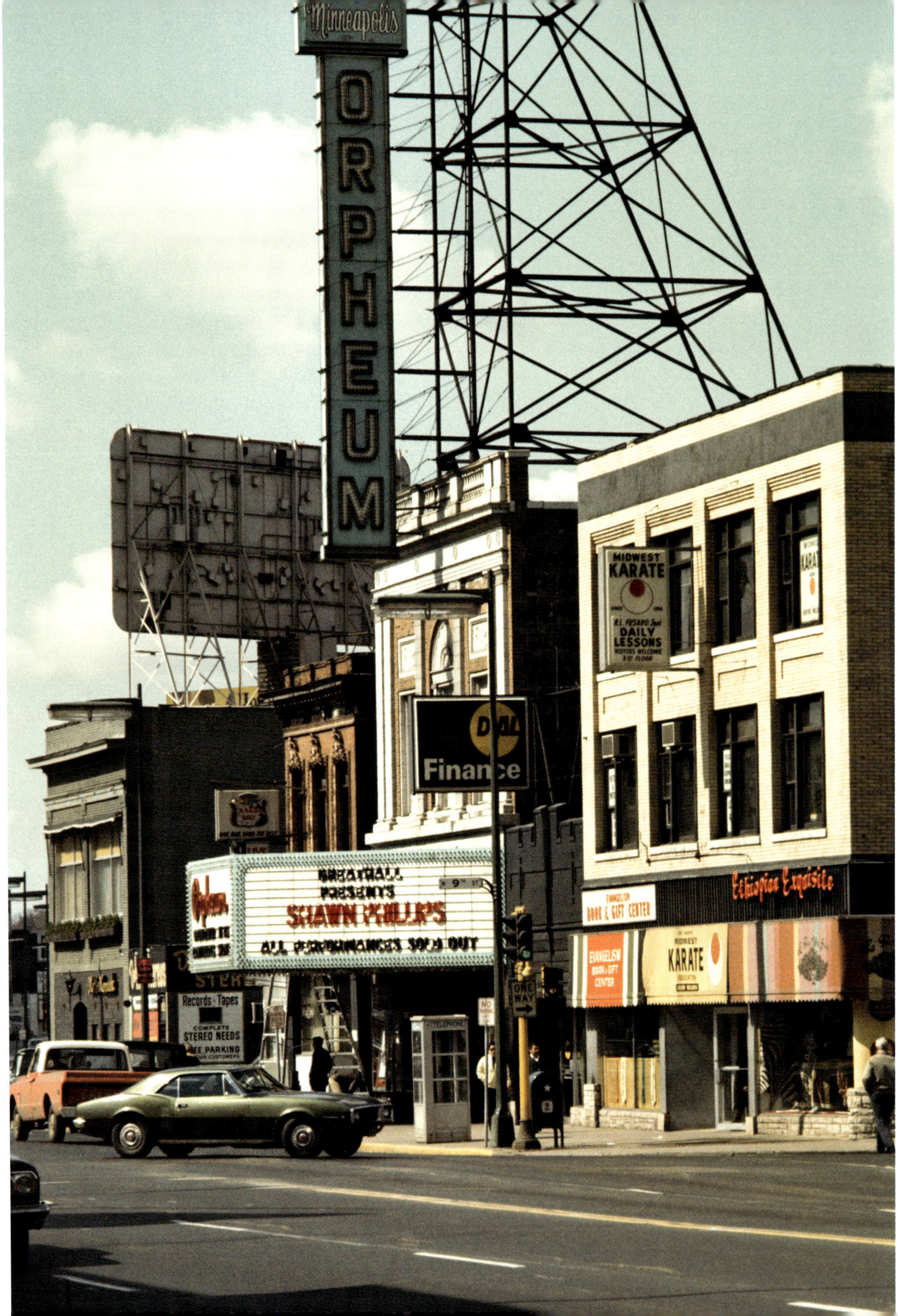
Minneapolis
ORPHEUM
MIDWEST KARATE
DAILY LESSONS
DML
Finance
GREATHALL
PRESENTS
SHAWN PHILLIPS
ALL PERFORMANCES SOLD OUT
Ethiopian Exquisite
EVANGELISM BOOK & GIFT CENTER
MIDWEST KARATE
Records Tapes
COMPLETE STEREO NEEDS
ONE WAY

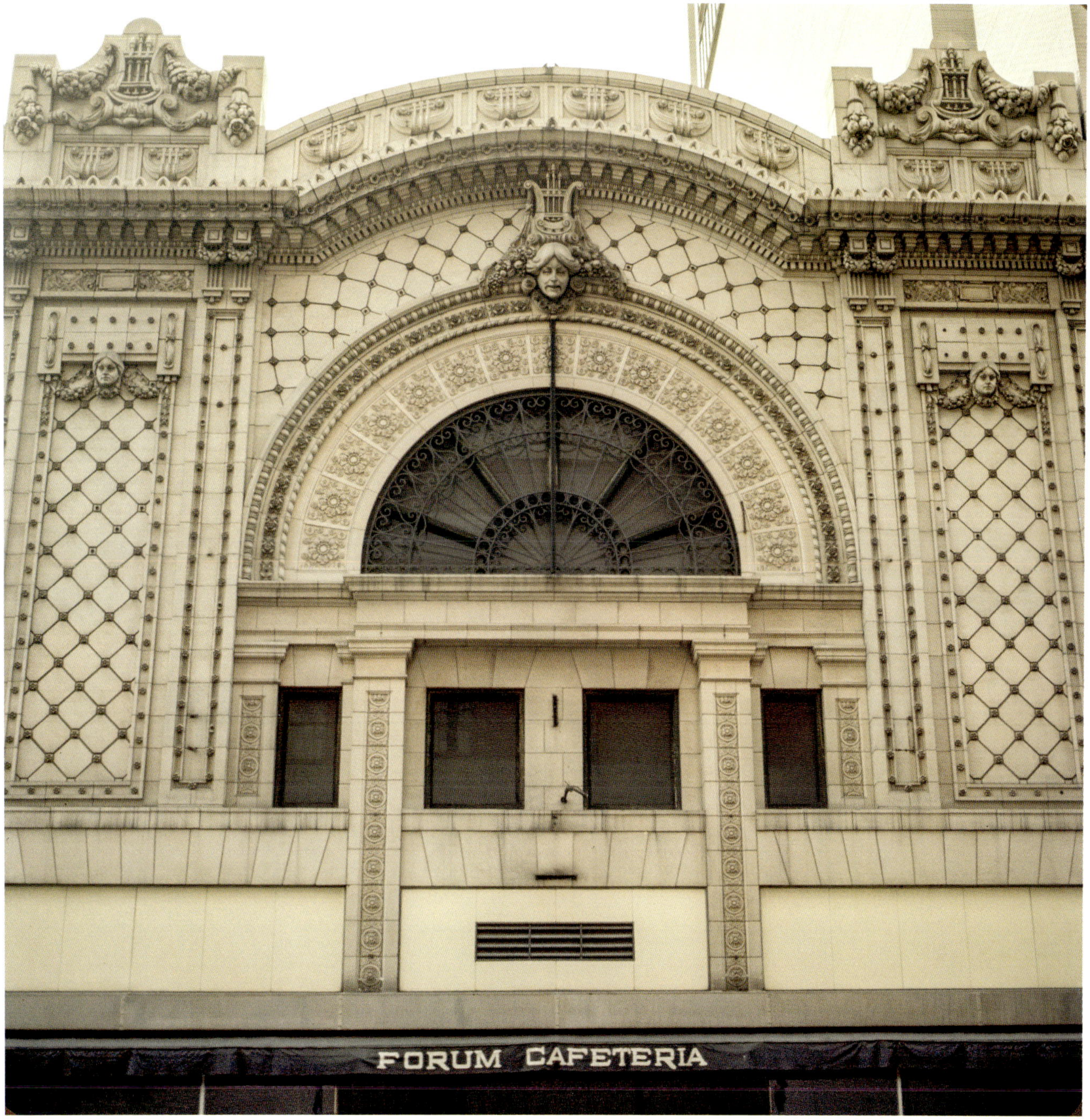

Above: The Forum Cafeteria (originally built as the Saxe Theater in 1914) on Seventh Street

Opposite: The Orpheum Theatre marquee featuring folk-rocker Shawn Phillips in 1973—"All Performances Sold Out." His theme for the remake of *Lost Horizon* was a hit that year.

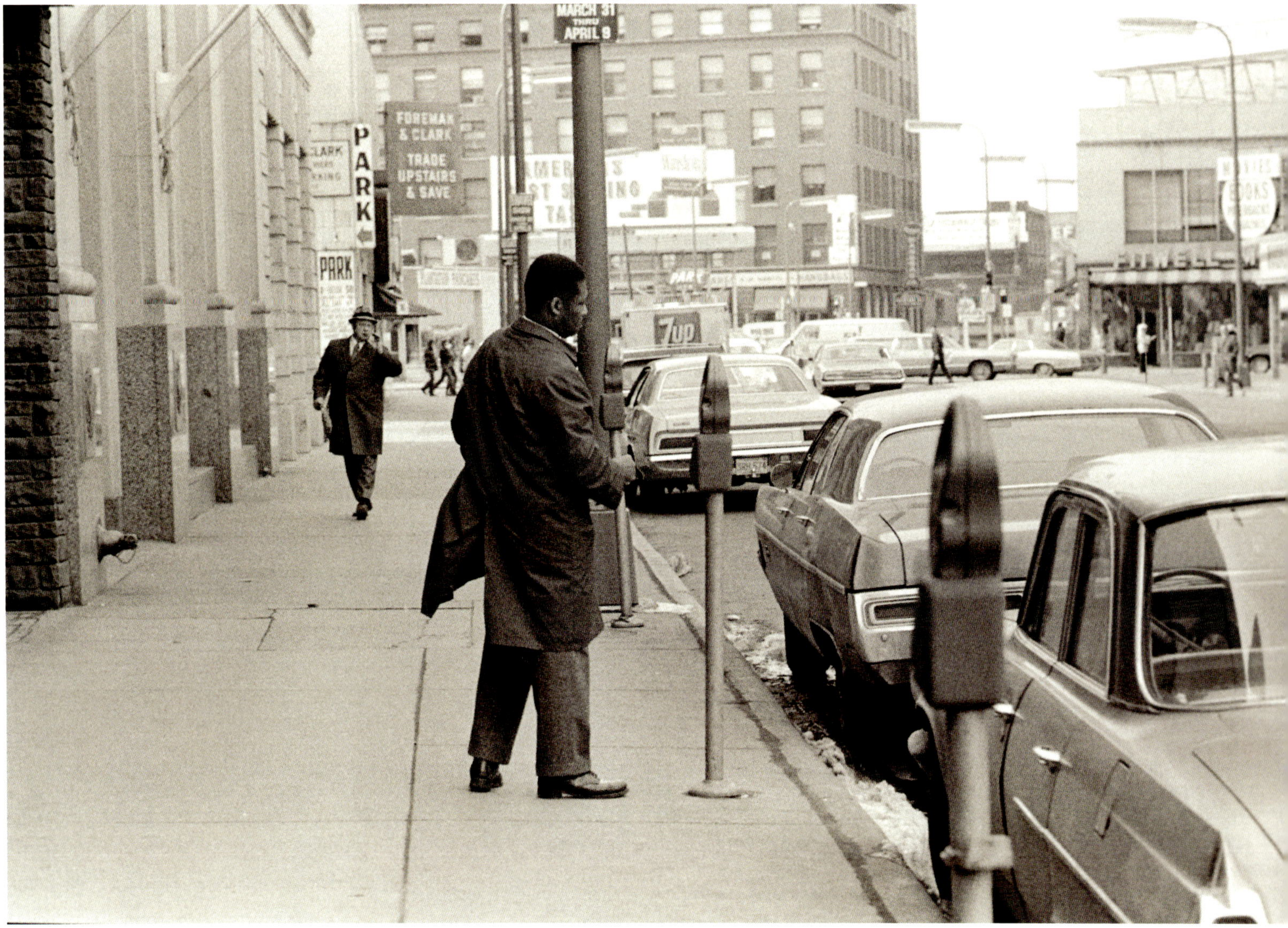

Plugging the meter on Fifth Street, near Hennepin Avenue

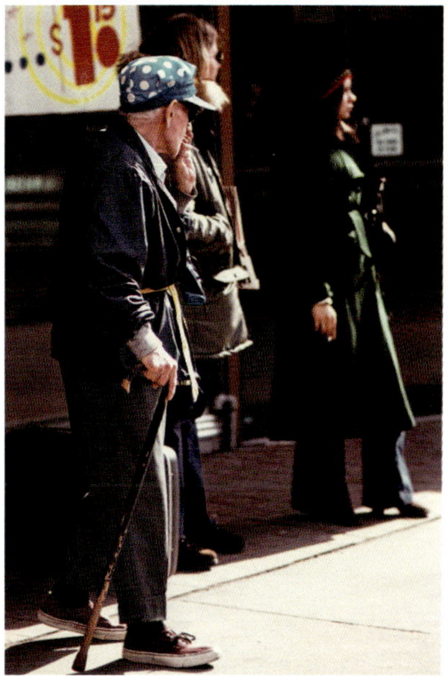

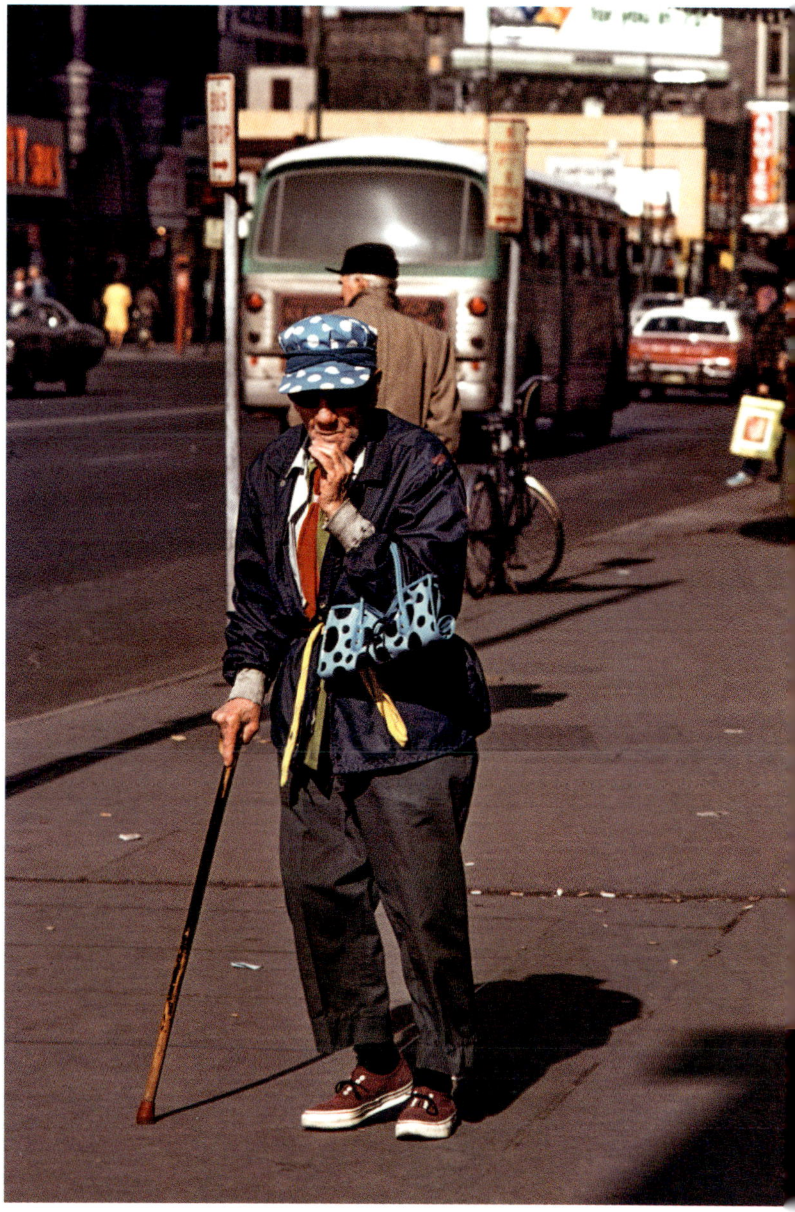

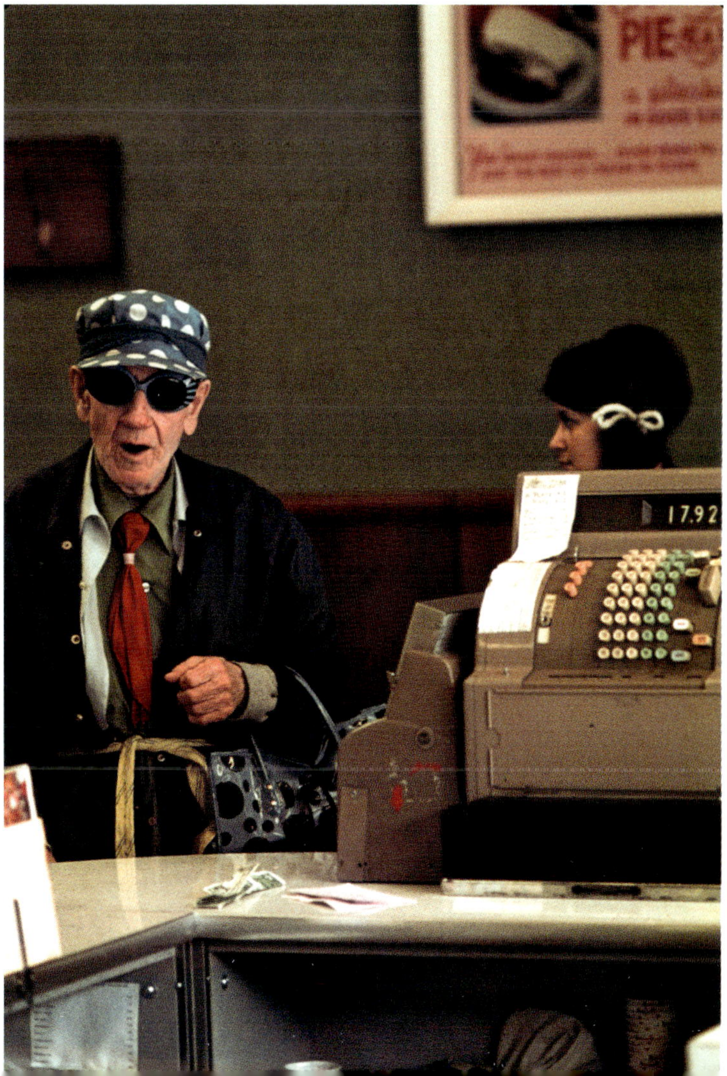

Among the unique characters to be seen in downtown Minneapolis in the 1970s was this fellow with the bug-eye sunglasses and blue polka-dot hat, gripping a matching blue plastic handbag. While some of the fashions in this book look dated from the perspective of today, this man's outfit is timeless—the universal costume of the urban eccentric. Alas, out of the thousands of members of the Old Minneapolis Facebook community, no one knew a thing about him. Whoever he is, he remains one of the great, unsung Minneapolis eccentrics.

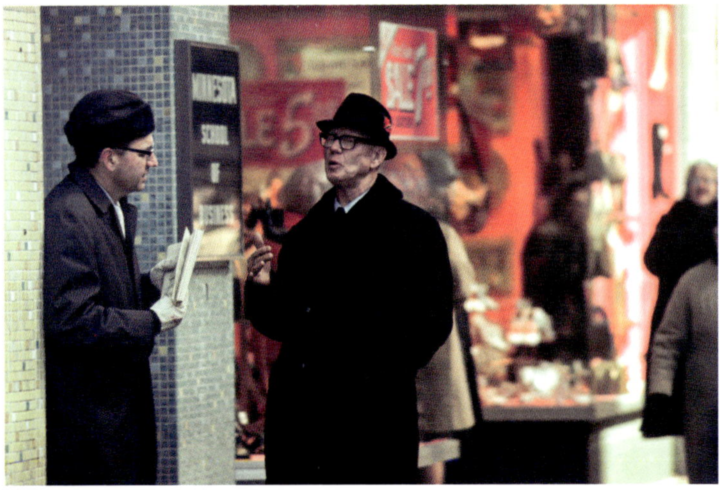

Left: Two men conferring outside the Minnesota School of Business on Seventh Street between Hennepin and Nicollet

Opposite: Man loitering downtown

Below: Panhandlers conferring on Hennepin

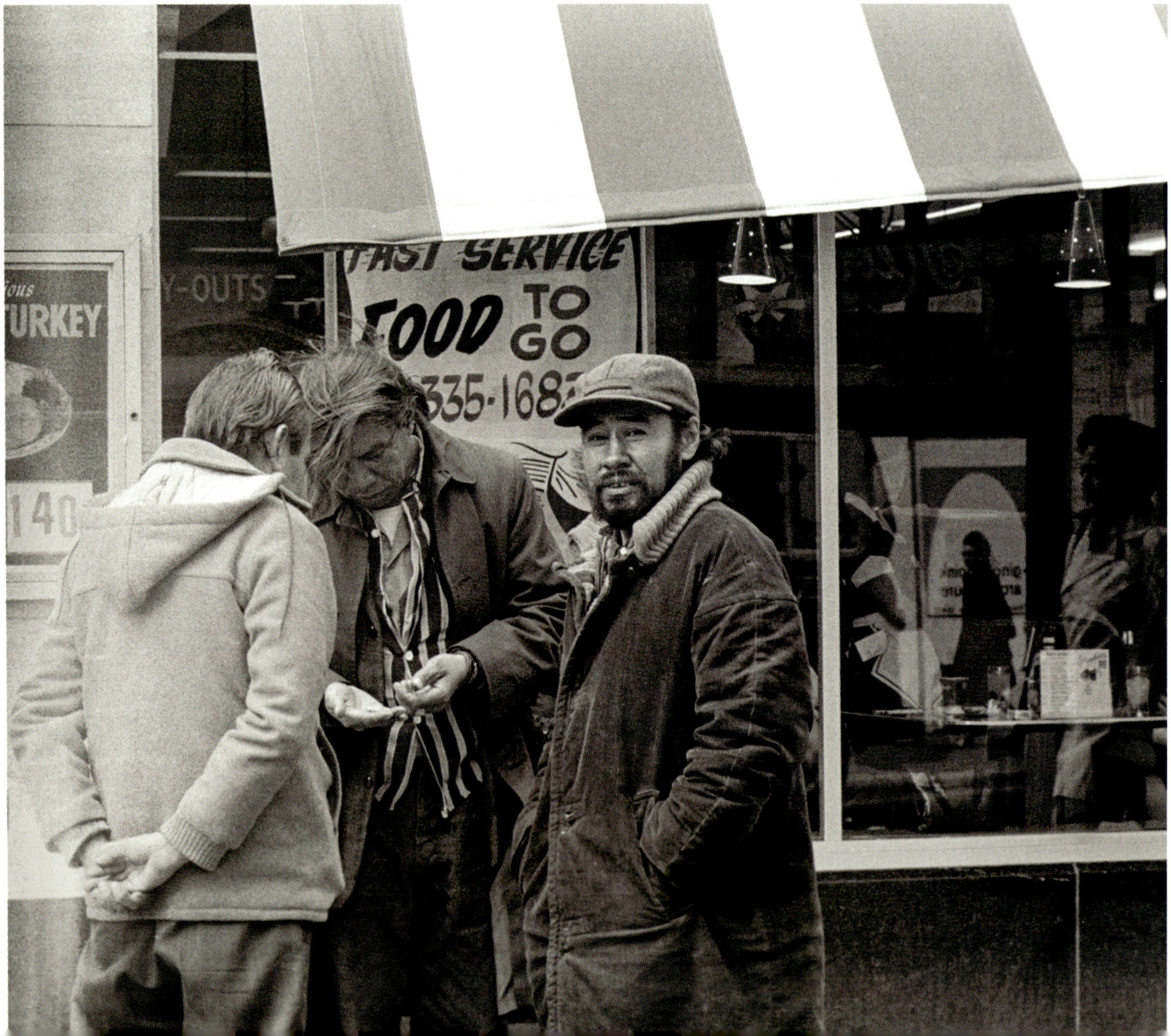

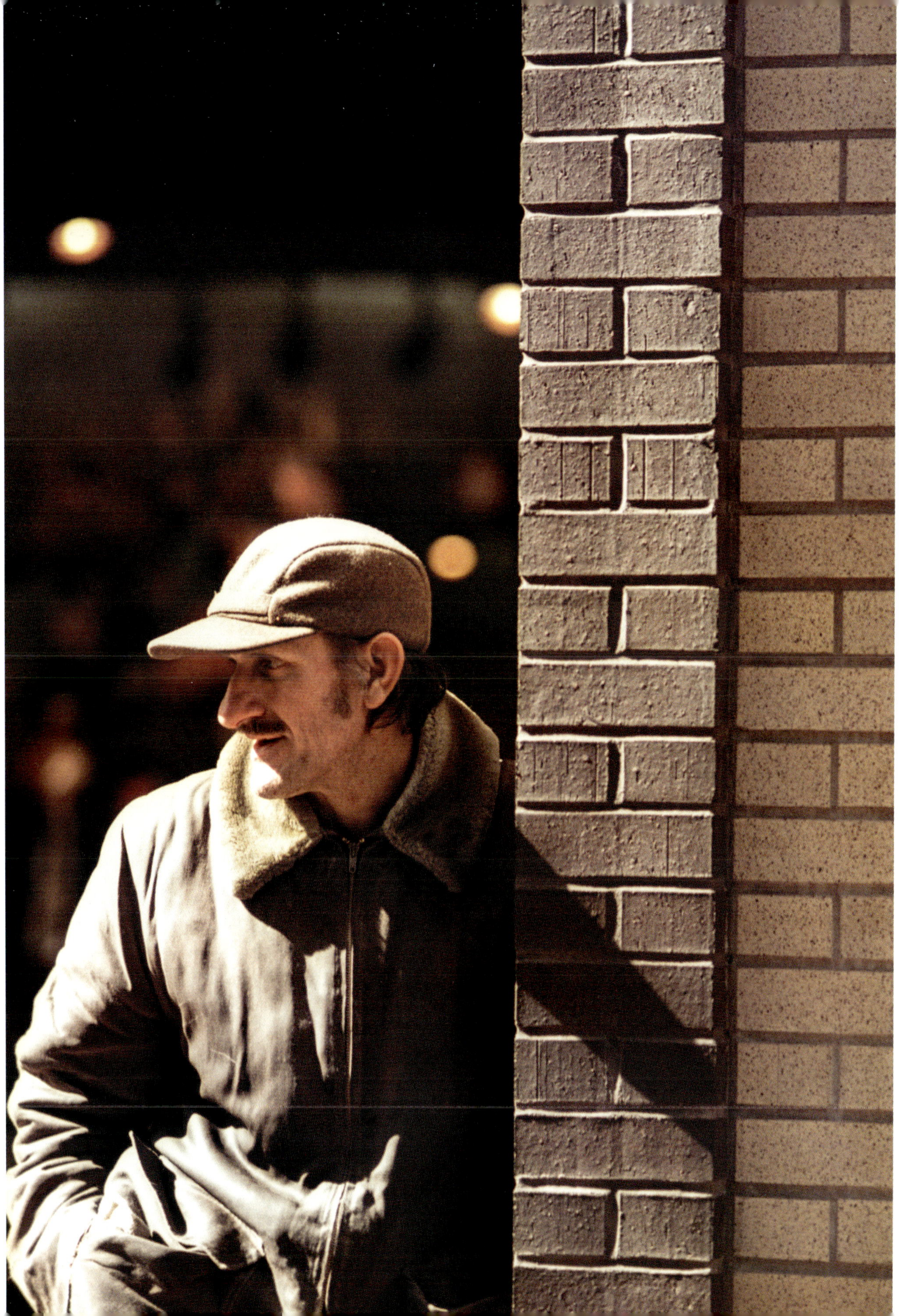

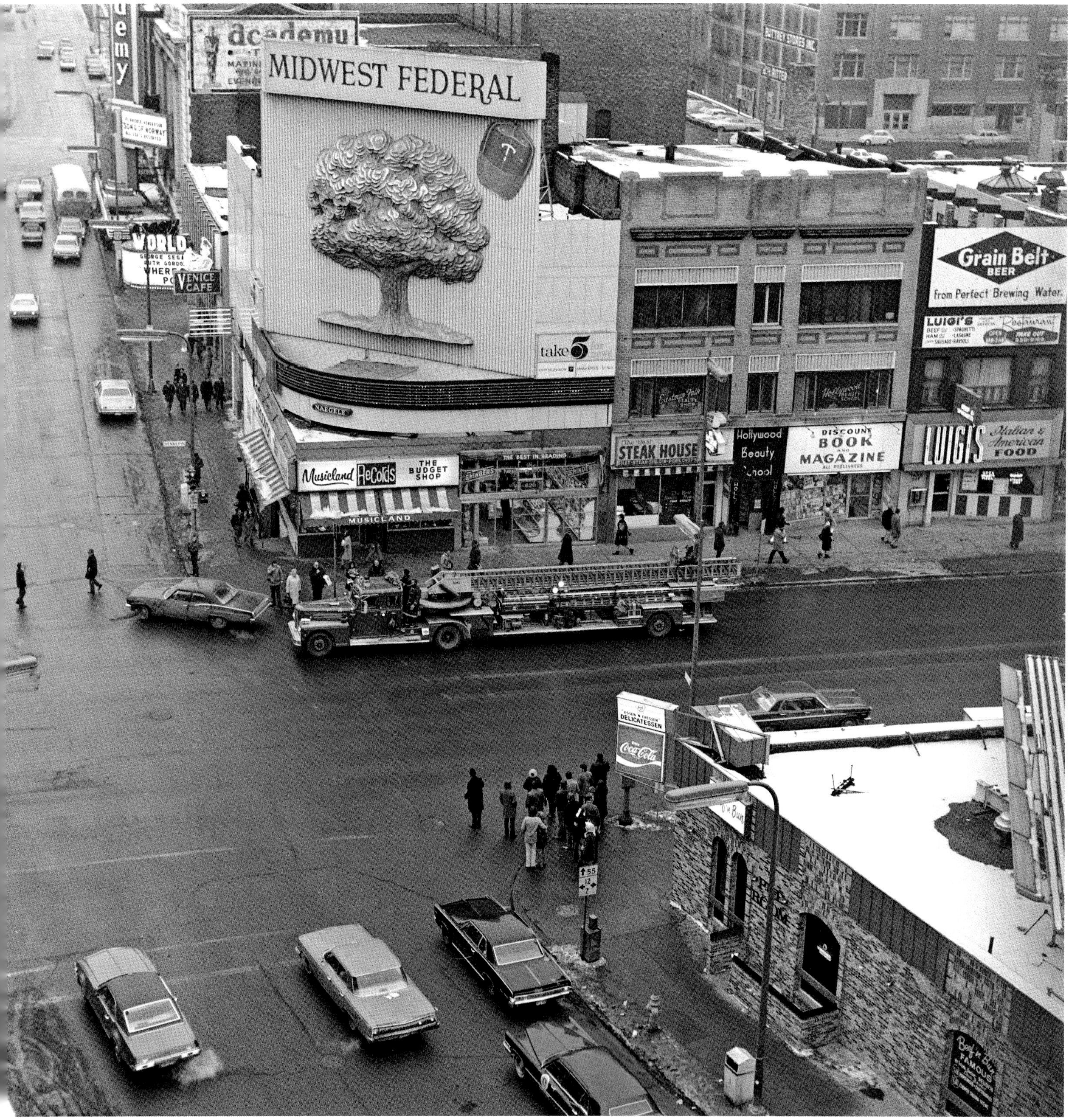
MIDWEST FEDERAL
Grain Belt
BEER
From Perfect Brewing Water.
LUIGI'S
Italian & American
FOOD
DISCOUNT
BOOK
AND
MAGAZINE
ALL PUBLISHERS
Hollywood
Beauty
School
STEAK HOUSE
Musicland Records
THE BUDGET SHOP
MUSICLAND
THE BEST IN READING
WORLD
VENICE
CAFE
take 5
DELICATESSEN
Coca-Cola

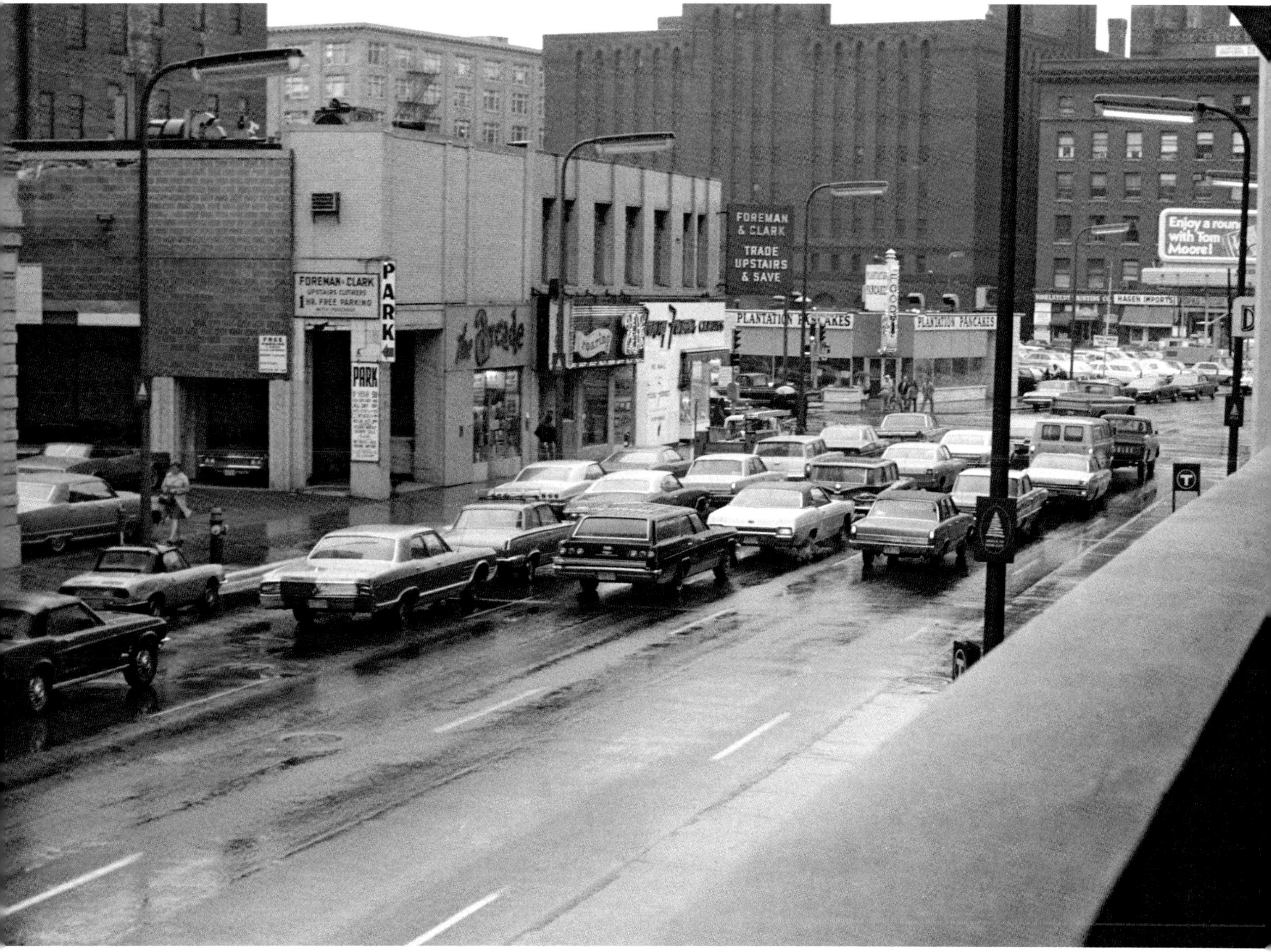

Above: Looking up Fifth Street toward the Hennepin Avenue mainstays Plantation Pancakes, Fanny Farmer, and Foreman & Clark, with Butler Square in the background

Opposite: Block E and the busy intersection of Seventh and Hennepin

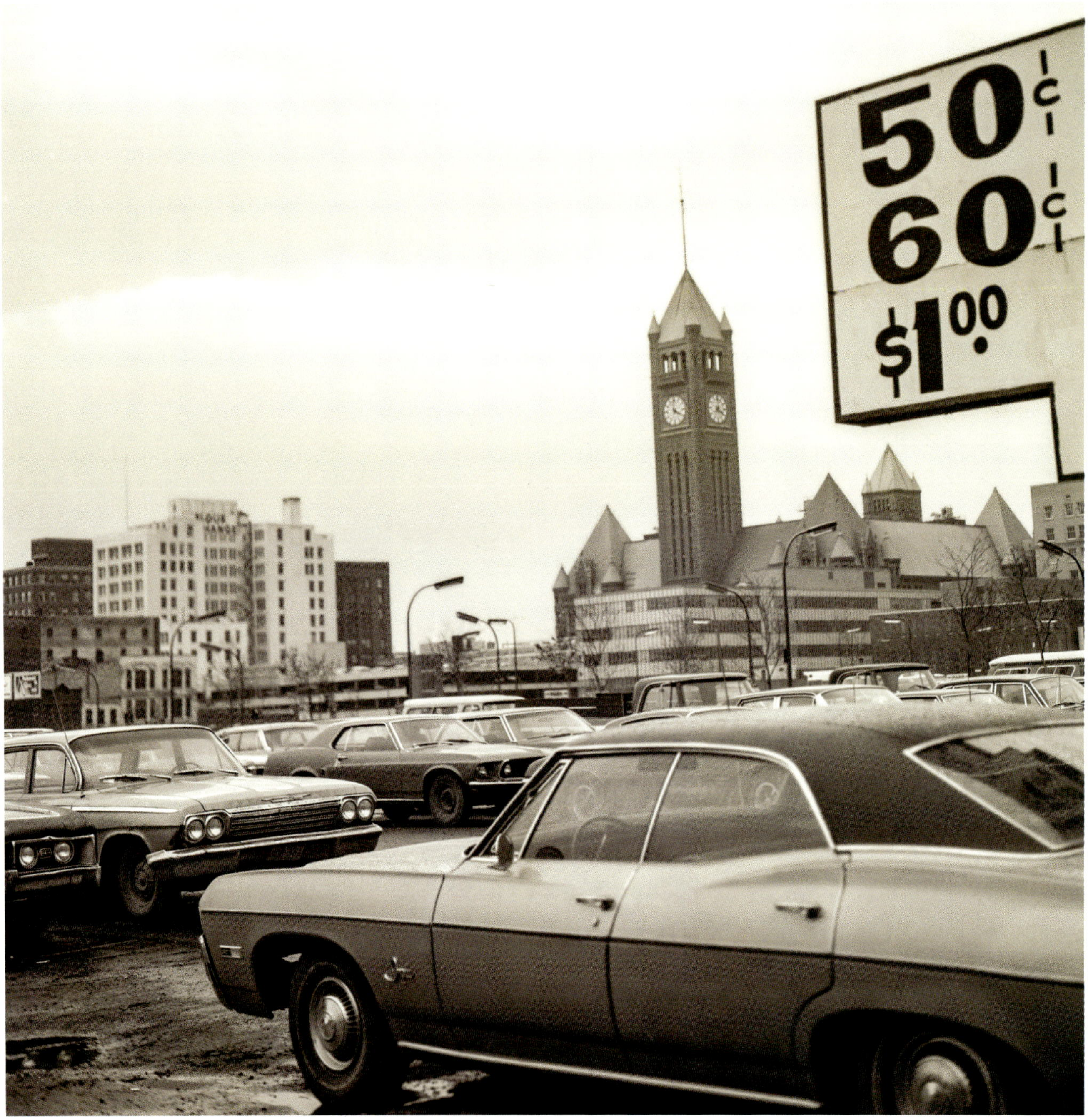

City hall, before it was hemmed in by taller buildings

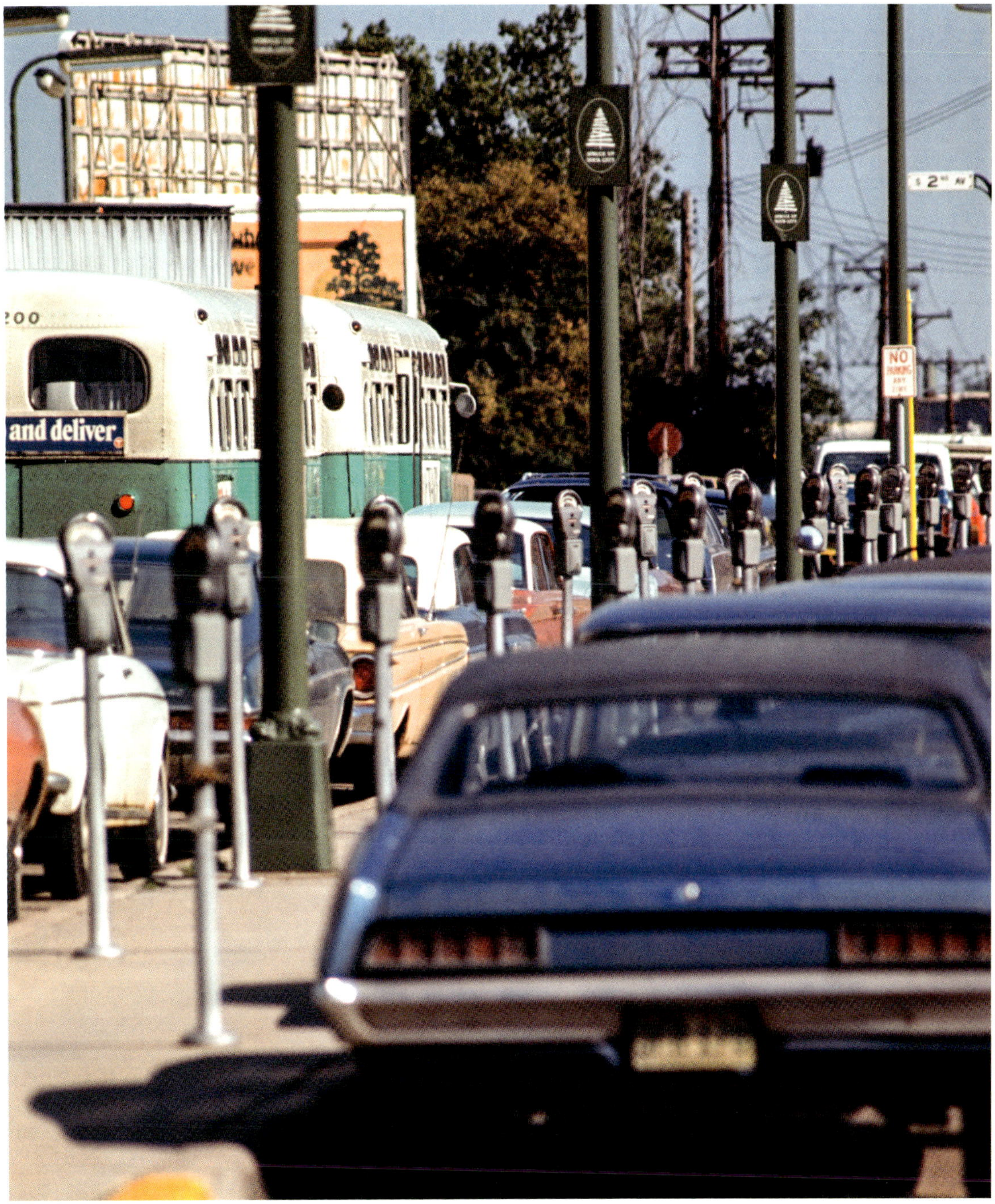

Old buses and parked cars downtown, autumn 1972

HITCHHIKERS

Of all the images Mike posted to Facebook and the Old Minneapolis group, this shot of two young hitchhikers looking for a ride on Hennepin Avenue proved to be one of the most popular.

What is it that people find so captivating? There is, from the perspective of forty years, an undeniably romantic quality to it. Young people have been warned against hitchhiking for so long now—not just hitching, but also picking up hitchhikers—that it's no longer generally practiced. The roots of this sense of hitchhiking being an unavoidably dangerous practice date back to right about this time.

Earlier books and manuals lionized the practice as a cheap, exciting, and immersive way to see the world. One such manual even determined the exact formula for successful hitching: 8 percent technique, 11 percent "good vibes, etc.," 13 percent luck, 17 percent appearance, and 51 percent sex. Some of these publications focused on the United States, but most of them stuck to Europe and Asia, where the practice was more common. "Vagabonding in Europe isn't the moral crime it is here at home, and the motoring public less often equates hitch-hikers with criminals, degenerates and worthless loafers," sniffed writer Ed Buryn in one 1969 guidebook.

In the early 1970s in America, there was indeed a growing sense of panic about hitchhiking, especially by young women. Locally, one of the most high-profile unsolved crimes of the era was the 1970 death of a twenty-four-year-old art student from Edina who was last seen hitching a ride from downtown Minneapolis to Des Moines for a concert. Her body was found on the roadside near Albert Lea, she having jumped or been pushed from a moving automobile.

When asked by the *Tribune* why so many young people felt safe hitchhiking, Dr. Robert Fulton, a professor of sociology at the University of Minnesota, pointed to the ideals of the youth culture. "The idea is that you love and you get love back—that kind of romantic dream," he told reporter Robert T. Smith. "Regrettably, it doesn't always pay to express high ideals with strangers." This article was followed up by another the next weekend, asking young people with some bewilderment why they insisted on hitchhiking in such large numbers.

Similar pieces appeared in the national press throughout the early 1970s, in mainstream publications like *Time* and *Good Housekeeping*. "A generation of young women seem bent on proving that they are formidable enough to take care of themselves," wrote *Time*, chalking this newfound assertiveness up to "Women's Liberation and youth's emphasis on freedom." In 1973 *Good Housekeeping* ran a lengthy article on the phenomenon entitled "Hitchhiking: The Deadly New Odds."

In that piece, a twenty-year-old from Chicago summed up her feelings about hitchhiking as a young woman, perhaps reflecting those of the two women in this photo as well: "I've been sheltered all my life. I grew up in a nice home but my horizons were so limited. . . . I want to spread out, meet the world, really know what it's like out there. For some girls, too, the very act of hitching, involving as it does an entirely new method of transportation hitherto barred to them by custom, offers not only a change but a new kind of excitement."

In 1974, a statute dating from the 1930s that limited hitchhiking was amended by the legislature to outlaw it completely in the state of Minnesota.

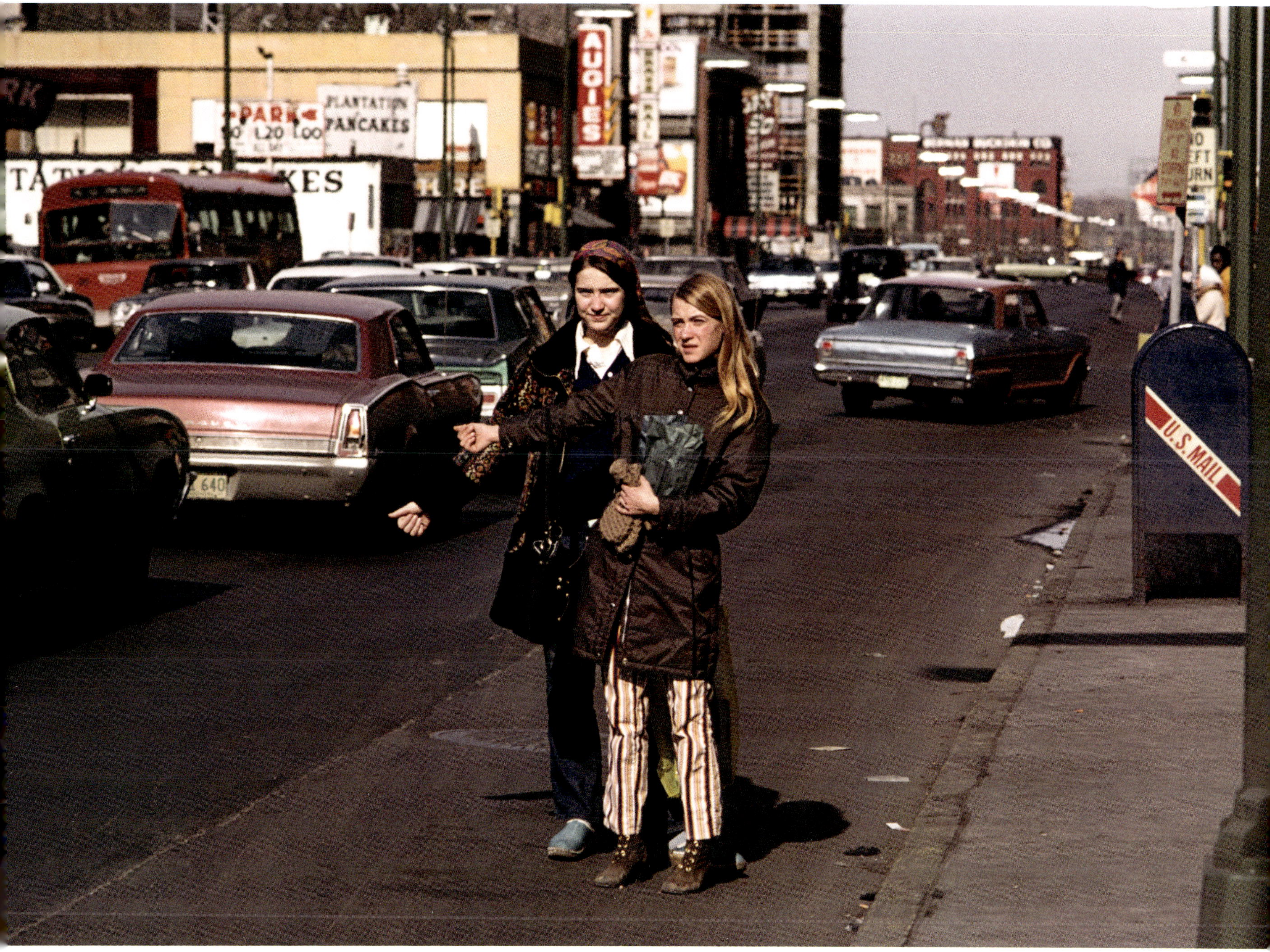

Young girls hitchhiking on Hennepin near Fifth Street

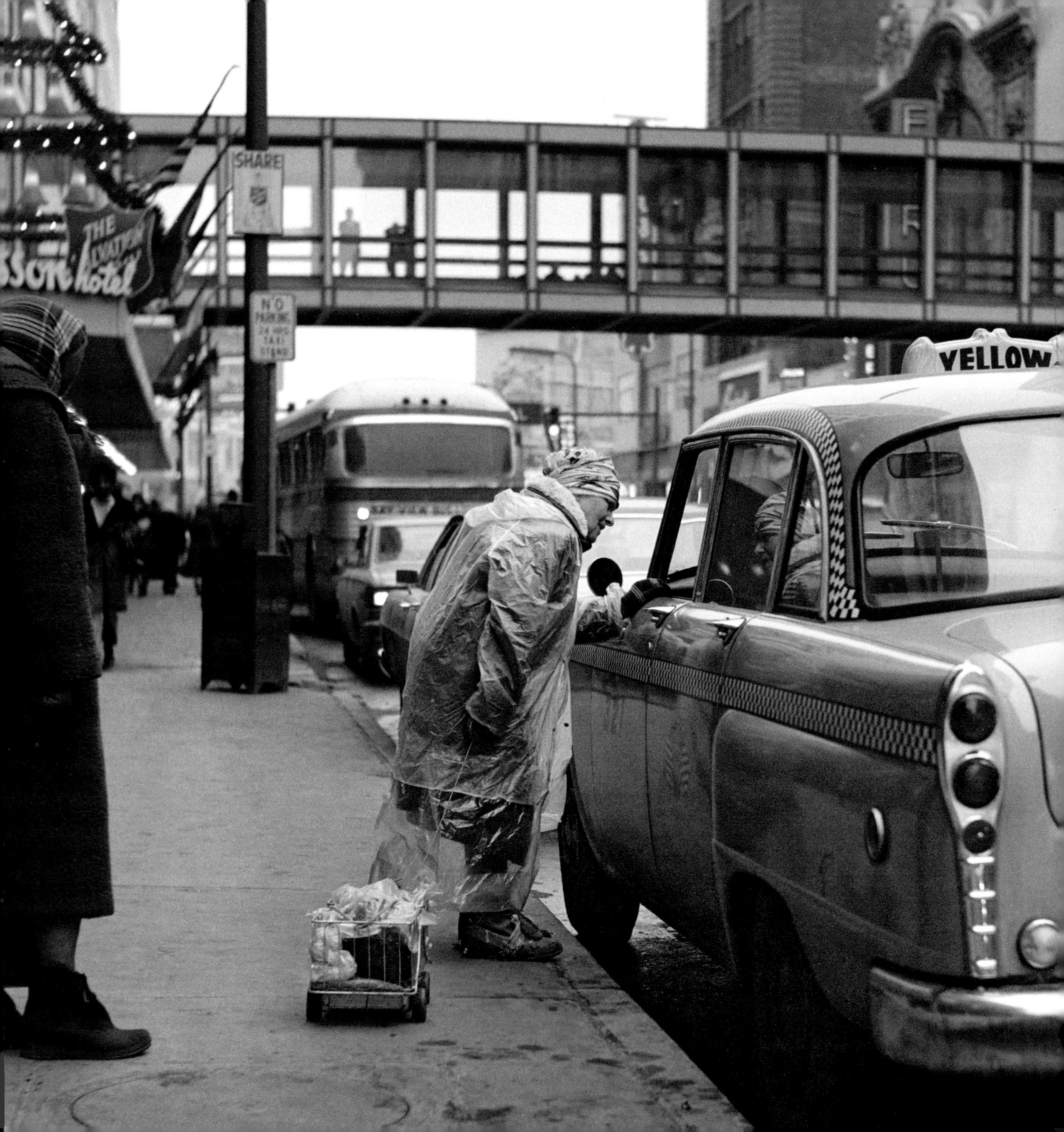
SHARE
NO PARKING
YELLOW

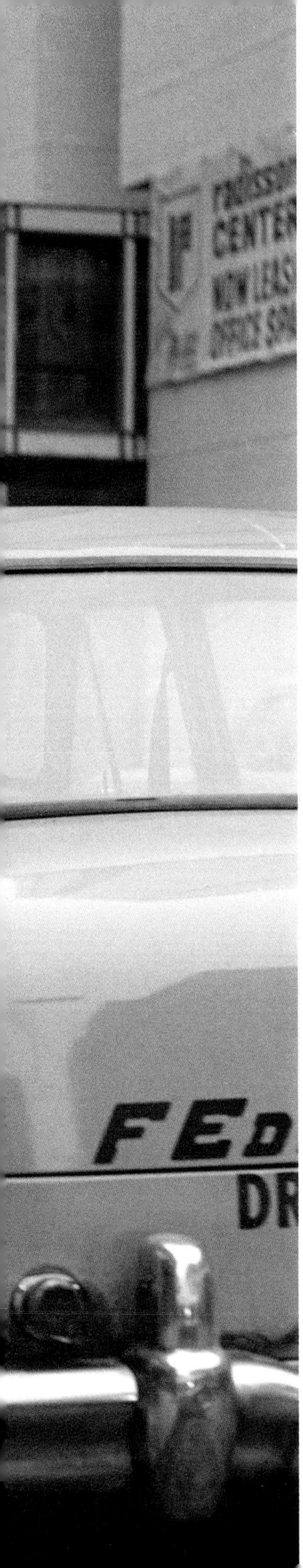

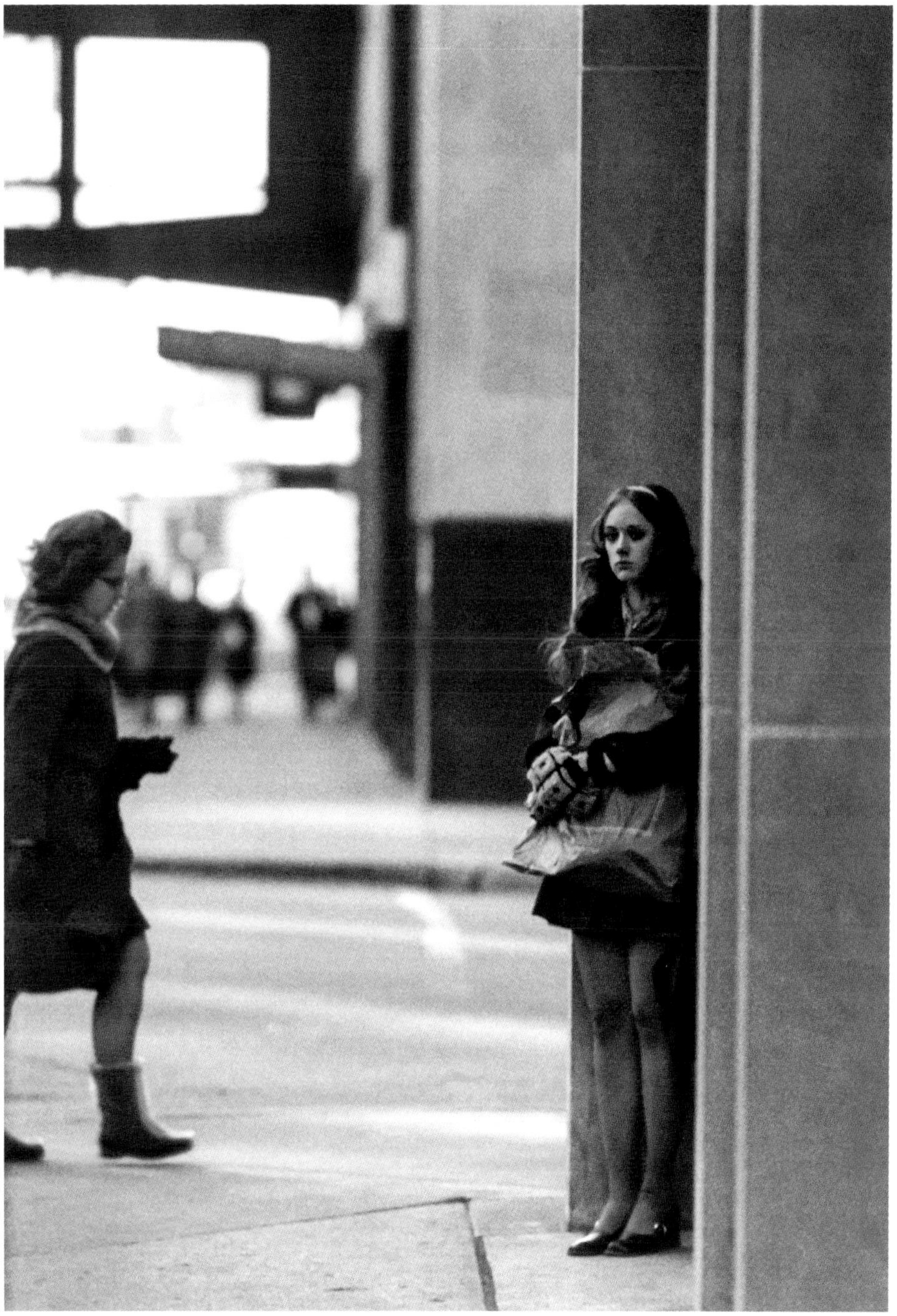

Above: Waiting at the corner

Opposite: Chatting up a cabbie on Seventh Street, in front of the Radisson Hotel

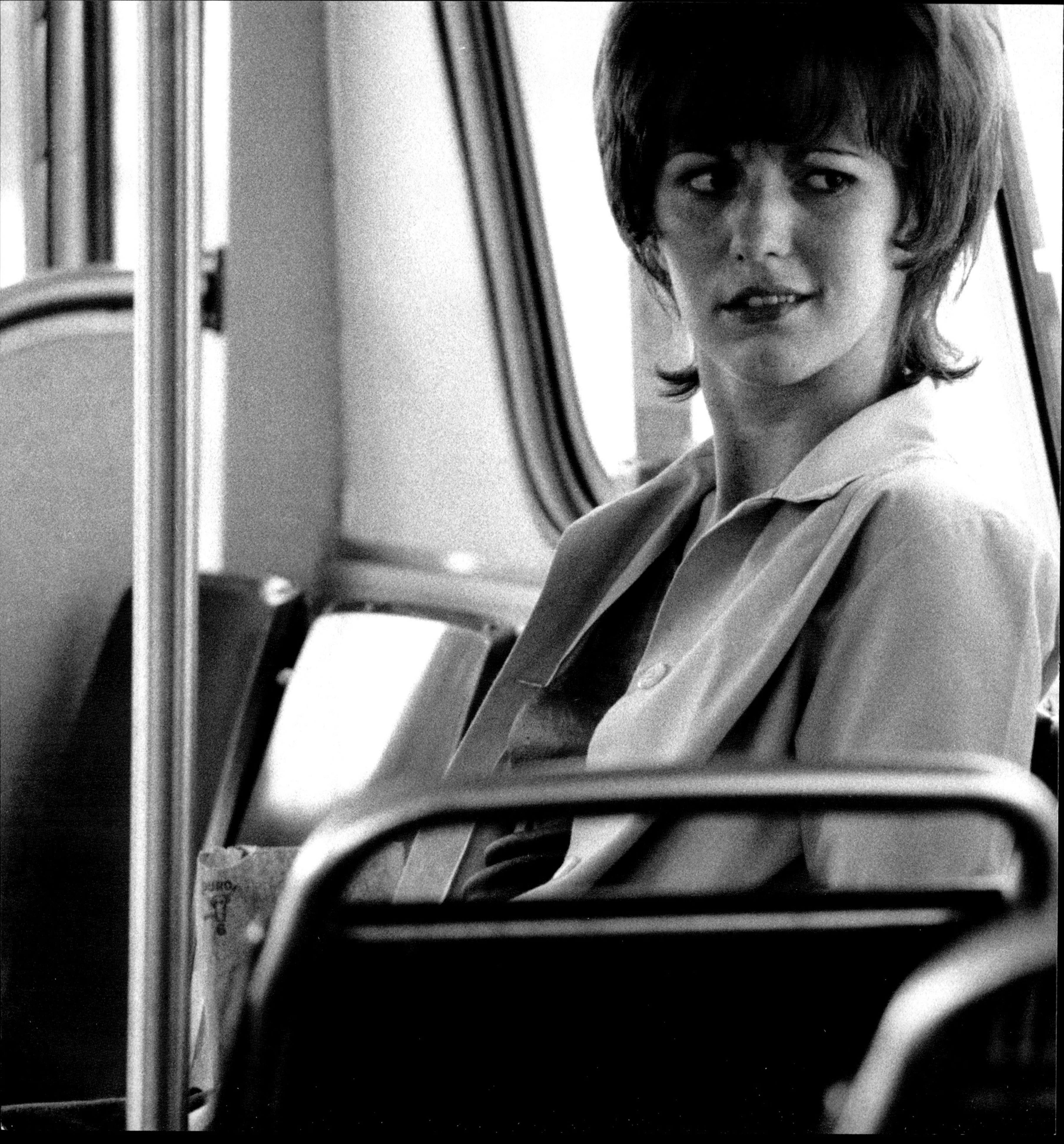

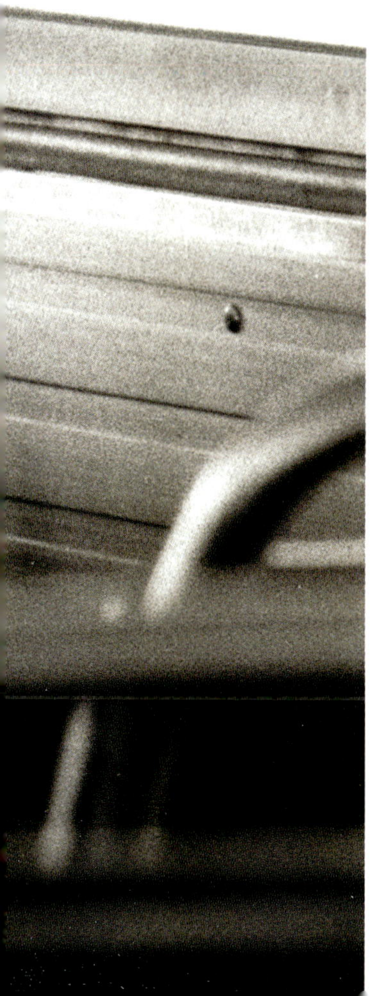

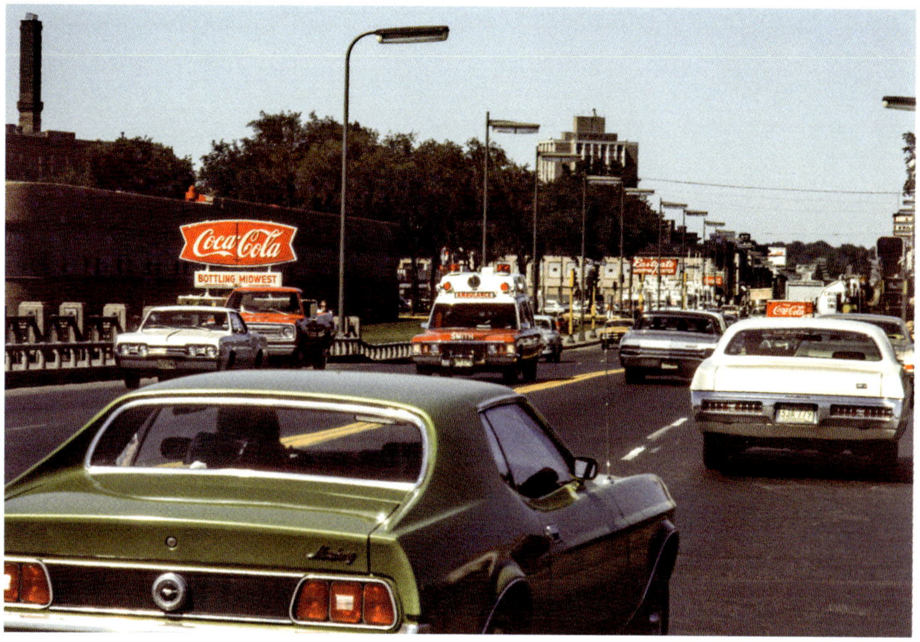

Above: Central Avenue, heading north just across the river from downtown—Mike's return trips home to the suburbs went this way

Opposite: "Seriously?"

THE PHOTO EQUIPMENT

by MIKE EVANGELIST

For the photographically inclined, here is a bit of background on the gear that I used to create the photos in this book and to get them into print.

THE CAMERAS

Nearly all the images in this book were shot on 35mm film. The earliest images were made with my first SLR camera, a Mamiya 500DTL with a 50mm *f*2 lens. I bought it new from Allied Radio in 1969, for $169. It was a great "learner's" camera.

In early 1971, I sold the Mamiya and bought what would become my primary camera for the next several years: a Nikon FTn with a 55mm *f*1.2 lens. This was a huge upgrade in capabilities and image quality. The majority of the photos in this book were shot with this trusty Nikon. Over time I added other lenses, most notably a 135mm *f*2.8 and 70–200mm zoom.

In addition, thanks to my involvement with the school newspaper and yearbook while attending Mounds View High School, I had access to a nice collection of gear that the school owned. I often borrowed their Nikkormat camera. This was convenient because the Nikkormat could use the lenses from my Nikon, and carrying two cameras allowed me to load black-and-white film in one and color in the other. (I shot far

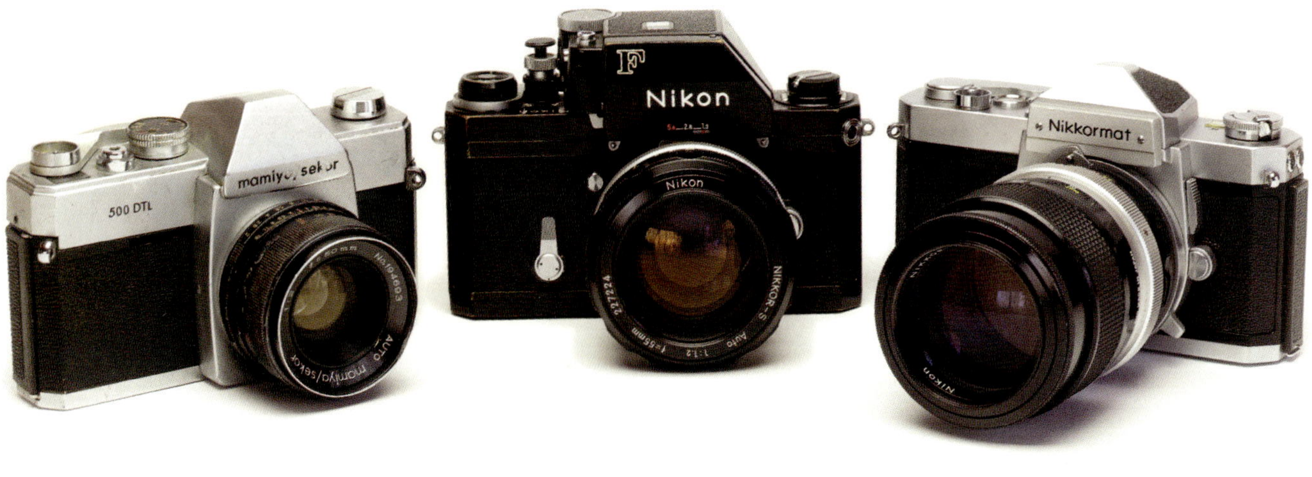

more black and white, simply because the film was less expensive and I could develop it myself; color was a rare luxury.)

I also occasionally borrowed a Mamiya 220 twin lens reflex camera from school. This was my first experience with medium-format cameras, and it opened my eyes to the higher quality that could be achieved. A few of the photos contained here were shot with that workhorse.

Through my connection at Brown Photo, I had the opportunity to use a bunch of other cameras and lenses over the years. Most of them were far out of my reach financially, so it was a special treat to shoot with them. Of those, I had the most fun with the Leica M5, the Pentax 6×7, and the Hasselblad 500C. Owing to the short time I had with each (typically only a day or so), I was forced to concentrate more on their unique attributes and how they allowed me to see my subjects differently. All three produced some of the images in this book.

SCANNING THE IMAGES

I scanned all of these images with a Nikon Coolscan 9000 ED film scanner. I was fortunate to acquire it: the model has been discontinued for some years now and is highly sought after for its quality. It can scan negatives and slides up to 6×9 (2"×2¾") format, at up to 4000 dpi. It has an automatic dust-removal function for color film, an incredible time saver. With black-and-white film, any dust or scratches have to be manually retouched in Photoshop. And no matter how careful I am, there is always some dust.

It takes about five minutes to scan each image, not including retouching. The images are saved as TIFF files, averaging about 50MBs each. I started on the pile of roughly ten thousand images about two years ago. I work on it from time to time, whenever the mood hits me. I'm about half done. •

"Reflections on the next chapter—me with my wife, Sandy, pregnant with our first child, seen reflected in a store window on Nicollet Mall"

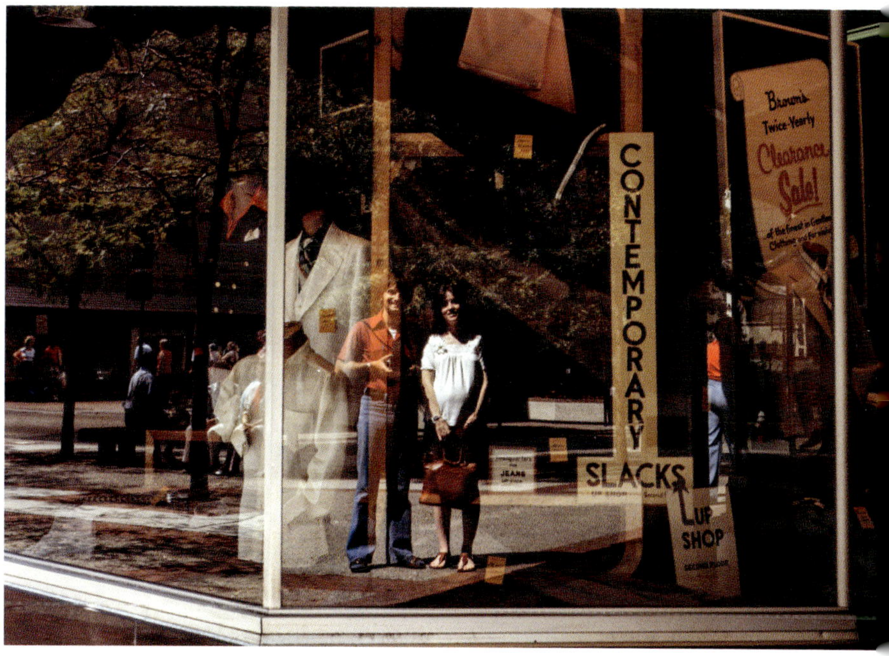

ABOUT THE AUTHORS

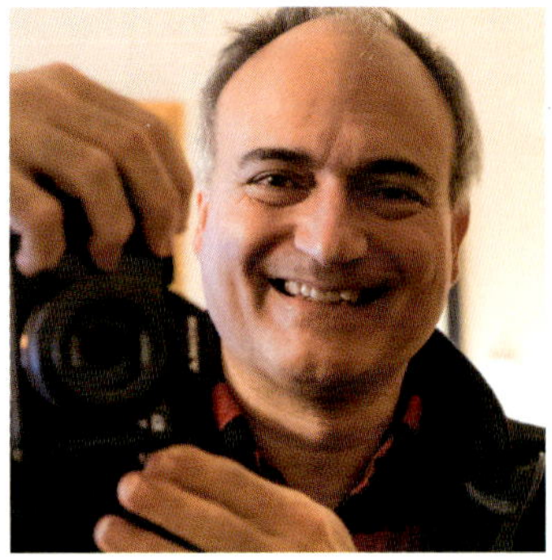

Mike Evangelist was born in Minneapolis and grew up in nearby New Brighton. He attended Mounds View High School, and it was there he discovered his love of photography, spending much of his time taking pictures for the school newspaper and yearbook. Even before graduating, he was getting professional work, and he attended the University of Minnesota fully intending to make photography his career. But life intervened, and he spent the next twelve years working in the advertising field as an account executive, with occasional photography work sprinkled in. He moved into personal computers in the late 1980s, creating and marketing a variety of products. He spent time at Apple as a director of product marketing and later became chief marketing officer at Code 42 Software. Since retiring in 2014, Mike spends much of his time taking pictures. His favorite subject is his grandson. Mike is married and has three adult sons. He lives in Birchwood, Minnesota.

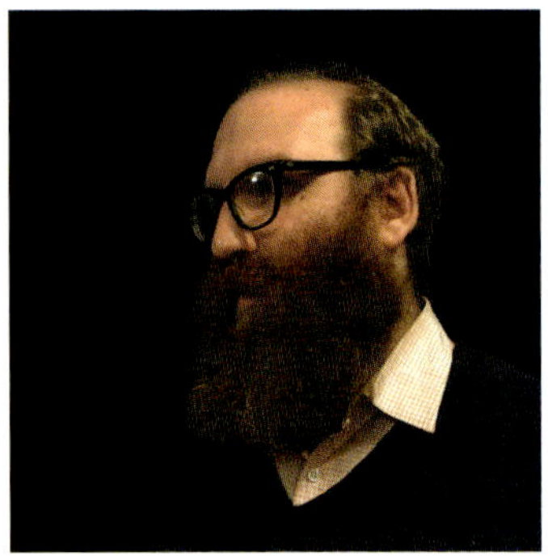

PHOTO BY PAULA MCCARTNEY

Andy Sturdevant is a writer and artist. His weekly column in *MinnPost*, "The Stroll," highlights the art, architecture, culture, historic sites, and visual miscellanea of the Twin Cities. He is the author of *Potluck Supper with Meeting to Follow*, published by Coffee House Press in 2013. Andy lives near Powderhorn Park in Minneapolis.